SILENTLY INTO THE MIDST OF THINGS

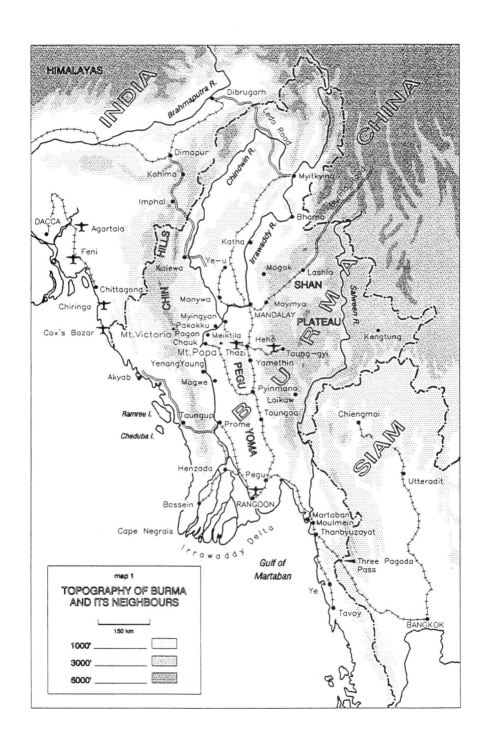

map 1

TOPOGRAPHY OF BURMA AND ITS NEIGHBOURS

150 km

1000' _____
3000' _____
6000' _____

SILENTLY INTO THE MIDST OF THINGS

177 Squadron Royal Air Force in Burma,
1943–1945
History and Personal Narratives

Atholl Sutherland Brown

The Book Guild Ltd
Sussex, England

The Book Guild Ltd.
25 High Street,
Lewes, Sussex

First published 1997
© Atholl Sutherland Brown, 1997

Set in Times
Typesetting by Acorn Bookwork, Salisbury, Wilts

Printed in Great Britain by
Bookcraft (Bath) Ltd, Avon

A catalogue record for this book is
available from the British Library

ISBN 1 85776190 1

For Doogie – lovely, loving, clever and strong!

Photographs

Photographer is generally unknown unless taken by the pilot of a described operation. Many photographs taken by 177 staff photographers.
Source of prints given in brackets.
* Indicates subsequently missing or killed in action.

CONTENTS

FOREWORD

By Air Chief Marshal Sir Lewis Hodges, KCB, CBE, DSO, DFC

Following the disasters in South East Asia in 1941–42 when the Japanese armies swept all before them capturing Singapore and overrunning Burma, the Allies were forced back in a long retreat to the borders of India. It then took time for the British and Commonwealth forces to recover and consolidate in preparation for a renewed offensive.

The pressure facing the Allies in Europe and the Mediterranean at this time meant that the South East Asia theatre had been starved of resources, particularly modern aircraft, and a great deal needed to be done to reinforce the Far East air forces with new equipment and to develop the airfields and infrastructure required.

By 1943 the situation was beginning to improve, enabling the Allies to go over to the offensive. The campaign for the recapture of Burma in 1944–45 has never received the recognition it deserves, and this is particularly so in the case of the air operations in support of the 14th Army in its advance from Imphal and the Arakan, driving the Japanese from Burma and, by May 1945, recapturing Rangoon.

The use of Allied air power was a vital ingredient in achieving victory, and in this regard the long-range Beaufighter squadrons played a key role in interdicting the Japanese communications and supply lines in Burma — road, rail and river — on which the Japanese forces depended for the provisioning of their armies in the field.

Furthermore, from 1944 onwards the relative freedom that our ground forces enjoyed from Japanese air attack was in large measure due to the continued harassment of the Japanese air force by attacks on the enemy airfields and bases — many of them in Siam; and in these operations the Beaufighter squadrons with their long-range and heavy armament played a significant part.

Silently into the Midst of Things describes the work of the air and ground crews of the Beaufighter squadrons, particularly 177 Squadron — following its fortunes from the arrival of its aircrews in India, having flown out with new aircraft straight from the factory, itself a most demanding task. The author has drawn on personal reminiscences of officers and men from many of the Commonwealth

xi

countries as well as the United Kingdom, which gives this book a freshness and authenticity that makes compelling reading.

Based in East Bengal on the Burma border, the Beaufighters carried out missions at low level, searching out targets in jungle country; often being subjected to intense anti-aircraft fire from Japanese ground defences and facing the ever-present danger of attack from enemy fighter aircraft.

From my own experience the major differences between operations in Europe and the Far East were the great distances involved, the rugged nature of the terrain, and the very mountainous and jungle-covered country making navigation extremely difficult, and the appalling weather conditions in the monsoon period between May and October.

The day-to-day squadron life is vividly portrayed; the problems of keeping the aircraft serviceable in the very primitive conditions prevailing and with minimum facilities; the very rudimentary living and working conditions exacerbated considerably during the monsoon, called for strong leadership on the part of the squadron commanders. The high operational sortie rate was certainly very demanding on the aircrews and groundcrews alike, and in spite of the losses incurred the morale and spirit in the squadrons remained remarkably high.

It is now half a century ago that the war against Japan ended, and this well-researched book is a most important addition to the literature of the Far East conflict. It will, I believe, be of great value to students of the history of this most important aspect of the Second World War, and of particular interest to those who took part.

PREFACE

Silently into the Midst of Things was written as a result of discussions between Donald M. Anderson of Perth, Australia and the principal author, Atholl Sutherland Brown of Victoria, Canada, prior to a reunion of 177 Squadron, Royal Air Force, in London in August, 1994. We felt that, as the one general history of the Squadron, *Mission to Burma*, was out of print and there were no plans to reprint it, a new history should be written in which surviving members of the Squadron would be encouraged to provide their own narratives to illuminate the account. This possibility was proposed at the reunion and was enthusiastically endorsed. I became the principal author and editor because I had previously written and published my own memoirs, *Indian Days — Burmese Nights*, of which the 177 Squadron section was published in the autumn 1995 number of the journal, *Canadian Military History*.

The Squadron members who survived the Second World War and 'time's arrows' to the present have contributed the unique aspects of this history — they have contributed narratives, photos, published works and encouragement as the volume evolved. The contributors include: Alf Aldham, Don Anderson, G/C P.H. Baldwin, Chas Bateman, Ted Bellingham, Bill Benneworth, Norman Bolitho, Noel Boyd, Henry Chew, James Denny, Reg Fox, Jack Harper, Hugh Howard, Alec Kappler, Reg Loffill's son Jeffery, Jim Marquis, George Nottage, Tony Rieck, Keith Ried, Eric Ruddell, Reg Wood, Dick White, and Joe Van Nes. Special thanks are due to Don Anderson, Noel Boyd, James Denny, Jim Marquis and Joe Van Nes for the volume of material they provided and Tony Reick for his help in London with publishers. I am in their debt. I would also like to acknowledge the critical support I received from Bill Rodney, Professor of History, Academic Dean and wartime Halifax pilot. Also my moonlight colleagues of the BC Geological Survey, Brian Grant, Dick Player, John Armitage and Sharon Ferris who helped with photos, maps and information. Finally, tribute must also be paid to the forbearance of my wife, Barbara, as it must to most authors' mates.

Canadian Content

The author is a Canadian and is aware that the Burma campaign of the Second World War seems remote to Canadians of the 1990s, but this differs little from that of Canadians of fifty years ago, or indeed of the HQ and senior personnel of the Royal Canadian Air Force during that time. The focus of Canadians was on the war in Europe and that of the RCAF Headquarters staff on the Canadian squadrons in Europe: Six Group of Bomber Command and the Canadian fighter Wings, 126, 127, 143 and 144, as well as other Canadian units. However, the Commonwealth Air Training Plan was an incredible success despite the politics and chauvinism of its beginnings (Dunmore, 1995). Canadian aircrew, particularly pilots, were produced at a rate that Canadian squadrons could not absorb, so they were dispersed all over the globe as reinforcements for Royal Air Force units. Two thirds of all Canadian aircrew were members of RAF squadrons but, once so placed, they seemingly passed beyond the ken of RCAF HQ as well as the contemporary Canadian media.

Canadian contributions did not stop at the provision of Canadian aircrew to bolster RAF squadrons, for the majority of Commonwealth aircrew also took at least some of their training in Canada.

In Burma there were three Canadian squadrons: a Catalina squadron (413) came to Ceylon in March 1942 and took a major role in finding and shadowing the Imperial Japanese naval task force that attacked Ceylon in April of 1942; and two Canadian Dakota squadrons were formed in India in early 1945 which, though late on the scene, played an important role in the air supply of the advancing 14th Army. However, the major Canadian contribution in Burma as elsewhere was the provision of aircrew for the RAF squadrons in the battles for Burma. The situation of 177 Squadron, Royal Air Force, was typical of the contribution Canada and Canadians made. As its history confirms, the Squadron was the most effective Beaufighter squadron on the Burma front. Again, most of the two-man crews were at least partially trained in Canada. 177 began operations in September 1943 and was disbanded in May of 1945. During its nearly two-year operational life a total of 77 pilots flew with the Squadron, of which 14 were Canadians. Five of those were missing or killed on operations. Two were awarded the DFC. This Canadian contribution was not unlike that to other RAF squadrons in Burma, the African desert or Italy but is not acknowledged separately by British official accounts and rarely by Canadian ones.

PART I

THE SQUADRON

Figure 1 177 Squadron crest and motto, *Silenter in Media Res.*

1

Background

'Silently into the Midst of Things' is the translation of *Silenter in Medias Res*, the appropriate Latin motto on the crest of 177 Squadron of the Royal Air Force. The crest itself shows a cobra ready to strike and coiled about two cannons (Figure 1). 177 Squadron was a wartime creation. In its short two-year history of operations, after a difficult beginning, it was remarkably effective in its role in the defence of India and defeat of the Japanese forces in Burma. Flying Bristol Beaufighters, the squadron had an assigned tactical role to interdict transportation: shipping, trains, and lorries, as well as to attack enemy airfields in Burma and Siam. The aircrew were recognised for their bravery, capabilities and dedication by the many decorations they were awarded. The groundcrew who supported them so effectively under difficult conditions received too little recognition. This volume is an attempt to portray the history of the squadron by the recollections of the people who made it. Individuals recount their experiences of operations and life on the squadron with their memories bolstered by their log books and photos. The historical framework is based primarily on the squadron Operations Record Book (ORB) and some published works. Unfortunately, survivors of war and time are now few and scattered and their memories, even with these aids, are often erratic. Nevertheless, many aspects are still surprisingly vivid. Not unexpectedly, parts of the composite memory panorama are missing because the key minds and hands are gone. This volume attempts to sketch in the vacant patches of the canvas.

Two histories of the squadron have already been written. *Mission to Burma* by F.H. Burton is out of print, while *View from the Cupola* by R. Loffill has not been published. Burton's book is particularly valuable for his follow-up trips to Burma and his research into the fate of missing crews. Unfortunately it is not available for quotation. Loffill's book is valuable as the view of an observer and of the later history of the squadron. We are in debt to these authors for their lead. *Silently into the Midst of Things* is different from the former books in that it is a mosaic of many individual reminiscences attempting to portray the history in a broader way. We also think

3

there are lessons for today in how individuals and an organisation met difficult assigned roles, not fearlessly or faultlessly, but with fortitude and accumulating skills.

In the half century since the events related here took place there have been major political realignments in the Indian subcontinent and South East Asia with consequent changes of name and frontiers. Pakistan was partitioned from India and later Bangladesh seceded from Pakistan; French Indo-China divided into Vietnam, Cambodia and Laos. Siam has been renamed Thailand, and Ceylon renamed Sri Lanka. Burma under its present military government has recently changed the names of the country and principal city to variants; Burma to Mynamar and Rangoon to its first name, Yangon. The Western world seems reluctant to adopt these names. Most other names in Burma have remained the same, and are shown on the maps of this volume. Generally we have stayed with the names current at the time of the history.

The squadron aircrew changed by attrition and by tour expiry. Casualties were responsible for much of the change because 35 percent of all aircrew went missing or were killed and only a few of these casualties occurred in 1945. Basically there were two sets of aircrew, the original from September 1943 until November 1944, followed by a separate group from then until the unit was disbanded at the end of May 1945. Irrespective of this, there was an incredible unity in esprit and attitudes probably in response to some of the ikons that left a mark on the original squadron aided by some crews that bridged the gap.

The pattern used for names and rank may seem erratic. Generally, in writing from the squadron Operations Record Book, the ranks current at the time and initials are used and occasionally decorations and Air Force (i.e. RAAF). In connective material, rank and initials may be omitted and first names or nicknames used. In narratives the latter were normally used. Nicknames were fairly general and had many sources; common contractions or diminutive versions of given names; nicknames brought by an individual from his past and commonly known by someone from training days; and occasionally, names attributed by the groundcrew. W/C J.E.S. Hill was Long John because of his height but mostly we called him Sir or waited for him to look at us. Harold Brentnal Hunt was called Mike by all, even the groundcrew, if not to his face. O.E. Simpson if one had lots of time was called Half-a-Sahib because of his compact stature, or Simmy in a hurry. R.H. Wood was invariably Timber. J. Lottimer was Lottie or even Auntie Lottie. F. Jungalwalla was Jumbo. N.F. Archer was Gummy. W.G. Herr was Gee. L.A. Clark was naturally Nobby. R.J.

Newcombe was Blondie for his yellow hair. T.C.M. Marshall was Pinky for reasons given later. S. Sinibaldi was Sinbad. J. Walsh was Holy Joe. The first Adjutant was Wizzie Westwood. The principal author was called Soggy, a variant of a family nickname. Most were just contractions such as Alf, Andy, Dickie, Don, Fergie, Joe, Kap, Mac, Matt, Rupe, Tony or Willy.

Time has also done something to the perception of the war; some have glamourised it, more have recently written of it in an unbelievably revisionist manner. George MacDonald Fraser (1992, p.xix) in a recent personal history of his experiences as a rifleman and lance corporal in the 14th Army in Burma has written:

> There is for some reason I don't understand a bitter desire in some to undermine what they call the "myths" of the Second World War. Most of the myths are true, but they don't want to believe that. It may be a natural reaction to having the war rammed down their throats by my generation; it may have its roots in subconscious envy; it may even spring from a reluctance to recognise that today's safety and comfort were bought fifty years ago by means which the intelligentsia find unacceptable, and from which they wish to distance themselves. I cannot say, ...[many of the revisions present views that are false and dangerous] and these may be taken as true by the uninformed or thoughtless, since it fits fashionable prejudice. And that is how history is distorted. You cannot, you must not judge the past by the present; you must try to see it in its own terms and values, if you are to have any inkling of it. You may not like what you see, but do not on that account fall into the error of trying to adjust it to suit your own vision of what it ought to have been.

This account avoids dwelling on the fear and agony of the combatants but it is here, nevertheless, and it takes little imagination to fill in the outline of the tragic aspects of the efforts of this small group of men in their attempt to secure no less than the freedom for the West and the world.

Another reason to write and assemble this history is that even the authors knowledgeable about the war in Burma still knew little about the role Beaufighters played in the defeat of a ferocious and tenacious foe. The war in Burma may not have been out of sight to the Australians but it certainly was to Britons and Americans, to say nothing of Canadians; yet we all fought there. If the 14th Army of General Slim was the 'Forgotten Army' then the 3rd Tactical Air Force, or more particularly 224 Group, was the 'Invisible Air Force'. So it is not too surprising to find that in the *Official History of the Royal Air Force*,

5

Volume III (Saunders, 1954) there are only two paragraphs and two poor photographs dealing with the Beaufighters of 224 Group in Burma of which 177 Squadron was a part. What is unforgivable is the presence of factual errors in the latter publication. Appendix XII, Order of Battle, Air Command, South East Asia, 1st July 1944 does not even list 901 Wing, the Beaufighter Wing (ibid., p.418); and worse, neither the Wing nor 177 Squadron are listed with their aircraft in the amplification. 27 Squadron was in southern India on that date, 211 is listed as a Beaufighter squadron in 169 Wing with no others, and 177 Squadron is not mentioned at all. In the text 177 is mentioned once, on page 347, for our attack on the convoy at Kalegauk Island on the Tenassarim coast of southernmost Burma. For a squadron that fought for two years in the worst of the Burma campaign, lost 35 percent of its aircrew, who altogether only totalled 150, and yet were awarded 4 DSOs, 14 DFCs, two DFMs and an MBE, this seems inadequate.

Perhaps as surprising was that General Slim himself clearly knew little of the tremendous damage we did, not only to traffic on the lines of communication, but to the enemy themselves. Beaufighters as such are not mentioned in his text (Slim, 1956) although of course 224 Group is in a minor way (on four pages). Certainly General Slim had a great understanding of air power and was an innovator in its use. He said: "Until a degree of air superiority, amounting at least locally to dominance, had been secured, neither air supply, movement nor tactical support could be carried on with the certainty and regularity our operations demanded. The fighter and the bomber between them had to sweep the skies and push back the enemy landing grounds," (Slim, 1956, p.545). However, it might be fair enough to say his views were coloured by the palpable use he was able to make of air supply, and direct air support; Slim has less to say about medium and heavy bombing and almost nothing about the tactical damage we inflicted on the Japanese at long range before they ever came into contact with the 14th Army. Had he seen them, a glance at the large-format, low-level photographs of the damage we did should have convinced him we had a significant role in the defeat of our enemy. So there is an element in putting the record straight in this volume.

2

The Bristol Beaufighter

The Bristol Aeroplane Company showed considerable foresight and initiative in developing the Beaufighter in the uncertain prelude to the Second World War. It filled a niche that was open in British armament, a twin-engined cannon fighter, and was from the start the most heavily armed fighter of the Allied arsenal (see Appendix 1, Evolution of the Beaufighter). There was a clear family progression from the Type 142, a private venture of the Bristol Company and Lord Rothermere, through the Blenheim I and the Beaufort torpedo bomber to the Beaufighter.

The Bristol Beaufighter was a remarkable aircraft. It was not a truly beautiful plane like the DeHavilland Mosquito but it had rugged good looks (Figure 2), great strength and power, good speed at low elevations and a most formidable and flexible armament. Its premier role was as a nightfighter but it was also intended from concept to be a long-range fighter. It also developed into an anti-shipping and ground attack cannon and rocket-firing fighter, torpedo plane and tactical bomber. Its versatility and heavy armament were the subject of a Wren cartoon in *Flight* magazine in 1944 (Figure 3), a humorous interpretation that sums up the aircraft's virtues in unique fashion. The development of the aircraft progressed from the Mark I with Bristol Hercules VI engines to the Mark II with Rolls Royce Merlins Xs or XXs to Mark VIs and Xs with Hercules XVII rated at 1,735 hp each. All Marks had four fixed Hispano-Suiza 20 mm cannons in the belly and most had six Browning .303 calibre machine guns in the wings. Later adaptations installed long-range fuel tanks rather than the machine guns and had a rear-firing Vickers gun in the observer's cupola. Various Marks or adaptations could mount rockets, bombs or a torpedo.

The Beaufighter layout consisted of a roomy pilot's cockpit in the snub nose with an unexcelled forward view, and an observer's cupola in the dorsal position with a good view aft. Pilot and observer were not in direct sight communication if the pilot's armoured doors were closed. The fuselage between pilot and observer was largely occupied by four cannons and their magazines which held 250 rounds per gun.

7

Figure 2 A Beaufighter over Arakan (P.H. Baldwin, King's College London).

8

Figure 3 Cartoon by Wren, *Flight* magazine, 7 July 1944; a humorous comment on the increasingly heavy armament of the Beaufighter (A. Sutherland Brown).

The observer was navigator, wireless operator and rear gunner. Primary entry for both positions was by hatch doors with ladders that folded flush with the belly when closed. The pilot had an emergency upper hatch and the observer's cupola opened.

177 Squadron flew the later Marks of Beau, VIs at first then mostly TFXs (Torpedo Fighter Mark X). Many of the latter were fitted with non-jettisonable rocket rails. Many pilots preferred the VIs to the Xs because they were faster and were not fitted with rocket rails. Actually, the difference in cruising speed between Beaus with fixed rail and jettisonable installations was supposed to be only 4 knots. However, many thought the average Mark VI was about 15 knots faster than the X with fixed rails. There was no denying that rockets were very effective against shipping and tanks. 177 was one of the few squadrons to fly XIs but there were not enough of these for pilots to have strong opinions about them. The main difference from the TFX was that they did not carry torpedo launching gear.

3

Training

To Make a Beaufighter Crew

Few pilots arrived on a Beaufighter squadron in India without spending two years or more in training and waiting. Flying training for pilots seldom started for three or four months after enlistment. Initial training on DeHavilland Tigermoths or similar light, single-engined craft was followed by secondary training for pilots destined for multi-engined aircraft on one of many types of twins: Avro Ansons, Cessna Cranes or Airspeed Oxfords. Passing successfully through these schools took at least eight months and about 200 hours of flying time. The fledgling emerged proudly with pilot's wings and a feeling that he knew how to fly. Those destined for Coastal Command duties then spent two months at a General Reconnaissance (GR) school where the emphasis was on navigation. During this training he would spend several months in transit to and from various stations of the Commonwealth Air Training Plan in the UK, Canada, Australia or southern Africa as well as waiting in pools. In the UK he would spend a month at an Advanced Flying Unit (AFU) probably flying Oxfords and then two months in an Operational Training Unit (OTU) learning to fly Beaufighters. The training here was intensive although the aircraft were pretty well worn out. Curiously, a deficiency of OTU training was insufficient air-to-air or air-to-ground firing. In most cases a pilot from OTU bound for India and his new observer would take delivery of a new Beau from a factory, test it and then fly it out to the sub-continent. Once in India they would more than likely go to an aircrew pool rather than directly to a squadron. It was a long process with lots of frustation while waiting but the product was a fairly well trained pilot with about 400 hours of flying and an equivalently trained navigator. Their real operational training, however came on the job in their first few flights over Japanese-held Burma.

Observers had a parallel training: usually Signal School in the UK followed by transit to Canada for Air Navigation School to learn navigation, bomb aiming, air gunnery and associated skills. This

11

would be followed, as for pilots, by GR school and a similar amount of waiting before arriving at OTU. The elapsed time for them was also about two years and they emerged with broader skills than ordinary navigators. They would need these riding in a Beaufighter's dorsal cupola.

Crews were formed about halfway through OTU. God knows how the partners were chosen, perhaps by dartboard, but the surrogate marriages were generally successful and the crews were mated for life — or death. As Jim Marquis (F/L J.D. Marquis, DFC), a navigator, says:

> The crewing up of pilot and observer at OTU was a bit of a hit or miss affair for neither knew much of the background or ability of the other. It is surprising how well most partnerships worked out. Certainly a very special relationship developed for both relied on the other for mutual salvation. When an observer lost his pilot for any reason it was traumatic, even more so if the pilot was killed after they had flown together for a long time. Crewing up with a new pilot in such circumstances was never easy but again mutual trust gradually built up. Any period spent as a spare navigator flying with various pilots short of their normal navigator was not a happy time.

It also spoke much for the men who were to undergo this experience.

Flying Beaufighters

Opinions differed about flying Beaufighters and whether they were difficult to handle or not. Bingham (1994, pp.67–69) gives the impression that they were easy. Most tyros thought they were fearsome. The pilots of 177 generally thought they were marvellous aircraft but not to be taken lightly at any time, not just when landing or taking off. This view was held by Mike Hunt (S/L, DSO and Bar, DFC) and George Nottage (W/C, DSO, AFC) who were far from being tyros. Bingham (ibid.) writes:

> A lot of nonsense has been written over the years about the take-off swing of the Beaufighter, which was in fact no worse than that of the Mosquito, and could easily be held. It is obvious that any aircraft whose CG (centre of gravity) is well behind the main wheels, with two powerful engines forward, is a natural for moving from the straight and narrow as soon as the engines are opened up. This

fault on the Beaufighter was easily corrected by some differential throttle control when opening up, maintaining the aircraft in the forward direction until the rudder 'bit' and full rudder control was gained — then moving the throttles to the gate and the Beau accelerated like a scalded cat.

On the other hand, Sutherland Brown (1992) wrote:

Flying Beaus was no piece of cake: their reputation for being hard to handle was deserved. The great torque generated by the powerful engines, connected to large three-bladed propellers winding up forward of the fuselage, tended to create wild swings on take-off. Also the high wing-loading dropped you out of the sky like a brick on landing. Furthermore in the air there was no hands-off flying because Beaufighters were relatively unstable: they needed constant trimming and had no auto pilots.

On the positive side these planes were otherwise nice to handle, responsive, silent on approach, powerful and fast at sea level. They were very rugged and had remarkably well-planned, roomy cockpits with unexcelled visibility. Instrument layout was logical and relatively uncluttered [see Figures 4 & 5]. The engines were trouble free, seldom overheated on the ground in the tropics and kept on producing even with severe damage from enemy action.

Figure 4 Pilot's roomy cockpit showing reflector gunsight in position, side vent windows, and pilot waving chocks away (permission of Chaz Bowyer).

Figure 5 Cockpit, instruments and controls. Flight instrument panel in front of control column; undercarriage, flap, engine, fuel, VHF controls on left; compass and trim controls on right (*Flight*).

On 177 Squadron the pilots were involved in long-distance flights at the limits of the aircraft's endurance so they cruised at high boost and low revolutions to save fuel — commonly flying at 180 knots except on target, when under fire or during evasive action when they might go though the throttle gate for short periods and might exceed 260 knots (300 mph) at sea level (see Appendix 2, Handling of Beaufighters and Performance).

The squadron pilots were not a demonstrative bunch and rarely beat up the field after a 'good show', possibly because they were nearly out of gas. So little did they perform egotistic manoeuvres that a Dakota squadron sharing Feni with them did not think they were fighter pilots on ops. Occasionally someone would blast over the mess or briefing room at about 20 feet which would certainly startle all inside. Whatever the origin of the sobriquet 'Whispering Death', it certainly was true that with such an approach one heard nothing on the ground until one nearly soiled one's trousers with surprise. A few pilots barrel-rolled Beaus, but not near the deck because none of the

14

Figure 6 Wing damage including loss of starboard aileron from hitting a tree during evasive action; pilot F/O Lottimer on right and observer, F/O Watson on left at Feni December 1943 (W.E. Bellingham).

observers liked it. A manoeuvre pilots did like was steep turns along the deck in humid conditions (most of the time) when the wingtip vortexes created vapour trails and a strong whistling sound to external observers.

The pilots also liked having a bulletproof windscreen, considering they were frequently diving at an enemy who was firing at them. However the plane-sloped surface of the windscreen was not designed for tropical downpours, when it became opaque with sheet flow. Pilots were saved flying along the deck under such conditions by opening the vent windows at the sides (Figure 4) through which, with the neck of a giraffe, one got a small glimpse of reality.

The ruggedness of the plane's construction was another thing Beau pilots all liked and to which many owed their lives. The photos of Beaus with trees in their wings, or missing wingtips, large holes in the airframe and engines, crashes and belly landings in which most of the crew survived made them all believers (Figures 6, 7, 44 & 63). They

15

Figure 7 Belly landing of a Beaufighter at Feni in 1944 with minimal damage (W.E. Bellingham).

might have been scared white at OTU, flying clapped-out Beau IIs at night but, once experience was gained on these remarkable aircraft, they flew the later Marks with bravura and confidence.

4

The Long, Confused Gestation of 177 Squadron, RAF

Assembling the Pieces

The authorisation, manning, assembly and equipping of 177 Squadron were lengthy and seemingly erratic ventures; about a year long, without certain direction towards role, initially without senior personnel and hustled from base to base like unwanted cousins. A poor way to start! Authorisation from the Air Ministry in mid-1942 was followed by a Formation Order (No.271) from Air Headquarters, India on 25 November 1942 when the groundcrew had already been assembled in the UK and embarked in a troopship from Liverpool (ORB, pp.1–2).

The Air Ministry conceived the need for Beaufighter squadrons in India to defend Calcutta and Ceylon from night air-raids and also for tactical operations against the Burmese transportation arteries and airfields. However, some confusion apparently existed because the evidence indicates the groundcrew for both 177 and 176 Squadrons were assembled in the UK and despatched by troopship before their final destination or role was decided: Middle East or India, nightfighters or tactical ground attack (Aveyard, 1976; Denny, this volume, Fox, ibid., Wills ORB, p.6). It is likely that 177, like 176, was originally intended to be a nightfighter unit, but before they were properly in place in India the strategic situation changed. The anticipated night raids against Calcutta were not mounted to any degree after the interceptions and destruction of Japanese bombers (Army 97s) in early 1943, so the establishment for nightfighters was scaled back. Hence 177 was slated for tactical operations and eventually became part of a Beaufighter Wing (901) of 224 Group, 3rd Tactical Air Force. The squadron's main duty was to sever and harass (interdict) the Japanese supply routes and attack Japanese-held airfields.

A contrast in methods of manning the squadron between the aircrew and the groundcrew is striking. The aircrew did not know they were joining 177 Squadron and from the history of individuals it is doubtful if there was any master plan beyond getting some aircrew to the squadron. In fact too many were actually assigned. Almost all

17

the aircrew flew Beaufighters to India that they either picked up at a factory in England or from a Maintenance Unit in Egypt. The groundcrew on the other hand were assembled in the UK and shipped by trooper to India.

Reinforcement Flights of Beaufighters to India

The newly qualified Beaufighter crews who were posted to Air Command, India had a testing start to their RAF operational history; an experience that was not counted as ops but in many ways was as challenging. The Beaufighters to equip the squadrons in India were chiefly flown from factories in the UK by aircrew who were assigned to the Command. This was a calculated risk, as they had first to brave the hazards of Junkers 88s patrolling the Bay of Biscay and then a difficult airport at Gibraltar. Along the changing route they had little communication with the ground and few navigational aids; they flew over remote areas of central or northern Africa, some of which were in enemy hands, and finally faced the hazard of the Arabian desert and the Gulf of Oman. Most of the crews had never done anything like this before, but their training was adequate for the challenge.

Apparently the hazards and delays of shipping were worse than the reinforcement flights by novices. Freighters had to run the gauntlet of the U-boat wolf packs in the Atlantic and the aircraft had to be broken down, transported and reassembled in India. Many Beaus on reinforcement flights also acted as freighters, being stuffed with spare parts, engine covers, rocket rails, tool kits etc.

The routes flown changed as the Axis forces were driven out of north Africa; initially flights started in west Africa but moved progressively farther north as the continent came under Allied control. The following accounts trace some of these changing patterns as well as the hazards and uncertainties of these flights.

F/L Joe Van Nes, DFC, from Flin Flon, Canada recalls:

> We still had no idea what our job would be until at the embarkation unit we were issued tropical gear. Our journey by ship from Liverpool to the west coast of Africa was long, wet and tedious. It was followed by an overland trip to Kano, then by Liberator to Khartoum, Dakota to Cairo to sit in tents at Almaza Transit Camp. This was finally relieved by a posting to Edku where we were eventually allowed to fly. Rumours circulated that our group was being readied to relieve the Malta Beaus as their numbers had

18

been drastically decreased. One day a Flight Lieutenant flew into Edku and addressed us with a breezy, 'Good show chaps, you are off to India to reinforce 177 Squadron'. This was our introduction to Mike Hunt, who became a 177 Squadron ikon, and it was our first knowledge such a unit existed. In no time we were at a Maintenance Unit to pick up aircraft and retrace our steps to Khartoum. The trip was uneventful but my navigator, Trevor Matthews, developed malaria and it was some time before he was well enough to fly to Karachi by Dakota to recuperate.

In the meantime my Beau was cannibalized to an alarming degree while it sat at Khartoum. Eventually orders came for me to accompany six Baltimores to Cairo to take the northern route to India. I now had no air intake filters, no radio and no navigator. The flight to Heliopolis was uneventful until I tried to land. Happily I let the Baltimores go first because when I let the wheels down only the tail wheel descended. The landing was under control but the bumpy gravel strip took its toll on the aircraft. It took two weeks to complete the paper work and longer to repair the Beau. The cause of the malfunction was that an oil return line had chafed the hydraulic line until it had slowly lost all the fluid. Back to Landing Ground (LG) 224 to pick up another aircraft; a bit like a game of snakes and ladders. I was slated to fly to India along the oil pipeline accompanied by a Spitfire and Beaufort; perhaps it was more like the Wizard of Oz. At Tel Aviv the Spit went unserviceable so the Beaufort and I trudged on via Habbaniya (near Baghdad), Bahrain, and Sharjah (near Dubai) to Karachi. Here I was informed that I landed with only a gallon of oil in the port tank. Happily I picked up my navigator and we flew on to Phaphamau.

James Denny relates his experience as follows:

In January 1943 I joined 176 Squadron in Edku, Egypt. I had not flown a Beau in three months and on my first flight I did my one and only swing (ground loop) in a Beaufighter. I think I opened the throttles too quickly, could not hold it on the runway and went haring across the desert before I could stop it and taxi back through clouds of sand to try it again. A humiliating but useful lesson, particularly when I was expecting later to be using narrow airstrips in semi-jungle with large trees close on either side of the runway.

Anyway we were off to India with only five Beaus and five crews with the rumor we would meet the rest of the squadron there. F/L Birt was the flight commander with the other pilots, F/O Newcombe, Sgts White, King and myself. On 28 January, 1943 the five of us took off for India. The first stop was Wadi Halfa on the Nile. I had a old Beau I, T4723, with rough running engines. After we landed at our next stop, Wadi Seidna (Khartoum), I had them checked and to my delight was given a new Mark VI, EL466, with dihedral tailplanes. We set off for Asmara in Eritrea next day, and as the airfield is 7,000 feet above sea level, it presented a unique experience. It had a fairly long runway and we needed it all. The following day, January 30th, was my 21st birthday but was more memorable for the flight to Sheik Othman (Aden). There was solid cloud to 10,000 feet so we flew above it until dead reckoning (DR) showed we should be above the Red Sea. Here we split up to let down through the cloud and find our way to Aden. Fortunately we broke out at 1,500 feet over the sea, and joined up with Birt and White, and made our way to Aden. King arrived soon after us minus his rear hatch and most of his observers kit. Newcome arrived a few minutes later; he had landed at an airstrip over the border in Yemen and realized his mistake when he saw a large party of horsemen galloping towards him brandishing swords. He turned the Beau around and took off down wind just in time.

We got away from Aden two days later after two abortive attempts because of bad weather. Everyone at Sheik Othman was intrigued with our Beaufighters — most had not seen one before. The CO asked us to give them a beat-up when we left which we did in spades. We then flew along the mountainous South Arabian coast to a refueling strip at Salaleh in Oman. The next day we flew to another strip on Masirah Island, refueled, had lunch of biscuits and jam, and took off across the Arabian Sea to Karachi, where we landed late on the afternoon of 2nd February.

On the 6th we flew to Jodhpur, there to learn that 176 Squadron had already been formed from another squadron and we were in limbo. On the 9th, we taxied our beloved Beaufighters across the airfield to 119 Maintenance Unit and wondered if we would ever see them again. On the 13th the bad news arrived — we were all posted to 42 Squadron to fly bloody Bisleys (Blenheim VIs). What a come down! F/L Birt tried to reverse the posting but to no avail.

F/L Jim Marquis, DFC, relates that he and his Canadian pilot, Wally Roberts:

...left Portreath, Cornwall, at 08:30 hours on 5th February 1943. We had been held up at the end of the runway for some time because a Wellington had crashed on take-off, killing all the crew. We were a few aircraft behind the Wellington in the queue. Eleven Beaus left Portreath, nine reached Gibraltar, the other two were never heard of again. Things were 'iffy' in the Med also. On the morning of the 8th, Wing Commander (W/C) "Killer" McConnell, with Wally standing in the well, and myself as navigator, did a 4½ hour trip from Gib to Cape Tres Forcas from where we flew south of west and then back on the reciprocals to check the feasibility of an alternative route to Cairo. McConnell was on the Air Staff at Gib and had been CO of a Beau squadron in the UK conducting shipping strikes along the Norwegian coast and fjords. On the 9th four Beaus left Gib individually to fly over the Atlas Mountains and land at Marble Arch Airfield in Tripoli. We ran into severe sand storms and bad weather causing us to fly by dead reckoning for a long time. After $6^3/_4$ hours Wally and I landed with 50 gallons in our tanks. Two other Beaus made Marble Arch, one landed safely, the other ran out of gas on approach and crashed. The aircraft was a write-off but the crew got out. The fourth landed at Castel Benito but its engines cut out while taxiing. Castel Benito was almost at the front at the time, not long having been taken.

On the 10th February we flew on to Cairo to LG 224. On the 11th we were instructed to fly to LG 222 to turn our aircraft over to 108 MU. We then had several moves about the delta but eventually picked up the same Beau to fly it out to 177 Squadron to which we found out we were posted. On 1st March we flew to Wadi Halfa, and successively to Khartoum, Aden, Salalah, Masirah, Jiwani, Karachi, Jodhpur and in March to Allahabad where we delivered our aircraft to a Maintenance Unit. We hitched a ride to Dum Dum, Calcuta, to pick up another Beau to fly to Agartala as part of 177's detachment with 27 Squadron.

W/O A.J. Kappler, DFM, relates that he flew in May 1943 from Portreath to Gibraltar, Tripoli, Cairo, Habbanyia, Bahrain and on to Karachi. 'We were briefed that the runway at Gib ran east–west and the wind always blew one way or the other. We were to fly around the Rock on arrival to decide which way to land. Forty-nine aircraft took off, the slowest first! Consequently a large number arrived about the same time. Some flew clockwise, others counter-clockwise. What a mess with many a near miss!'

F/L A. Sutherland Brown, DFC, relates (1992, p.10):

On 23 August we got a written order to fly the new Beaufighter, LX996, [which we had picked up at the factory at Filton] to India for reinforcement and to remain in the India Command. It was a sparkling day as we flew south down the Irish Sea from Islay to Portreath, here to refuel and arm for the flight across the Bay of Biscay on the morrow. We seemed to be treated especially well at the mess and the thought of ' lambs to the slaughter' barely crossed my mind. The next day, also sparkling, we took off at dawn in a loose gaggle of three expecting the air to be full of JU 88s. However the flight turned out to be an uneventful cruise down the Portuguese coast within sight of Lisbon and on to land at an airfield at Fez, Morocco.

A kaleidoscope of impressions and change enveloped us on leaving Britain! We had left behind a drab, battered and warworn England suffering a cool and rainy summer with blackouts and boring rationed food. We arrived in Fez to find an ultra-modern French colonial city with good restaurants and excellent food; we visited the Casbah that exuded Berber life; we swam in the warm dusk in a clear palm-fringed swimming hole in an oasis near the airfield. So far it was stimulating adventure.

After three days in Fez we took-off to fly across the Atlas Mountains and the Sahara to the newly captured Castel Benito airfield at Tripoli. The Italian base was also a contrast to UK wartime fields for, even with some damage, it had an airy, comfortable mess and a profusion of Bougainvillia blooming in the grounds. The next day we flew to Cairo across the desert etched by tracks of armoured corps maneuvers and littered with burnt out hulks. Incredibly the circuit of our designated airfield at Cairo included the Great Pyramids. After a day in Cairo we were off successively to Baghdad and Bahrain to finish the third day in Karachi. The welcome there was not what we expected. As I shut down the engines the hatch door in the belly opened and a petty official climbed up to douse the interior and us in a fog of flytox from fear of importing yellow fever. So much for greetings! This incident was followed in good time by the news we were to be separated from our aircraft and to leave by train in the future for an aircrew pool in Poona. We had thought that we would immediately be dispatched with our aircraft to a squadron and operations.

Not so — we languished for three months in Poona followed by three months in Delhi flying an assortment of aircraft, Lockheed 12A, DC3, Hudson, Argus, Anson, Harvard and Puss Moth, with South East Asia Air Command Communications Squadron before we were posted to 177. While I chafed at the time, in retrospect it was valuable experience, flying all over India, including the Arakan and Imphal, in such a variety of types and weather.

Groundcrew to India

The groundcrew experience was quite different. They knew they were going to India but not much beyond that. C.R. Fox, a wireless operator mechanic at that time, relates his view of the events:

Although we did not know it at the time, the motley crowd that was assembled at Hednesford in September 1942 was destined to be the groundcrew of 177 Squadron. The aircrew we learned had preceded us via Takoradi (West Africa) and the Middle East, some picking up aircraft on the way.

It was a right old tub of a troopship on which we groundcrew embarked at Liverpool at the end of September. Its pre-war name was the *Empress of Japan* but it had diplomatically been renamed the *Empress of Russia*. In her heyday she was one of the Canadian Pacific liners that were designed to rush raw silk and passengers from Yokohama to Vancouver. She was past rushing now, a coal burner which shed soot all over the deck when the wind was not strong enough to carry it away. The original crew — Chinese we were told — failed to re-appear when the boat was due to leave and a scratch crew of embittered seamen from around the dock was 'hijacked' as in the navy days of sail. The Chinese left their cockroaches and bugs behind however. It was not a complete crew so volunteers (you, you and you) were detailed from among us passengers for odd jobs around the ship; such as stoking the boilers and working the galley.

Being a wireless operator mechanic, I felt lucky to be detailed to take shifts standing by one of the two motorized lifeboats which were equipped with a radio. I was to be an emergency operator should the ship's wireless operator fail to make it in the event of a shipwreck, e.g. a U-boat attack. I had to insist on having a look at the equipment that I might have to operate and was horrified to find an old spark transmitter, but no receiver! With the bottom of the boat awash in water even before it was launched, it seemed to me that the choice would be between drowning or electrocution.

We encountered a terrific storm in the Atlantic and, being on the slow side, the old dowager was always at the tail end of the convoy steering as straight a course as she could while the rest of the convoy zig-zagged in true wartime style. When it was in view we looked longingly at the *Durban Castle* and the lucky devils in it. Several mornings when we came on deck there was no sign of the rest of the convoy, only a Navy corvette signalling to us to hurry and catch up. Whether the captain took a short cut or the rest came back to us I do not know.

And so the old tub staggered into Freetown for re-fueling. Coal barges appeared alongside with hundreds of natives who loaded coal in baskets then carried them on their heads to the side of the *Empress* and tipped the coal into the bowels of the ship. The steady rumble of coal seemed to go on for days. When fully fueled, the old *Empress* had a list to starboard. This gradually changed to a list to port as the coal was burned (or was it the other way around?).

Then down the west coast of Africa we sped to make an approach to Cape Town. When in clear view of the town and docks, with Table Mountain in the background, the ship veered away and off we went to Durban. The "Lady in White" sang *Rule*

Britannia as we docked. We had several days in Durban and what a time we had after war-torn Britain.

Then unaccompanied, we crossed the Indian Ocean until we encountered some mechanical problem. The boat circled a few times before the engines stopped. We drifted around a bit and then struggled into the nearest port which was Mombassa where repairs took a week; we were allowed ashore on certain days. The last leg took us to Bombay. Is it surprising the journey lasted almost three months?

Halley (1989) states under the heading 177 Squadron, '...[it] was formed on the 28 November 1942, but at the time of formation the personnel of the Squadron were still at sea enroute from the UK.' That, I think, puts it in a nut shell!

The draft of airmen (No.4765) that arrived in Bombay on 6 December 1942 had four non-aircrew officers with it including the Engineering Officer, the Adjutant and an RAF Regiment officer in charge of security and airfield defence, and one other. On arrival they and the technical and non-technical groundcrew were dispersed to a variety of stations; some to assemble aircraft in Karachi, some to guard duties at various sites and some to temporary clerical duties elsewhere.

Squadron Formation and Training

Within a short time the groundcrew had lots of experience of India's railway system. Most of the troop train carriages in which the airmen travelled to their postings were Indian Third Class with old wooden benches and anything but clean. W.E. Bellingham remembers:

> ...the washing facilities were almost non-existent. When the train stopped to take on water, we all showered from the water tank. The locals were startled by the sight of 250 naked Sahibs dashing along the station platform for a shower. Also the carriages were infested with bedbugs and roaches. A knowledgeable medical orderly with us concocted his own anti-bug spray. We used it throughout the train when stopped at a station, leaving the carriage doors open. The spray was so effective that literally thousands of bugs hurled themselves through the open doors on to the platform. I hope the orderly remembered his formula to make his fortune after the war.

Despite the early dispersal of personnel they began to be reassembled in early 1943 at Amarda Road, in Orissa. Flying Officer A.P. Wills, who had operational experience on Beaufighters in the UK and

Middle East, was the first aircrew officer assigned to the squadron on 11 January 1943 and was in nominal charge. It must have been suggested that the new squadron send a detachment to Dum Dum airport, Calcutta, to bolster the nightfighter defence. Wills had to point out to 221 Group Headquarters (HQ), to which the squadron was initially attached, that he was not trained as a nightfighter pilot but as a general reconnaissance (GR) pilot, and that arriving new crews would be the same and freshly out of Operational Training Units (OTU). Also the squadron had not been properly worked up, their Beaus did not have radar and the technical groundcrew were not conversant with Beaufighters (ORB, p.6). The established strength of the squadron was reputed to be 340 but as of the beginning of February it had only 117 personnel including one pilot.

Forming the squadron continued in a fitful way. In the beginning of April the squadron was moved to Allahabad to a tented site whilst groundcrew continued to arrive as well as some aircrew. The latter were mostly seconded to 27 Squadron for training and familiarisation. As David Innes relates (1985, p.57):

> During February (to April) seven aircrews of 177 Squadron had joined us at Agartala (near Comilla). This new Beaufighter squadron was to be based at Phaphamau and pending the airdrome being prepared for Beaufighters and the groundstaff being established, these aircrew were given the opportunity to participate with their No.27 counterparts and learn what to expect when their squadron began operations. Some flew with us as passengers whilst others flew as operational crews, and sadly this was not a very successful experience. Within a very short time they had lost three of their seven crews, including that of the commanding officer elect, Squadron Leader (S/L) I.G. Statham, AFC, and his observer, Pilot Officer (P/O) K.C. Briffett.

Statham was an experienced pilot having received his wings in 1930. He was posted to 177 to be CO in November 1942 but on arrival at the end of February 1943 went directly to 27 Squadron on loan and went missing on 26 March. Also one of the missing crews, F/L McMichael and Sgt Dodd, survived a crash and were imprisoned in the beastly gaol in Rangoon until the end of the war.

The squadron had another short move across the Ganges at the end of April with the advance party moving by road on the 24th. The unit occupied this station at Phaphamau for three months while it was training (Figure 8). Unfortunately there were only four aircraft when these were delivered to the squadron on 11 May. The aircrews included F/L Hunt DFC, F/O Wills, F/O Weston, P/O Taylor, Sgt

Figure 8 Camel train passing 177 Squadron Beaufighters at Phaphamau airfield near Allahabad, May 1943 (J.D. Marquis).

Pilots Boniface, Highfield, Herr, Moffat and Copeland, and Sgt Observers Davies, Morris, Mearns, Gibson, Read and Smith. F/L Hunt became the acting Commanding Officer (CO) and he appointed Wills as a flight commander. Many other aircrew began arriving directly to the squadron. At long last 177 had become an entity but it was far from operationally ready or complete.

Training in the monsoon was difficult enough, but the shortage of Beaus, poor maintenance because of a lack of spares and trouble with fuel tanks, and a sudden superabundance of crews meant that each one got only four to five hours aloft during May, June and July. Training consisted of low flying, dummy attacks, evasive action, single-engine flying, wireless and navigation exercises but no airfiring as no range was available. Wing Commander (W/C) P.H. Baldwin arrived on 4 June to take command. At the end of June the squadron had 31 crews and 11 were declared surplus — as a result many were posted away, some to return later (Appendix 3A).

In August the squadron moved to the front — again not simply but in two stages, first by rail and ferry to the seaport of Chittagong for a week and then 50 miles north to an airfield at Feni which was to be the base for nine months. Training continued for a while including dummy squadron attacks and, at last, airfiring at a range on a low, barren island at the mouth of the Padna (Brahmaputra) River. Operations commenced from Feni on 10 September. A difficult period of losses, poor aircraft maintenance and the worst of the monsoon lay just ahead.

Establishment and Composition of 177 Air and Groundcrew

The squadron was composed of two Flights, each with eight Beaufighters and sufficient aircrew to man these and allow for leave and sickness. Normally there were 20 to 22 aircrews. The nominal strength of the squadron was 340 persons of all ranks. The groundcrew were never up to this strength even though they had to carry out major repairs unlike the squadrons in the UK.

The aircrew were young; most just 20 to 22 or 23. The CO and flight commanders were old, 25 to 28. The adjutant and the IO were really old, in their thirties and had the wisdom, and got the respect, due their age and experience. The groundcrew had a broader spectrum of ages, up to 40 but most were still in their early twenties (Figures 9, 34). Not more than a handful of the Squadron were per-

Figure 9 Some groundcrew at Phaphamau, July 1943; left to right, Les Sakne, Jock Robertson, John Hill, Ted Bellingham, Joe Sheard, Joe Sowerby and Tich Sherris. They are still wearing UK tropical issue including topees (W.E. Bellingham).

manent RAF or even Volunteer Reserve. They were new volunteers yet they maintained the highest traditions of excellence, valour and devotion to duty of the Royal Air Force.

Among the aircrew all the observers were from the UK except F/S F. Jungalwalla who was an Indian in the RAF. Over 30 percent of the pilots were either Canadians (14), Australians (8), or New Zealanders (2). The commissioned ground staff consisted of five to seven: an Adjutant (Adj), Engineering Officer (EO), Medical Officer (MO), Intelligence Officer (IO) and Signals Officer (Sigs), and at times an RAF Regiment officer in charge of airfield defence and an Army liaison officer. For much of the time the Adj was an Australian (W.S. Ferguson) and Sigs was an Indian (Z.A. Aziz) in the Indian Air Force (IAF) otherwise all were British. Appendix 3A lists the squadron aircrew at the end of June 1943 before operations started, 3B lists them as of August 1944 after the move to Chiringa in the middle of the squadron's history and, finally, 3C lists them in April 1945 before the squadron was disbanded. Appendix 4A also lists in chronological order all of the aircrew who served on the squadron (160 in total).

The non-commissioned groundcrew were almost entirely from the UK and styled at the time as British Other Ranks (BORs). The exceptions were some unenlisted followers: bearers (servants) and 'lascars' (cleaners) who were Indians. When first reassembled at Amarda Road there were 221 BORs and on the eve of disbandment there were 254. Appendix 6A lists the groundcrew as of August 1943, and 6B as of the beginning of July 1945. The members of the original draft that came out on the *Empress of Russia* were mostly still there at the end. They were expected to serve in India for four years. The groundcrew may not have suffered some of the stresses of the aircrew nor the casualties but they had little except their own efforts to leaven their lives; no expectation of the expiry of a tour and little relief from the heat, poor food, tropical diseases, isolation and tedium of the routine of a squadron on the Burma front.

5

The Setting in South East Asia

The Terrain

Burma is a country of diverse topography (Map 1). The western
boundary of the country extends from the eastern end of the
Himalayas southwest to the Ganges–Bramaputra delta, along the
Bay of Bengal and a third of the way down the Malaysian peninsula. Its eastern boundary is relatively close to the Salween River
throughout its course but only for a short distance does it follow
the river. The Chin Hills, a south-trending bow-shaped range of
mountains with peaks to 10,000 feet, form the border between
India and Burma. Eastern Burma is an upland, the Shan Plateau,
which has elevations between 3000 and 6000 feet. Between this and
the Chin Hills is an area of plains and low dissected hills through
which the branching system of the Irrawaddy and the Chindwin
Rivers flow to form a major delta in the south. The Chin Hills
(Arakan Yoma in the south and Naga Hills in the north) consist
of long linear ridges with steep slopes formed of folded mainly
Tertiary sedimentary rocks. They are clothed in jungles to near the
ridge tops where narrow grasslands with trails, villages and scattered clumps of bamboo and rhododendrons occur (Figure 10). In
contrast the sharp valleys are sites of torrential streams and little
culture. The central lowlands in the north consist of low hills
covered with dry teak forests grading southwards to semi-arid hills
with areas of rice field on the flood plains near the rivers in
central Burma (Figure 11). In southern Burma highly dissected,
low, brushy hills (Pegu Yoma) in the spine are flanked by plains
and delta of the Irrawaddy (Figure 12) and Sittang Rivers. A
remarkable feature of central Burma is a single symmetrical
volcanic cone of 5000 feet, Mount Popa, rising like a pyramid
from the plain. The Shan Plateau, underlain by uplifted old Paleo-
zoic metamorphic rocks, is covered with grassland interspersed with
scattered clumps of bamboo and mixed trees (Figure 56). Deep and
narrow internal valleys such as that of the Salween River are
clothed in tropical jungles.

29

Figure 10 View across the Chin Hills ridges near Mt Victoria (10,018 feet). Note slash and burn agriculture of the ridgetop fields (J.C. Van Nes).

The Climate

Burma's climate is driven by the monsoons. The rains of the Southwest Monsoon begin in May, are most intense from June through August and decline towards the end of October. The cloud masses in the intense monsoon extend solidly from a few hundred feet above the ground to more than 60,000 feet. A cool season of the Northeast Monsoon follows until February during which small cumulus clouds with a common base elevation build up during the day over the plains and greater masses over the mountains. March and April are dry with increasing heat and generally sparse clouds until the approach of the wet monsoon when isolated towering cumulo-nimbus storms become increasingly common.

Temperatures, humidity and rainfall vary with elevation and site. Central Burma is in a rain shadow and so is semi-arid. The flanking hills, plateau and mountains receive many hundreds of centimetres of rain a year and the delta well over 150 centimetres. Temperatures in the plains may reach 45° C whilst some of the northernmost mountains have permanent snow.

30

Figure 11 River Mu of the central dry belt during northeast monsoon. Beaufighter shadow on the dry river bed (A. Sutherland Brown).

The Infrastructure

Burma of 1940 exported rice, teak, gems and the metals lead, zinc, silver and tin and was self-sufficient in petroleum. About half of all the supplies the Japanese invaders needed were available locally. In comparison with its neighbours, Burma was a rich and fortunate country. It may have been unhappy with its colonial status, particularly when it was relayed through Delhi, but the country was flourishing in most senses. The commercial and political capital was Rangoon, an active city of more than a million with, for Burma, a polyglot population of Burman, ethnic tribes from the hinterlands, Sikhs, Hindus, Chinese and British. It is a young city although the Shwedagon Pagoda and some parts near it go back to the Kingdom that ruled from Pagan in the eleventh century. Mandalay, at the edge of the Shan Plateau and on the Irrawaddy River, was the most important internal city and the capital of upper Burma. It is a young

31

Figure 12 177 Beau over the Irrawaddy deltaic plain (N. Boyd).

city also, Victorian in age, but it is adjacent to the old capitals of Amarapura and Ava. It was concerned with the governance of central Burma and with trade in teak, gems, metals and rice. The plains of Burma were dotted with small towns and villages with a well-developed transportation network.

As in India, the British built a network of railways with more than 2500 miles of track (Map 2) that was primarily oriented to resource extraction. In addition the Japanese forced through a railway from Bangkok to Moulmein as their main strategic supply route to Burma. The Burma railways consisted of a main line from Rangoon up the eastern side of the plains along the Sittang River to Mandalay and from there north to Myitkyina. Six lines branch from the main line; three to the west through the plains to termini at Kyaukpadaung near Chauk and Pagan, one to Myingyan in the centre of the oil fields and one through Monywa to Ye-u. Two of the eastern branches climb into the Shan Plateau, ending at Lashio, terminus of the Burma road to China and one to Taung-gyi. The other eastern branch leaves the main line at Pegu and doubles back south to Martaban across the mouth of the Salween River from Moulmein which was the terminus of the Bangkok railway. Another line covers the delta; it leaves Rangoon to travel 160 miles northwest

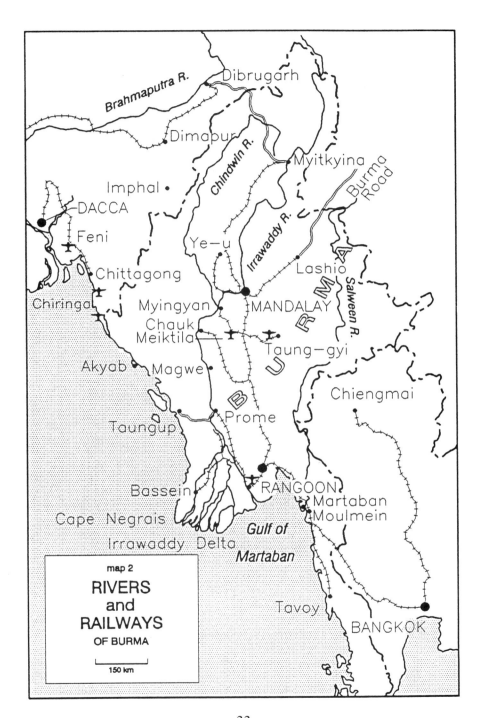

map 2

**RIVERS
and
RAILWAYS**
OF BURMA

150 km

to Prome on the Irrawaddy and, across the river, doubles back to Bassein.

There was an extensive network of roads in the plains and Shan Plateau. Most railway lines were roughly paralleled by roads, some of which were paved. The secondary network covered the plains and extended eastwards into Siam. There were almost no roads through the hog-back ridges of the Chin Hills, only mule tracks. The main Japanese road to supply the Arakan crossed the hills from Prome to Taungup on the Bay of Bengal. The main road under Allied control left the railhead at Dimapur in the Brahmaputra valley and wound its way over the hills and valleys through Kohima to Imphal. The Americans began building a road from Ledo in the north towards Myitkyina with the idea of connecting with the Burma road to supply China.

The Irrawaddy and Chindwin are navigable well to the north, the Irrawaddy to Bhamo in the dry season and to Myitkyina in the monsoon, 700 miles from Rangoon. The Chindwin is navigable in the monsoon a 100 miles or more above its confluence with the Irrawaddy. The Salween is only navigable for 125 miles above Moulmein. The rivers were truly the main transportation conduits of Burma before the war, and freight was carried by all manner of native craft as well as shallow-draught steam boats, paddle wheelers and barges.

The oil fields of central Burma extended north from Yenangyaung for about 100 miles roughly parallel with the Irrawaddy. Tank farms existed at Chauk and Yenangyaung and a pipeline followed the river south to Prome and then to Rangoon.

The features of topography, climate and infrastructure played pivotal roles in all calculations of strategy by the Allied and Japanese High Commands, as well as tactics by all subordinates. The grain of the sharp ridges of the Chin Hills governed all attempts by the Japanese to take India, and by the Allies to break out into Central Burma. They prohibited road making and forced movement and supply to be by mule or air. The monsoon rains turned the roads of Burma into impassable quagmires and prohibited tank deployment. They also created unbelievable difficulties for ground attack aircraft and for maintenance of aircraft in the open. The established lines of communication, rivers, rail lines, roads and oil pipelines, were the arteries of Japanese war-making and, because of their governance by topography and limited distribution, the targets for tactical air operations that were obvious but difficult to defend.

34

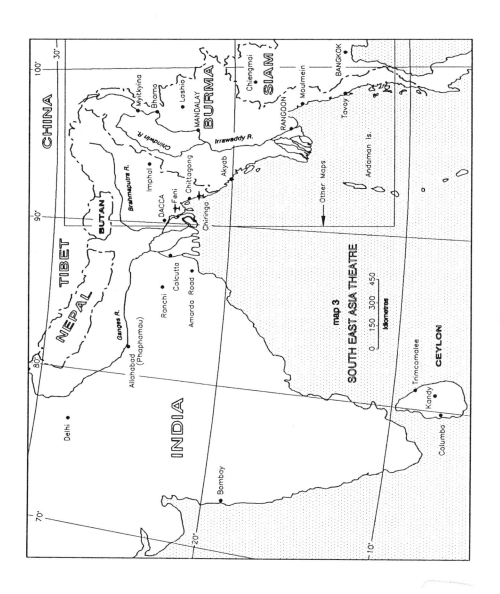

SOUTH EAST ASIA THEATRE

map 3

kilometres

0   150   300   450

36

6

The Strategic Canvas

The setting into which the new squadron, 177, was launched was very different from that of the European or Pacific theatres: as different in the stage of conflict and in the sinews of war as it was in topography, climate and infrastructure (Map 3).

The strategic situation in the Far East in mid-1942 to early 1943 was calamitous for the Allies. The severe British defeat and withdrawal from Burma was completed by mid-year at great cost in men and the poor equipment in the air and on the ground with which they were burdened. The Japanese were consolidating their positions along the natural border between India and Burma. In April a major Japanese carrier taskforce approached Ceylon, severely bombed Colombo and Trincomalee and sank two British cruisers, an aircraft carrier and two destroyers in the Bay of Bengal. The Royal Navy then, in effect, temporarily withdrew to the western Indian Ocean. However, in the course of the engagement the Fleet Air Arm and the RAF inflicted fairly severe casualties on the Japanese aircraft and damaged three carriers to such an extent that the attacking forces did not press home their advantage. Furthermore, the encounter left the Japanese with only two operational carriers at the Battle of the Coral Sea which cost them dearly (Churchill, 1950, pp.151–188).

On land the defensive forces available to the Allies were minimal. The best trained and experienced units of the Indian Army were in the Middle East, and the RAF in India had a only a minimal strength of second-rate equipment. However, the Japanese supply situation was also poor, Burma being the most remote theatre of their greatly expanded field of war. Hence late in the monsoon of 1942 the current situation was a temporary stalemate. The Indian Army occupied defensive positions concentrated in the Arakan and the Chin Hills around the Manipur valley; fighting was limited to some penetrative patrols in the former area. Kachin irregulars fought limited guerrilla skirmishes north of Myitkyina. A Chinese army from Yunnan, which was sometimes entirely under United States General Joseph W. Stilwell, retreated to the Shan Plateau. In contrast, the Japanese occupied Akyab and its hinterland with moderate force

37

(Slim, 1956, p.149) but nurtured the hope of a major build-up to take India soon. The Arakan and the Chin Hills, with their sharp jungle-clad ridges separated by abundant parallel mountain torrents, or tidal rivers, and nearly devoid of roads, was not a terrain that encouraged modern land warfare. It was a terrain for which the Japanese had developed suitable tactics, but one the Allies had yet to master (Slim, 1956).

Debate at the highest levels of the Allied Command ensued about the relative merits of the various theatres and the awarding of assets (Churchill, 1951, pp.553–581). India was usually accorded the fourth priority after the UK, the Mediterranean or the Pacific. Landing craft and naval forces assigned to South East Asia, for example, were withdrawn to the Mediterranean. United States assets for the East went to the Pacific or to China. India was thus in a perilous situation.

At the end of 1942 and early in 1943 Japanese bombing of Calcutta created an immense panic in a public that considered the war as little of their business. Many thought the Japanese would, in fact, free them from colonialism and include them in a fraternal group of the Asian Co-prosperity Sphere. This was a hope that many Burmans also held, only to be quickly disabused of it by Japanese behaviour and demands (Thakin Nu, 1954). It was apparent in Britain that if India was to be held its air defence had to be strengthened quickly with more effective aircraft. As a consequence a flight of five Beaufighters was detached from 89 Squadron in the Middle East and flown to Calcutta in January 1943 to form the nucleus of 176 Squadron. Immediately after they arrived they severely mauled Japanese night bombers (Army 97s — Sallys) that were ill-prepared for radar-aided interception (Aveyard, 1976).

In February 1943 the first of three Beaufighter ground attack squadrons formed in India (27 Squadron) became operational. Saunders (1954, p.300) states: '...this type of aircraft proved of the greatest use in offensive operations because of their range, which allowed them to penetrate deep into Burma, and the fire power they were able to bring to bear on such targets as, rivercraft, rolling stock, locomotives and mechanical transport. There were too few of them in the air, however, to achieve any marked effect before September 1943' [when 177 Squadron became operational]. 211 Squadron followed in January 1944. These squadrons formed 901 Wing of 224 Group, 3rd Tactical Air Force. They were not typical Tactical Air Force units because, although they took part in some direct army air support, their main role was the destruction of the enemy transport systems and attacks on enemy airfields that were carried out up to 700 miles behind Japanese lines — as far south as Tavoy on the Tenasserim coast and east, as central Siam (Probert, 1995, p.258). In many ways these squadrons and their work were unique. They flew great distances behind Japanese-held positions at low level, singly or in pairs, using tactical weapons, but they really played a strategic role; one more analogous to the bombing of bridges by the Liberators of Strategic Air Force than the Hurribombers of the Tactical Air Force blasting Japanese bunkers. They were appropriately called the 'Lone Wolves' of the RAF in Burma in an article in *The Statesman* of Calcutta on 31 January 1945. No squadrons played exactly comparable roles in the war in Europe.

In November 1943 a Wing equipped with Spitfire Vs arrived and quickly brought an end to daylight raids on Calcutta, the use of forward airstrips by the Japanese and the use of Mitsubishi Dinahs for photo reconnaissance. These air activities formed the one hopeful sign early in the war in South East Asia. The advantage continued, for by late 1943 mastery of the air over Burma had been firmly established by the Allies at minimal cost.

In contrast, after the monsoon of 1943 the ground forces were rebuffed in a limited offensive to take Akyab and its strategic airfield, and the Royal Navy was skulking around Ceylon. Already these events revealed the immense importance of air supremacy combined with a large capacity for air transport and air supply in such a terrain. Support for these elements in the high commands did not come easily, but was eventually established and proved pivotal in the defence of India and the war against the Japanese in Burma.

The Japanese moved quickly in 1942 to try to improve their supply lines. Japanese Railway Regiments were ordered to design a railway from Bangkok to Moulmein and to supervise its construction. The Japanese Imperial Army's High Command, with characteristic disregard of Geneva Conventions and of human life, ordered PoWs to be brought from Singapore, Java and Malaya to build a railway which was routed through Three Pagoda Pass in difficult, virtually uninhabited mountainous jungle between Bangkok and Moulmein. Construction was carried out mostly by hand labour, with savage discipline, minimal tools, shelter or food, and with complete disregard for health of the forced labourers. Twenty percent of the PoWs, mostly British, Australian or Dutch East Indians, died and the health of the rest was forever compromised (Dunlop, 1990: Bowden, 1984). In the jungles they died of malnutrition, overwork, dysentery, tropical ulcers or cholera. Employed Tamil labourers moved from the rubber plantations of Malaya fared even worse as they had no discipline, medical staff or caring supervisors.

Much of the trackage on the railway was poor, some of the grades were over-steep and the rails, engines and equipment were cannibalised from Malaya, Indonesia and Burma to the eventual detriment of the whole transportation system. For example, the second track from Rangoon to Toungoo was taken up, which later had serious implications for the Burma main line (Kinvig, 1992 p.51). The Burma–Siam railway was started early in 1942 and was completed at the end of October 1943. It was supposed to be able to carry 3000 tons per day but rarely exceeded a third of that (ibid., p.176). Nevertheless, the Japanese built up their forces in Burma to two armies late in 1943; moving them by the railway and coastal shipping. The reinforcements were drawn from elsewhere in South East Asia and the Pacific theatre. The goal was to capture India.

7

Developing the Tools

Procedures for Operational Sorties

A crew was notified that it was due for an operational flight and given the time of the briefing by the Intelligence Officer. Commonly the CO, the IO, the Flight Commanders and the Squadron Navigation Officer were present in the briefing room. This was not as some might envisage like the ops room of Fighter Command with Air Chief Marshall Sir Hugh Dowding, Prime Minister Churchill and a dozen WAAF moving pieces on the board. Rather it was a small basha with silhouettes of Japanese aircraft on the walls and a small group of sweating aircrew (Figure 13). Briefings for daylight operations commonly preceded take-off by several hours whereas those for night sorties were usually held in the late afternoon. Discussion took place in front of a large composite wall map of Burma and Siam with the primary target and the alternative marked. The crews and aircraft assigned would be identified, the section or flight leaders designated, the weather forecast, the signal data and colours of the day, known hazards and expected defences all discussed. Much of it was pretty routine. The observer and pilot would prepare their maps with tracks to be followed, turning points and landmarks. The observer fussed with calculations regarding wind speed and direction and estimated times. The feelings of the crews were seldom evident except by occasional excessive sang-froid. The CO and the IO were entirely businesslike although sometimes there was some rough humour. On one occasion we had all seen pictures of the Cardinal of New York blessing the American bomber crews in front of their carefully lined-up planes before they were off to bomb Rome. A local service padre came to the briefing room next day and said to Mike Hunt that he would like to bless us before we departed. Mike's reply was, 'Throw a blessing at them as they leave. They're in a hurry'.

Before night operations a crew seldom had more than a drink or two before dinner; it wasn't like the movie *Dawn Patrol*. For attacks at first light, crews retired as usual and were awoken by their bearer, by the duty officer or NCO. Normally you evacuated your bowels

Figure 13 Ops or briefing room, Chiringa. Note Japanese aircraft silhouettes on wall, aircrew with back to camera wearing escape money belt, F/O Mac Mackay* at one post and F/O Noel Boyd at the other (N. Boyd).

and felt pretty tense as you emerged from sleep and dressed in flying gear. The latter would vary depending on choice and temperature from a light one-piece drill flying suit full of pockets and escape boots to normal khaki shirt, trousers and battledress tunic. This was followed by gear to aid in escape of downed aircrew including a belt full of silver rupees, a kukri (Gurkha knife) and revolver on a belt, a silk two-sided map of Burma, a compass, a goulee chit (Figure 14) and a Mae West (inflatable vest). A leather helmet, goggles and oxygen mask or an open headset would complete one's personal equipment.

A cool trip in a fifteen-hundredweight truck to dispersal followed. There your Beau was ready on the hard standings of interlocking steel plates that served for tarmac. A crew of five or so groundcrew was present to expedite your departure; they often used carefully phrased humour with you and commonly presented you with a mug of tea. You donned your parachute with a hard and uncomfortable inflatable dingy that formed the seat and which was guaranteed to

မိတ်ဆွေကြီးခင်ဗျား။

ကျွန်တော်သည် မဟာမိတ်စစ်သည်တော်
ဖြစ်ပါသည်။ ကျွန်တော်သည် မြန်မာပြည်သူပြည်
သားများ ကို ရန်ရှာ ရန်လာ သည် မဟုတ်၊ ရှုဖက်များ
ကိုသာ မြန်မာပြည်မှ လျင်မြန်စွာ မောင်းနှင်ထုတ်
ရန် ်သာ ပါ သည်။ အကြုံ ်းဆုံး မဟာမိတ်စစ်တပ်အား
ကျွန်တော် ကို ပို့ပါ လျှင် ကျွန်တော်၏ အစိုးရက
ဆုလာဘ်တွေများစွာ ပေးပါလိမ့်မည်။

မူးတစ်ယောက်တင် ဆ ကိုး သုံ့ ၏

[second column Burmese text]

ကင်ဘျုမ်ိစ်လုက်သိုက်တပ်မရှ မိတ်၏၊ ကင်အဖူး့လတ်ခိုင်
ခွံပတ်ပိခ္ဂင်ကိုး၊ ဂင်းကင်တံ၊ ကင်အဖူး့ကာတွက်တော်
လှကြျုမာ်၊ ကွက်ရှုအင်ကိုးဝါင်တံ၊ ဂွိုးသေ့ပ်ဆိုးဘ။ ၌ဂတ်
ဟာ့းလု့ယ့်ခံးသေဝါယ်၊ ဖေုံကြာ်တက်ဝ်ကိုးရှ သုင်ပယာ့း
တီတပ်မရှုဝိတ် ကမ်ထိုးဝံဝေဝ်ဂိုးဝ်အံ ၍ ကက်ဝ်ဟတ်
ရ ်တ်ပတ်သုံ့ဝှံး။သုင်ိ သုလ့ဝိဝ်ိ မိုးကမဝါ်ယ်ဝ်။

Dear friend,

I am an Allied fighter, I did not come here to do any harm to you who are my friends, I only want to do harm to the Japanese and chase them away from your country as quickly as possible. If you will lead me to the nearest Allied Military Post, my Government will give you a good reward.

Figure 14   Goulee (ball) chit in Burmese scripts and English (A. Sutherland Brown).

keep you awake. You climbed the ladder of the hatch door in the belly, grabbed the bars on either side of the perspex upper hatch and swung into your seat. One of the crew followed you up the ladder to help you with the Sutton Harness (safety shoulder straps); they then signalled clear to start and removed the starter trolley after both fans were going. By now the business at hand had absorbed the last of the tension and apprehension. You ran up the engines, checked the instruments and fuel gauges glowing in the dark, the settings of gills, flaps, fuel tanks, altimeter and caged your gyro compass. When your observer was also ready you signalled chocks away, taxied out to the end of the runway, and after a vital action check, a green signal light from the tower, you opened the throttles, accelerated down the runway and climbed into the black sky.

On a normal return you taxied in to the waiting crew, picked up your maps etc. and descended the ladder, dumping your chute as soon as you could. You discussed briefly with the fitters and riggers the performance of the aircraft, deficiencies or damage. The debriefing followed immediately. Normally you got a rum-laced cup of strong tea after a night sortie. The whole flight was carefully reviewed; flight paths, targets sighted, attacks made, damage observed, flak experienced and any unusual aspects. The nose-camera photos were quickly developed to check the results claimed, but not before you returned to your mess and, depending on time, to your charpoy (string bed) (Figure 30).

Navigating Beaufighters in Burma

Jim Marquis (F/L, DFC) describes the observer's environment as follows:

> The Beaufighter navigator entered the aircraft through a hinged hatch ladder that folded aft flush with the belly towards the rear (Figure 15). Space was restricted; everything compact. The navigator sat in a swivel chair, above him a perspex cupola that was close to the head of any six foot occupant. Looking forward he saw the cocking mechanism for the four 20mm cannons, the belt magazines for the ammunition and the butt ends of the guns. A hinged table could be pulled down on which he could write or put his maps and charts for navigating. If the hinged armour plate doors were open he could see the back of his pilot's head and shoulders in his cockpit at the bow of the plane. These doors could be opened or shut from the navigators side but getting to them or the pilot was a difficult crouching crawl over the cannons and magazines. On the starboard side just aft of the navigator was the Marconi wireless set and Morse key.
>
> When we started operations in September 1943 there was no rear gun and no armour aft of the navigator. If you were attacked from the rear by a Japanese fighter the navigator had to give the pilot a running commentary on where the fighter was, its range, judge

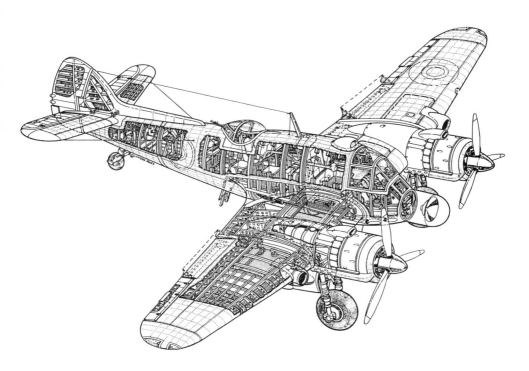

Figure 15 Cutaway diagram of a Beaufighter TFX with radar dome nose which was replaced on 177 by a normal nose-cone housing a Fairchild F24 mapping camera. Notice navigator's entry hatch and rear gun. By Lyndon Jones in *Bristol Beaufighter* by Victor Bingham, Air Life Publishing Ltd.

when it was about to fire and tell the pilot to break right or left as appropriate. You felt rather naked with no gun or armour.

Later modifications made on the squadron cut a hole in the back of the cupola to mount a machine gun which made the office draughty. A metal rod interrupting the traverse of the gun was supposed to stop us from shooting off our tails. Those navigators who hadn't done a gunnery course picked it up on the job. If the pilot after making an attack, pulled up sharply and banked steeply, the navigator could also open up on the target and keep the enemy's heads down.

Later aircraft reaching the squadron had rear guns fitted with sliding doors which cut down the draughts and also had rear armour. The arrival of VHF (Very High Frequency) voice transmission for the pilot cut down on the navigator's wireless operations considerably.

During an attack, if any of the cannons jammed, it was the navigator's job to recock them as it had been in early Marks with drum ammunition to reload the heavy magazines. These jobs usually had to be done while the Beau was in a tight turn pulling out from a diving attack, the air full of hot cordite fumes and your head below your body as you struggled not to puke. You were as quick as possible so you could get your head back in the cupola to keep a lookout aft.

According to Alf Aldham:

Navigating a Beaufighter over Burma was rather different from training. In fact it was best to forget most of the rules, and find your own system. Mine consisted of dead reckoning based on weather information from base briefing to lay out courses, regular drift readings while flying and a dogs leg (60° off course and the same back to the flight line) now and again to accurately check wind speed and direction. But the main method day or night was map reading with crossed fingers. This was not easy while looking backwards from the bubble and we relied on our pilots for clues. We mostly knew where we had been but had to guess where we were going.

Flying just above the trees as we did this system seemed to work in central Burma. When our ammo was expended we would often just turn west, map reading casually as we went but picking up a definite position on the coast and then head back to base.

Southern Burma and the Gulf of Martaban were a little different. We had to be sure of our position when leaving the coast of the Bassein Delta. As my pilot flew so low it was impossible to get drift readings or see the wind lanes on the calm surface of the water. He often flew so low I could see the wash astern of the aircraft made by the propeller's slipstream. Hunting shipping here was a hit or miss affair and at the end of a strike our position would be a little uncertain. We tended to take a wide berth, keep well out to sea, and check our position upon hitting the coast well west of Rangoon. Always remembering that these were long trips and a shortage of fuel could be a problem. Once I can remember we had to land at an American base well south of Chiringa as we were virtually dry.

Jim Marquis basically agrees:

While the Beau navigators were highly trained, a lot of the navigating over Burma was very much by the seat of the pants. The pilots usually cruised to and from the target areas at 180 knots so that for each minute flown you covered three nautical miles. ETA (estimated time of arrival) was then dividing the distance by three to get the time to go. Dead Reckoning was occasionally used, mainly over the sea, e.g. square searches for missing aircraft. Overland in the monsoon when you climbed to 10,000 feet to get over the hills and your pilot was continually changing course to avoid the worst of the gut-wrenching cumulonimbus storms, DR was impracticable. Once down to the plains you flew at 50 feet or so and navigation was map reading and terrain recognition. A lot of operations were offensive patrols over a length of rail, road or river with definite points on and off patrol. This meant Leading Lines could be used effectively. Navigators could aim deliberately to the left or right of the starting point so that when they reached the road etc. (leading line) they knew which way to turn.

The GR-trained pilots were more proficient than most in navigation and map reading and so were a considerable help to their observers. Should they survive the first few operational flights, both crew members soon became familiar with the landmarks — railways, rivers, roads, hills and flak nests of Burma — and expert in safely finding their way around. In the monsoon it was much the same but more difficult. However, in solid cloud many flights were made by DR at heights to clear any intervening topography with reliance placed on letting down in level terrain and breaking out at a reasonable elevation — sometimes rather scary!

Radio homing was used on return to base especially in bad weather at night, and a course was followed well out into the Bay of Bengal where the aircraft would let down gently by altimeter readings. Even in the worst of nights the sea could be identified by the different very dark grey of breaking waves from the black of the sea. The plane would then fly the reciprocal course until the shore was identified by a dark grey band of surf against the black land behind, and then grope home in familiar terrain. At times this was a hair-raising procedure. About radio homing, C.R. Fox has this to say:

> As a fully fledged wireless fitter, not long out of RAF apprentice school full of enthusiasm for my trade, I found it somewhat disconcerting to find pilots seemed to have little interest in their radio. At an inquiry on how a particular aircraft performed, the engine and airframe fitters would discuss with the pilot the fine details of engine revs, mag drops, oil pressure, the vagaries of undercarriage warning lights, some strange stiffness in the stick, and so on. But when asked about the radio the answer more often than not was 'Oh ... mm ... yes OK ... I think'! Navigators were quite different; they could bend your ear on problems with the transmitter 'click stops', and how difficult it was to get the trailing aerial off its stowage. They also knew how they could tune the receiver to find

the American Forces Network with its steady diet of Glen Miller and Tommy Dorsey etc.

The day came when the Squadron, on its forward Arakan airstrip, acquired a radio vehicle fitted with VHF receiving equipment and a direction-finding aerial. With the aid of the compass-swinging crew, we set it up on clear ground just off the strip. One of the RT operators was given instruction on how to operate the equipment; such things as tuning the receiver to the crystal monitor, using the signal strength meter, how to rotate the aerial, and most importantly — the use of the aerial switch to distinguish the real bearing from the reciprocal.

There was no operational flying some days due to weather, but an aircraft just out of service needed an air test. I approached the pilot, Joe Van Nes (F/L, DFC, RCAF), and asked if he would like to try out our new acquisition. After a few words to tell him on which channel to call, and to hold the transmit button for a little longer than usual; he would receive a bearing back to base. He was asked to repeat the action a few times to give the operator some practice.

I watched the take-off then returned to my job in the workshop. Some time later I heard the familiar sound of a Beau flying overhead, above low cloud. I hastened to the the DF wagon where I found the operator, who because he was wearing headphones, had not heard the aircraft; and as he had not made regular checks with the aerial switch had continued giving the same bearing, which was now the reciprocal.

No more calls were received while I stood by but shortly I heard a Beau landing. It was with some trepidation that I approached the pilot, but I got an enthusiastic response. 'What a marvellous piece of gear that is, I followed the bearings given and when I dropped down through the muck I was directly over Comilla (another airstrip 50 miles from Feni) — I knew my way back from there so I did not bother with more bearings.'

I was too taken aback to tell the truth, and he went off to the mess with a glowing report to the other pilots on what a wonderful new navigational aid we now had. The RT operator got a right earful from me — he never made the same mistake again. I like to think our DF wagon proved helpful on many occasions afterwards.

Tactics of Beaufighters in South East Asia

The tactics developed by the 224 Group Beaufighters were similar to the interdicting ground attacks in other theatres but were adapted to the Burmese terrain, the weather, transportation infrastructure, the Japanese style of deployment and radar capability. 27 Squadron was the first in the air and 'learned by doing', at some cost to themselves. 177 and 211 Squadrons were guided by their experience and adapted their own variations relatively quickly.

The targets for the Beaufighter squadrons were principally trains and locomotives, followed by motor transport, river and ocean shipping and barges, oil pipelines and installations, airfields and radar stations. Initially river steamers were the principal targets but the large vessels known from before the war were soon all sunk or burned (Figure 16). Thereafter railways received the most attention, particularly the main line north from Rangoon (Figure 17) and the Bangkok line which just became operational at the start of the dry season of 1943–44. Initially it was too remote for the Beaufighter Squadrons to attack but, as aircraft with long-range tanks in the wings came into service, it received increasing attention from February 1944 onwards. Airfields, although risky targets, were frequently attacked in the first year (Figure 18). Motor transport, Japanese army trucks, (Figure 19) staff cars and fuel trucks were always priority targets but, although the results of daylight attacks were usually obvious, during the night when they were most active, results were much less so. Oil installations and pipelines (Figure 20) were common targets; the first were dangerous because of intense flak arrayed in defence. Coastal freighters (Figure 21) became a fairly common target after September 1944 when a major attack at Kalegauk Island in the Gulf of Martaban took place. When the Japanese occupied Burma they commandeered all native vessels, as they did the trains, and set about constructing wooden coasters and hundred-foot steamers (Saunders, 1954, p.346). Hence in the Gulf and the delta, seagoing Tavoy schooners (Figure 22), newly built river steamers (Figure 60) and self-propelled barges became important targets. These increasingly carried troops and supplies because of the shortfall of troop and freight delivery by the Burma–Siam railway through both poor engineering and airforce attacks. Also the Japanese were rapidly losing normal freighters in the Pacific and Indian Oceans and none attempted the passage to Burma but transferred their loads at Penang, Malaysia (Kinvig, 1992, pp.177–178). Secondary targets included country river craft, junks and smaller sampans, (Figure 23) which carried large quantities of freight for the Japanese, demonstrated when they frequently burst into flames with towering columns of black smoke when attacked (Figure 24). Actually pilots were even supposed to attack convoys of bullock carts in central Burma, for they too carried freight and food for the Japanese. These were unpopular targets to most pilots and were generally ignored.

Figure 16 S.S. *Maha* paddle steamer on the Chindwin near Monywa on fire after the fourth cannon attack, 1 October 1943 by F/O J.C. Van Nes in VL628. Two smaller boats alongside used for overloads at low water (J.C. Van Nes).

Figure 17 Locomotive boiler blown during an attack of a train in central Burma (P.H. Baldwin, King's College London).

Figure 18 Two Oscars in revetments on Lashio airfield under attack by S/L H.B. Hunt, 1944 (W.G. Herr).

Figure 19 Japanese lorry on fire after attack, Beaufighter shadow in foreground (A.H. Reick).

Figure 20 Oil pipeline set alight at Okkan north of Rangoon, 15 December 1944 Beau shadow in foreground (A. Sutherland Brown).

Figure 21 Small coaster in the Gulf of Martaban under attack, February 1945 (J.W. Harper).

52

Figure 22 Seagoing Tavoy schooners carried freight and troops for the enemy (J.D. Marquis).

Figure 23 Sampans sailing up the Irrawaddy carrying freight (J.D. Marquis).

Figure 24 Sampan carrying oil drums for the enemy, burning after attack (A.H. Rieck).

Avoidance of radar was a major factor governing the style of operations of the Beaufighter squadrons. Japanese radar stations were apparently fairly widely dispersed and may not have been technologically very advanced. Burmese terrain lent itself to disciplined aircrew avoiding early warning by flying low and using topography to advantage. Beaufighters crossing the Chin Hills for offensive patrols in central Burma barely crested the ridgetops even in bad weather and sped down the eastern side at tree-top height out of radar view. When fuel endurance was not a problem crews attempted to confuse potential ground observers in the hills by course changes. Along the plains and lowlands most pilots barely cleared the trees. However when one intersected the railway to follow it, one had to assume the enemy would be alert. The evidence confirmed that they were, because we were met by light flak at most stations. We were thankful that flak was rarely mounted on the trains. To thwart warning we generally did not just stooge down the line but frequently would switch from the main line to branch lines or roads. In operations along the rivers there was little warning to the river boats of impending attack. Most of the fleet of big river boats was sunk during early strikes.

On operations against southern Burma, shipping along the Arakan or Tavoy coasts or along the Bangkok railway, pilots generally flew down the coast at wave-top height just out of sight of land to Cape Negrais west of the Irrawaddy (Bassein) delta before laying a course for their target area; again to foil radar and observers. However, we generally flew past the lighthouse at Oyster Island near Akyab at the start of our sorties to avoid a fuel-wasting wide circuit, so we assumed information was broadcast that operations were under way even if they could not know the destinations.

The Japanese transport system was soon driven to operate mostly at night because of the intensity of Beaufighter attacks. Hence operations had to be geared to take advantage of the night and the moon periods. Thus the two weeks bracketing the full moon were the time of greatest activity for Beaufighter crews when over half the sorties were flown at night. In addition, strikes against trains, motor transport and airfields were commonly mounted at first or last light, necessitating a long flight at night along the deck one way or the other with or without the moon. Ground attacks at night with a veiled moon or during the monsoon were hazardous undertakings but most pilots felt comfortable and somewhat protected by the night.

Most sorties were mounted against targets of opportunity (sometimes called rhubarbs) related to a specific area with a secondary target designated in case of low clouds or other reasons. Initially operations were mostly conducted by sections of two aircraft but as the war progressed more and more were flown by single aircraft. On some occasions flights of four would fly to an initial point together, there to split up and patrol in opposite directions. Operations requiring four or more Beaus were rarer and would be mounted at specific major targets such as airfields or marine shipping. Some unusual operations were conducted, such as low-level night attacks against searchlights at Rangoon while Liberators were bombing from above, or searches for radar stations or intruder operations at night around major airfields such as Meiktila, looking for vulnerable Japanese aircraft landing or taking off. Sorties were also flown to try to find missing aircraft crews at sea or on land and to protect convoys bound for Calcutta or Chittagong.

During low flying patrols, pilots would pull up sharply from tree-top heights to a couple of hundred feet to observe ahead and to aid map-reading navigation, then dive back to the deck again. On finding a target — locomotive, boat or motor transport (MT) — the pilot would also pull up sharply, manoeuvre for a line of attack, then dive while firing the cannons or rockets. Normally we would pull out in a steep turn to observe damage, to prepare for another attack or to take evasive action. Imagine the feelings of the navigator facing backwards in the dorsal cupola during these manoeuvres.

The style of attack against different target types varied and most pilots followed similar patterns after experience had accumulated. Against shipping the most effective method proved to be shallow dives from amidships firing at the waterline followed by quarter attacks raking the superstructure to set it alight. Unless a ship was docked, flak was seldom intense so that attacks could be made until the ship was destroyed. Steeper dives were advantageous in rocket attacks because of the curved trajectory of the projectiles (Figure 59). Locomotives were generally attacked in fairly steep dives (up to 30 degrees) from the quarter until steam emission indicated that the boiler was blown or the fire box was destroyed (Figure 45) and then the carriages or box cars were raked. Even small railway stations were protected by flak and the larger ones on the main or Bangkok lines provided intense defence. Nevertheless pilots generally made two to four attacks.

Locomotives in shelters forced Beaufighters to attack along the railway line which increased the hazard from flak and made cannon attacks less effective (Figure 65). Motor vehicles on the open plains in daylight in the dry season were readily sighted and attacked (Figure 56) but most were encountered in forested hilly terrain or at night. Haste then became important, as vehicles would get off the road and under tree cover quickly and at night would extinguish their masked headlights. Attacks had to be made immediately at whatever angle was possible. Oil production and storage facilities were protected by batteries of heavy to light flak and could only be readily attacked at night and then with only one pass. Pipelines were only defended haphazardly but they could only be attacked where they crossed small gullies (Figure 20). Airfields were invariably well defended, so attacks were generally made at dawn by four to six Beaus in line abreast at low level out of the east. Initially pilots made more than one pass but this later changed. The airfields commonly had enough warning to get their Oscars in the air which caused an additional hazard.

Japanese passive defences included extensive camouflage by nets and leafy branches covering river boats moored at the banks or parked MT; the building of bamboo earth-filled loco shelters at stations; dispersal of freight cars of stationary trains, and operating transportation systems at night. In addition, tracks led to hides and by-pass loops in heavily forested jungle, (Kinvig, 1992, p.175). Their active defence was dominated by light flak, 50-calibre machine guns and Bofors type AA. Heavy flak was mostly positioned about major airfields, oil installations or docks. The Japanese soldiers were normally brave under attack and commonly aimed automatic weapons and rifles at us rather than ducking for cover. Many returning Beaus had random shots through them from this stubborn defence and some were almost certainly shot down. A serious additional hazard for attacking aircraft was isolated trees such as palms which could be hit while the pilot concentrated on the target during the pull out of a diving attack or during evasive action at low level. Japanese fighters, mostly Nakajima Ki.43 Hayabusa (called Army 01s or Oscars), were scarcely faster than Beaufighters unless they jumped us by diving from well above. They had radial engines, clean lines and great manoeuvrability but were lightly armed and unarmoured. They were not particularly feared by us because of their lack of a real speed advantage and the fact that they were unlikely to be vectored on to us. Furthermore, they were pretty well driven out of the forward airstrips by the end of 1943 and thereafter only came up for specific operations. Nevertheless they did shoot down some of our aircraft and a few of them were shot down by Beaufighters or destroyed on the ground. A more deadly plane was USAAF Lockheed Lightnings in the hands of pilots not well trained in aircraft recognition. They shot down at least two Beaus from our Wing over the Tangup Pass.

8

Life and Death on the Squadron

Morale

> The aircrew of 177 Squadron had no qualms about who the enemy was or how we were contributing to his defeat (Sutherland Brown, 1992, p.25). We probably had a weaker sense of aiding in the freeing of Burma or the protection of India. You don't ask twenty year olds to be philosophers and if you did, you would probably not have very effective warriors. We did not talk or think about it much but we knew Nazism was evil although at the time the full extent of the depravity was unknown. We also knew the Japanese were aggressors who had been trying to enslave and pillage eastern Asia for more than a decade. Countries like Burma that at first welcomed them to some degree as a means to end colonialism, within a year were resisting them passively and by guerrilla tactics. (Thakin Nu, 1954).

Our life on the squadron was motivated by these scarcely discussed attitudes but it was driven by routine, by a love of flying, by companionship, by a sense of fun, and more personally, by hope and by fear. The morale of the aircrew under the stress of severe losses always appeared to be good. Although it was supported by conviction of the rightness of our efforts, these other aspects, partly frivolous, played a major role. George MacDonald Fraser (1992, p.73) reveals a widely perceived attitude when he says of his service as a rifleman in the 14th Army, 'My parents knew I was in Burma and that (with the possible exception of air crew) it was generally believed to be the worst ticket you could draw in the lottery of active service.' This attitude was not held by the aircrew of 177, and a search for the reason must consider the excitement, especially for pilots, of limitless low flying. The aircrew were barely adults and the rewards of this excitement to most of them must have outweighed the risks. Friendship was a support but less than might be imagined. Amongst those at the frontline airstrips, friendships tended to be sincere but shallow, inhibited by a fear of possible loss. Friendship among many survivors today is much stronger and deeper. We were thrown together by

59

Figure 25 Aircrew at dispersal outside Ops room, Chiringa, November 1944 (A. Sutherland Brown).

chance, having no common geographic origins and not much of common background, except flying. Still we probably had our share of pride in not wanting to let the side down.

The record of aircrew was not perfect as regards courage, how could it be when danger affects people so differently? A few were overcome with fear that was part of our daily lives. W/O James Denny wrote the following:

> It was while I was on 177 Squadron that I encountered the so called 'LMF' (Lack of Moral Fibre) for the first time in my RAF career. During my time there we had two cases of pilots who felt unable to cope with Beaufighters, particularly at night. Both had apparently asked to be transferred to operations on other types of aircraft but they were court marshalled and reduced to the ranks and posted. This treatment seemed harsh at the time but without being in possession of all the facts, one is not in a position to judge.

Separation of the aircrew into commissioned and non-commissioned ranks was accepted generally as a British fact but it was almost certainly detrimental to morale and efficiency. On multi-engined aircraft with crews of seven or so and with stratification of skills it was not as difficult to accept, but with two-man crews it separated us on a basis most of us could not understand. That it was not based on education, social standing or graces was proved by the continuous flow of non-

60

commissioned aircrew on the squadron to commissioned rank. What the division did was to separate us in our messes and in broader friendships. It certainly did not help for crews of mixed status, who were dependent in the air on their cohesion, to be drawn apart on the ground. Generally in our life at dispersal (Figure 25), in briefings, at lectures or on leaves, little attention was paid to it.

Groundcrew morale appeared to be generally good considering the restrictions placed on them, particularly on leave in India. Discipline was very relaxed at the forward airstrips; no saluting, rare parades and no real formality. The groundcrew appreciated the relaxed attitude on an operational squadron and responded to it. As Ted Bellingham, a former WT mechanic, points out:

> [The need for discipline] was overshadowed by morale and pride. This was borne out when Lord Louis inspected the Squadron lined up on the runway, shirtless, some hatless and none too clean. While he was actually carrying out his inspection, aircraft returned from an operation. Without a word and with no hesitation, the groundcrews of those aircraft broke ranks to greet them. As far as they were concerned their loyalty and duty to their crews came before even that to the CinC.

Later Lord Louis gave an informal talk to the squadron outside the briefing room (Figure 26).

Figure 26 The Supreme Commander, Lord Louis Mountbatten, talking to Beaufighter squadrons, December 1944, outside 177 Ops room, Earl of Bandon, AOC 224 Group second on his right in a bush hat (W.E. Bellingham).

The air force was not like the army or the navy where small units operated and fought together as officers and men, sharing common danger and experiences. The aircrew were exposed to danger regularly as crews off by themselves. They knew they were very dependent on the knowledge, skills and diligence of the technical groundcrew but they had relatively little shared experience with them. Most aircrew had a good relationship with the ground-crews, with much joshing and mutual respect. However this scarcely extended to friendship and only the most sensitive aircrew were seriously concerned with their welfare. Another reason for the lack of strong bonds between air- and groundcrew on 177 was that no aircrew had a 'private' aircraft. You might have a favourite Beau, but you shared it with others and flew whatever plane you were assigned. Even the COs flew a variety of aircraft. This prevented close relationships being established with specific groundcrews, but had other benefits such as general aircraft readiness and 'democracy' rather than privilege. As Norman Bolitho reports:

> George [W/C Nottage] has emphasised recently that he did not want to have a particular aircraft designated as ours. His attitude was that he should fly any aircraft that was serviceable and therefore no one could say that we had one that was specially looked after... One drawback to this was that I certainly did not build up any relationship to our 'erks'. When George and I returned to the Squadron after our walk [escape from behind enemy lines] we were immediately surrounded by members of the Squadron and he spotted one of the airmen who seemed to him to be looking a bit worried so he found the opportunity to go over to him and talk. It turned out that this man serviced the aircraft we had flown and was concerned that he had in some way failed in the skill he had used and that we had crashed because of an aircraft defect. He was cheered immensely when George told him that it was Japanese fire that had caused the problem. I for one had never realised that our groundcrew could be so concerned when their aircraft failed to return.

For a similar view from a sister Squadron (211) one can quote A.M. Browne (1995, p.30):

> As I have said, the Squadron was a happy place and so was the Wing. For every man who actually fired at the enemy in the Second World War there were said to be forty in uniform supporting him. Combatants were sometimes apt to resent non-combatants, who in

turn counter-resented their arrogance. This was not so at Chiringa. The ground-crews were devoted and thorough, working always in the open, in withering heat or pelting rain, and delivering our aircraft in as near mechanical perfection as one could get.

Part of the lack of personal relationships between the air- and groundcrews was because the former were so young and had enough of their own worries. Welfare and concern for the groundcrew rested upon the older officers, CO, Adj and MO, as well as some younger ones that had auxiliary duties for sport and recreation. The administration facilitated the other ranks in their leaves, encouraged them in outlets such as sport and recreation and provided sympathetic hearings for problems and grievances. However the Adjutant, a free-spirited Australian, aided squadron efficiency and morale by unilaterally posting personnel who were a problem either way to pools in western India. With the poor efficiency of low-class communication in the Command it was months before questions could be raised.

The airmen's own efforts were the driving force in sport and recreation but the whole squadron was the beneficiary of these activities. As the squadron matured, the level of these activities increased so there were several choices most evenings and standdown days. We were all hundreds to thousands of miles from friends, relations, pubs and regular entertainment. The forward airstrips were seldom the recipients of visits by ENSA, the British Forces entertainment organisation, or other entertainers, although Vera Lynn visited us twice. Her performances were highlights. As the war progressed into Burma and towards a culmination, the squadron had more visits by entertainers and a real basha cinema. However, the airmen were mainly reliant upon themselves. They produced a magazine at irregular intervals (*The Gen*) full of poetry, satire, cartoons (Figure 27 and cf. Figures 51 & 52) and fiction, most of which reflected their situation (Appendix 7). The administration and the aircrew were not a prominent target of these activities. They also had a band, concerts and fairly regular if raunchy plays, classical record recitals, 'housie-housie' evenings and French lessons. All ranks enjoyed the brief reversal of roles at Christmas when the officers served the airmen their Christmas dinner (Figure 28). However it would be going too far to say there was no grousing or negative attitudes among the ground staff.

The morale of both aircrew and groundcrew was affected by the threat and occurrence of tropical diseases, ranging at the mild end

Figure 27 177 groundcrew's life from *The Gen.*

from the discomfort of prickly heat, tinea and diarrhoea to serious illnesses like dengue fever, jungle sores, malaria, dysentery or sprue. It is fair enough to say that we were seldom 100 percent fit. We hardly went for a month without some form of intestinal disorder and frequently flew when we were in considerable discomfort. Jokes about corks and bungs were not appreciated. Almost all of us, no matter how frequently we bathed, were seldom completely free of fungus infections such as tinea which could be very irritating. Many had serious lesions called jungle sores that could develop at any cut or abrasion. Fevers were also common, even though mepacrine controlled malaria to such a degree that persons getting it were charged with self-inflicted injury. We all had dengue fever at some time or another and it was as bad as malaria if not repetitive. These tropical disorders certainly had a noticeable negative effect on morale although for most it was accepted as a reality of life on the Burma frontier.

A factor that was even harder to evaluate was the remoteness from family, old friends, female company, dances, decent dinners

Figure 28 177 airman's Christmas menu. The vignette shows the CO serving a talker whilst a bored airman and an anxious one wait.

and the aspects of civilised life such as the ability to drop into a pub, cinema, library or museum. We were 'on' the squadron all the time except during our regular leave periods.

Daily Routines and Mess Life

On 177 Squadron each crew flew a sortie about every third day. The squadron had a stand-down with no operations about every ten days to two weeks and aircrew had a two-week leave after three months of operations. Between sorties the schedule was fairly relaxed. Those not on operations travelled in the morning by transport from their messes to the strip and hung around dispersal (Figure 25) and the briefing room awaiting any flying duties such as air tests of aircraft after repairs, ferrying, airfiring practice or swinging (correcting) the aircraft compasses. Some would, depending on their attitudes, spend time reading intelligence reports that could add to their knowledge of the sites of flak batteries, radar stations or possibly Japanese aircraft capabilities or distribution. After lunch there would be more of the same if one did not have administrative or auxiliary duties related to fire prevention, sports, security, bar supplies or mail censorship to perform. Late afternoon saw the crews return to their messes and their bashas where they might read or write letters until near dusk, when the ritual bath was taken to remove the sweat and dust and to fight tinea and more unpleasant skin diseases. Bearers would heat petrol tins of water over an open fire and carry them with their asbestos hands to your bath at the rear of your basha. There one would bathe in a puddle of water in a camp canvas bath like F/O Noel Boyd, RNZAF (Figure 29) or more rarely in the deep luxury of a galvanised tub. Drinks and dinner followed in the mess, and then to bed and perchance to sleep in the humid heat under a mosquito net undressed in a lungyi (Burman sarong) or a towel. Suspended from the roofs were traditional punkas, old carpets attached in line by cord to a reclining punka walla (man) at the end of the basha. Usually the cord was tied to his foot or big toe and he would cause the punkas to swing and creak in unison by raising and lowering his foot. Should he fall asleep while anyone was still awake, a coarse cry of 'Punk you bastard', was likely to ring out. The movement of air was quite substantial and cooling.

Officers, NCOs and airmen at Feni and Chiringa lived in orderly camps near the airfields in bamboo and palm-thatched huts called bashas. The camps were similar in appearance to the local villages although more spacious, (Figures 47 and 51). The rooms in the bashas were fairly commodious (Figure 30) and, if we thought of it at all, we realised we lived in luxury compared to the troops at the front.

A comical view of a routine day was written by Dick White:

66

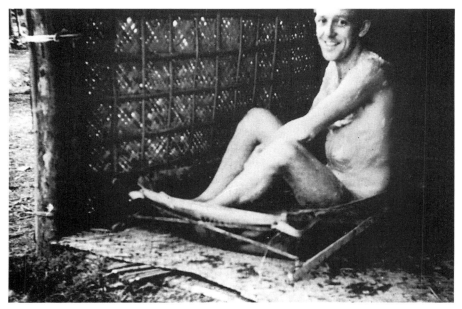

Figure 29 Noel Boyd, RNZAF, enjoying the regulation three inches of hot water in a camp canvas bath at Chiringa (N. Boyd).

Figure 30 Tony Rieck and Tommy Allen's basha with charpoys etc (A.H. Rieck).

We were usually awake when we got to the runway, but not for long. Some of us stayed awake to use our time dutifully to write letters, some had a walk around to see what was going on, some got detailed for a compass-swinging which was an unwelcome interference, but most just lounged in the warm sunshine until we saw the clean white dhoti of the catering contractor pushing his barrow loaded with goodies towards us — then we all assembled for the feast of custard tarts and other wads (buns) and char (tea). We marvelled at the brilliant aerial exploits of the kite-hawks who, having a bird's-eye view, were even better than us in spotting the approach of the tum-tickling delicacies; the birds gave us a display of wheeling, dipping, stalling, dropping, climbing, enough to catch your breath in admiration, but were shut out by the contractor from the feast as they had no rupees or annas to pay for what they took. They had to concentrate on the food we were holding in our hands, and they knew how to do that — just look the other way for a moment, hear the whirring of wings, and the custard tart is out of your hand and up in the sky. Marvellous birds.

Evenings at the messes involved a moderate to large amount of drinking before dinner and possibly after; a few played bridge, shove ha'penny or darts. The majority were drinkers because we knew that intestinal bugs were less likely to strike us. Sometimes we would raise our voices to the tune of a scratchy gramophone singing what would now be called cult songs, *Uncle Bill Has Much Improved* or the like. Dinner may just have been bully beef or spam curry but was conducted with some formality, partly Indian military tradition and partly because we had a fair number of bearers standing behind our chairs in the officers' mess. Occasionally we produced by our own skilled marksmanship black buck venison or green pigeons for dinner. Even rarer was an issue of frozen Australian beef or mutton.

The booze we drank was not our real choice but the best we could get. Beer would have been the first choice of most but little was made in India and the best, Murree beer, was produced in the hills of what is now Pakistan — it never found its way to the Arakan except as rations to the Sergeants' or Airmen's messes. On rare occasions we got an issue of Australian beer which was heaven. Mostly we had to put up with young American rye whiskey or the least poisonous Indian spirits, their gins, Carew's or Hayward's. We managed to test their products nightly, none of us went blind and we were not concerned with long-term effects.

Although the officers in the mess drank a lot, they seldom had a wing-ding because always there were some crews flying at night or early in the morning. The exceptional times were when it was announced that the squadron would be standing down the next day. Then there was sometimes excess. Jim Marquis (F/L, DFC) says of such an occasion:

> On the 22 January 1944 we were on stand down. I had spent the evening at the RAF Regiments Officers Mess, comprising one officer, F/O Jimmy Ashton whom I had known at Agartala with 27 Squadron. He invited me to dinner and we had had a convivial evening so that I got to bed rather late and a bit the worse for wear. I was woken in the dark to be told there was a panic on and I was on ops. When I got to the Mess S/L Gandy, DFC, my pilot at the time, was hanging on to the side of the truck that was to take us to the strip. He needed to, as he and the other crews had all been drinking copiously the night before. The fourth crew were both NCOs and the only ones of the four crews who were completely sober. Apparently one or two large paddle steamers had been sighted on the Irrawaddy. We took off at 07:05 and started to patrol at Mandalay coming down river to Pakkoku, centre of the Burma oil field. My log book reads 'Bofors from Chauk'. We had been flying down the river in two pairs, Gandy and I in the lead, flying as usual at low level, in a day of clear blue sky and brilliant sun. Gandy had just asked, 'What's that ahead Joe?' and I had just replied, 'Oh, it's insignificant', when all around us black puffs rapidly appeared as the Jap flak batteries open up. I was later told by the NCO crew that Gandy had been flying perfect evasive action all the way from Mandalay. In any case we all got back.

With our derated Beaufighters we did not have oxygen, because theoretically we weren't supposed to fly over 10,000 feet and need the gas. Our masks just contained VHF microphones, so we did not have the advantage of the traditional pilot's steadier and hangover cure.

In the Sergeants' Mess a different but parallel life co-existed. Dick White's remembrances, *Bliss in Bengal* put it as follows:

> What can't speak, can't lie: there are photographs showing 177 aircrew living it up, enjoying a good life during their time on the squadron when they're supposed to be enduring wartime hardships. Figure 31 taken on the verandah of a basha at Feni: Maurice Bunn, back to the camera, is kneeling, pumping strongly at a primus to get a tea brew-up going. Maurice's backside is the main part of him pictured; you can't see his face but the calf-length shorts give him away. He likes to be in charge, does Maurice, doesn't mind organising and working while others are lounging, watching and criticising. His reward is to have tea made to his liking. Actually at the time the picture is taken the kettle he is putting on must be the second one preparing for fill-ups because Cyril Hennel, Dick White,

Figure 31 Tea party at the Sergeants' Mess, Feni; left to right, Royce Rayner*, Dickie White, Cyril Hennel, Don Anderson, Vic Vallentine, ? and Maurice Bunn kneeling (D. White).

Royce Rayner and others are already holding mugs. Don Anderson is enjoying a Woodbine free-issue fag. The scene is one of relaxed, luxurious contentment.

The verandah overlooks a pond [a rectangular tank dug below the water table] where a little raft made of boards fixed across a couple of overload fuel tanks is floating gently on the water, and on it are aircrew dozing; exposing every inch of themselves to the rays of the tropic sun. From the distance the scene is one of sleepy, happy airmen with the details obscure.

[Other] nature scenes were created by airmen enjoying a swim in a larger tank to the south; again sans costume, but no one minded except the MO who woke up after several weeks to the fact that the water in that pond could have germs capable of giving us several mortal diseases at once. Didn't worry us — I suppose we thought, if we thought at all, that we could be splashed over the Burmese countryside before the germs had time to incubate. Anyway the MO put the pond firmly out of bounds — not that anyone showed signs of dying as a result of being in it. We reckoned he was a spoil sport, enjoying taking one of our pleasures away...

70

[We would return from Flights] and then pile into the Sergeant's Mess for a tasty meal of soya links or corned beef, whichever was on the day's menu. Then a couple more hours of civilised recreation playing bridge, the mental effort eased by a couple of Murree beers if you hadn't already had your ration, otherwise South African brandy, Rosa rum or Carew's gin. If the dust [thrown up by the ride from dispersal] had given you a sore throat, you cured it instantly by sipping Indian whisky, the fiery germ-killer which left penicillin standing.

A bridge game would mean there were at least 12 airmen in the mess — four to play and eight to watch and criticise — so enough for a session of the Mess Choral Society to finish off the evening singing well-known songs; the start of the concert was the cue for decent members to leave, because the words used were such as came into our heads, not the originals, and not the ones suitable for the hymn-tunes.

The lives of the groundcrew revolved around the routine of the aircrew so as to maintain operational readiness. Some trades had a standard daily routine such as the fitters (engine mechanics) and riggers (airframe mechanics) involved in major repairs. There were no adjacent Maintenance Units. Most of the technical groundcrew were geared to the same rhythm as the aircrew, they were there to see you off and to receive you no matter what time and they had to work on daily inspections (DI), regular maintenance and normal repairs (Figure 32). There were of course no hangars, so they worked in the blistering sun on the heat-reflecting metal hardstand-

Figure 32 Minor inspection of a Beaufighter at Feni (H. Howard).

71

ing tarmac, normally wearing just a pair of shorts and a slouch hat, or in the drenching rain in much the same gear. They had deep tans aided in part by the inadvertent application of engine oil. Their meals were not so elegantly served as those of the officers and they had to line up to get them (Figure 27 and 52) but they had much the same fare, perhaps more Soya links and less bully beef. Their mess hall was commodious and was the site of much of the recreation, housie-housie, bridge, flicks. Their bashas were open bamboo barracks. The cartoons from *The Gen* (Figure 27) illustrate the airmen's life and routines with some humour and cynicism; the confused arousal, the 'sharp pencil' DI, the chief action of the day — to hurry to the char wagon, the sonorous trip to Flights and the haute cuisine.

Leaves

Leaves were eagerly anticipated by the operational aircrew. We received two weeks after each three months of ops. Commonly we flew a Beau into Alipore airfield in downtown Calcutta with two crews aboard for some returning crews to fly back depending on the status of aircraft maintenance. There were rarely any other types of flight from Feni or Chiringa to Calcutta. The only alternative was a tough two days by rail, bus and ferry. We commonly did not have an exact date for leave and in any case it was not the mental attribute of those on operations to plan ahead. Consequently we were always scrambling for accommodation and transportation. Usually we got to Calcutta without difficulty, where you might hitch a flight to Allahabad to go to Nainital or catch a train to Siliguri for Darjeeling. Needless to say train and ferry was the way the groundcrew went most the time.

Oh Calcutta was OK for a day or two with its many clubs, restaurants and nightclubs but most of us preferred to proceed by train to popular Himalayan destinations. India was, and is, a beautiful and interesting country, if somewhat soiled. The hill stations in the Himalayas could be very attractive with their views, temperate climate and scope for activities. Leave for officers offered a full range of these at clubs etc., it was more restrictive for NCOs and very much more so for other ranks. At Nainital the town was wrapped around the kidney-shaped lake with a view from almost everywhere out to the plains or banks of clouds far below. Sailing, riding, tennis, fair restaurants and a social life were all available. The latter consisted largely of drinking at various bars with other service personnel on leave, but at least it was a change. Darjeeling was spread along a complex ridge and much of it had splendid views of Kangchenjunga. Memorable things there, besides the life at the Gymkhana Club, included the ride up the mountain by the toy, narrow-gauge railway that switchbacked its way up at walking speed, wraiths of cloud swirling on the tennis courts and views of orange-coloured Himalayas soaring into the evening sky.

In India there were a few good facilities open to the groundcrew, organised by church groups or military institutes, but mostly they were on their own. They still looked forward to their less frequent leaves and mostly came back in good order.

Dick White's view of a leave of an aircrew NCO was as follows:

Leave in Calcutta made a change from the fascination of life on the squadron. The busy metropolis had a race-course which fielded fine bloodstock and bookies; never saw grey toppers there but anyway the solar topee was the accepted Anglo-Indian style of elegance. Or take your time strolling around the maidan, the open green space dotted with hundreds of Calcuttans taking their ease; then pick your way between the bloodstains on the sidewalk — bloodstains? no, we found that the red splashes were the expectorations of Calcuttans who chewed betel-nut; finally to arrive at Firpo's, the big, lushly-furnished restaurant on Chowringhee Street here to pass the evening enjoying a slap-up meal cooked to any style you wanted.

We didn't spend every evening at Firpo's; the AFI (Auxilliary Forces Institute) always had an attractive bar — more attractive than some of the armed-forces characters you met there — and ran dances most nights; well-played rhythmic dance music, and a good selection of young ladies keen to ease the hardships of suffering aircrew by dancing with them.

Lower Circular Road was out of bounds to the Forces; I looked into one of the brothels there in the course of an innocent enquiry into life in Calcutta but didn't stay long; a black American soldier in the reception room where I was sitting drew a knife from under his coat — blade about four inches long — so the Scottish soldier I was talking to and I left without further enquiry.

Aircrew travel through Bengal wasn't always by Beau — sometimes we had the treat of a free rail–river–road tour of the Indian countryside. The estuary of the River Hoogly between Calcutta and our airfield at Feni needed skirting by rail north-east to the boat quay, then by ferry down to the road head on the eastern side of the delta. When squadron aircraft were not available to carry us back we loaded our luggage on to the train at Sealdah station and settled down to watch the paddy fields pass the window at 15 mph for 10 hours or so. We were not escorted on these tours by a

73

courier, it being wartime, though we didn't lack for company — there were fellow passengers lining the foot-boards of the carriage and some on the roof.

The highlight of the tour, I suppose you would say, was the six hour cruise down the Padma River. A modern (1930s) ferry driven by petrol motors chugged at 4 knots along the placid yellow water teeming with bird life and the occasional water snake lifting its head above the surface. We settled down on the crowded wooden decks; below was unbelievable. No refreshment facilities, but our fellow passengers were well prepared with a mass of little brass bowls carrying home-cooked meals which they obviously found delicious, swallowing their food with the help of chapatis and providing a wealth of spicy aromas to form a true India ambience. Most of us had never been away from our home environment before the war; we found our experience in close contact with India eye-opening though quite unlike the alluring mystic East portrayed in our boys' books.

The final part of the journey in a jolting four hour lorry ride along the rutted roads of east Bengal, unlike any trip in a tour coach. We sat or stood under canvas holding any framework that was available to avoid being thrown to the floor, shouting to be heard, eating and being coated in the pink dust of the flood plain thrown up by the lorry.

Tours of Duty, Losses and Reinforcements

That the aircrew of 177 Squadron had a hazardous operational life is confirmed by the ratio of losses to total number of aircrew. They acquitted themselves exceptionally well, judged by the number of awards for gallantry they received. A tour of operations in the Beaufighter squadrons of 224 Group was nominally 50 sorties or the equivalent to 200 to 250 hours of operational flying. To complete a tour with leaves and allowance for sickness would take 10 months to a year. Only occasionally was a pilot or observer tour-expired with less than 50 sorties, unless they were invalided for sickness or wounds close to this limit. Sickness was one of the factors related to operations; almost all personnel had fairly serious intestinal or skin diseases at some time in their tour that forced them into hospital. Original members of the squadron were starting to become tour-expired by about September to October 1944 and the complexion of the squadron started to change fairly rapidly. All the originals had left by December 1944 and yet the squadron remained very much the same. The culture and attitudes of the old guard was substantially handed over to the new.

The squadron had 160 aircrew that served on operations not counting the detachment to 27 Squadron (Appendix 4A). Of these, 54 became primary aircrew casualties: missing (43), killed on operations (6) or in non-operational accidents (5), and in addition two ground-crew who died from illnesses (Appendix 4B). Not counted among the missing were those captured by the Japanese including the W/C J.E.S. Hill, and his observer F/O G.W. Broughton, F/O C.O. Kidd whose pilot, F/O A.J. Platt, did not survive, Sgt F. Jungalwalla, and F/Lt McMichael and Sgt Dodd from the 27 Squadron detachment. All were found among the released prisoners in June 1945 and had been held at Rangoon without notice. They had been treated by the Japanese as war criminals rather than PoWs. These figures show that a new crew's chance of surviving a tour was one in three. In 1943 and 1944 their chance was actually much less because only two crews were lost after the beginning of 1945.

The relative roles of luck and skill were evaluated differently by different aircrew members. Skill and knowledge were of fundamental importance if a crew was to have a good chance of survival. There's the word — chance. Undoubtedly luck was of equal importance and most successful crews thought they were lucky. Although subject to intense fear at times and a low subliminal level of apprehension all the time, practically no-one thought they would be dealt the card. We all considered ourselves immortal. If we hadn't, our behaviour would scarcely have been as 'press on regardless'.

In most cases the cause of the loss of our aircraft can only be speculated upon. Many sorties were carried out by single aircraft but even during an attack by two or more it was seldom during the intensity of ground attacks that the loss of another Beau was actually seen. Without a doubt, a major cause of loss was intense light flak met at most target areas, particularly railroad stations and airfields. Another probable important cause was the hazard during evasive action at low level of hitting an isolated tree like a palm. Only a handful of squadron planes were intercepted and attacked by Japanese aircraft and only a few were definitely known to be shot down. Most interceptions occurred in the first four months of squadron operations when attacks were relatively numerous.

A.M. Browne (1995, p.24) said of 211 Squadron, '[Losses] were usually unwitnessed, and only the lost crew would ever know, and that momentarily, whether their end had been caused by flak, fighters, the sometimes terrible weather, the mountains, mechanical failure (rare) or simple error of judgement at low level. Very few indeed survived as prisoners. To fall into Japanese hands as air-crew was a fate to be avoided.'

The list of awards granted to aircrew and officers of the squadron is imposing for a new squadron in the hinterland of India with less than two years of operational service (Appendix 5). It included 4 DSOs, 14 DFCs, 2 DFMs and an MBE. The awards single out many individual acts of fortitude but this history attempts to record the skill and bravery of all the aircrew of the squadron and the diligence of the groundcrew.

PART II

OPERATIONS AND
PERSONAL NARRATIVES

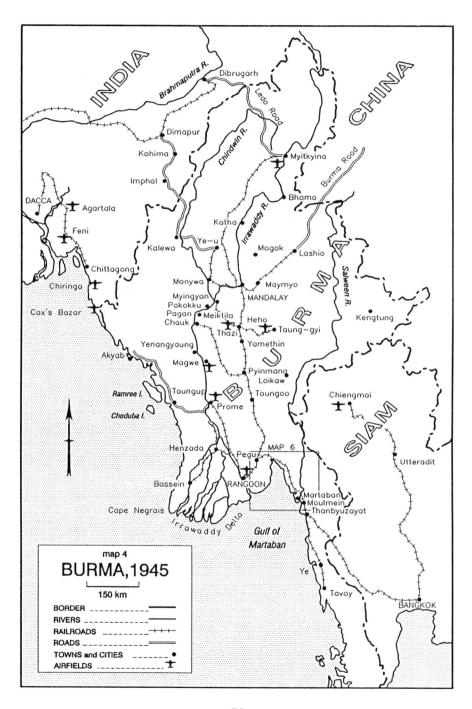

map 4

BURMA, 1945

150 km

BORDER	——————
RIVERS	——————
RAILROADS	———+++—
ROADS	══════
TOWNS and CITIES	———•
AIRFIELDS	——✦

9

The Squadron at Feni, 1943

The Start of Operations, September 1943

The squadron had been at Feni since mid-August and had been training more intensively now that it had an adequate number of aircraft and a range for airfiring. Operations actually started with relatively easy patrols by two Beau VIs down the north coast from Hunter Bay to Taungup on 10 September piloted by the CO, W/C P.H. Baldwin and F/O J.C. Van Nes, RCAF, to attack any shipping or other transport (Map 4). Little was seen except some large native craft used for freighting which were attacked and damaged. Some light flak was encountered near Akyab. Two other aircraft took off later in the day for a similar mission, one had a similar result, the other was damaged by hitting a bird on take-off and aborted the sortie.

Now that two Beaufighter squadrons were interdicting Japanese transportation, a division of labour had to be established between 27 Squadron flying out of Agatala north of Comilla and 177 based at Feni well to the south. Naturally 27 operated mainly in northern Burma and 177 mainly in south and central Burma. The Beau VIs of this period did not have long-range tanks in the wings, so distant operations were conducted by aircraft that landed at one of the advanced fighter strips in the south near Cox's Bazar (correct spelling) or at Imphal to top up with fuel before heading out. Most sorties were only about three and a half hours long, much shorter than those conducted later when the six machine guns in the wings were replaced by long-range fuel tanks.

Feni is a fair-sized village with a few brick buildings (Figure 33) situated on the Ganges–Brahmaputra delta about 15 miles north of Sandwip Channel, the easternmost channel of the rivers, and about 30 miles west of the westernmost of linear ridges that compose the Chin Hills. It is on the railway line between Dacca, Comilla and Chittagong. The airfield was a single paved runway surrounded by mixed fields and woods. Figure 34 shows the technical crew for an aircraft adapted to the Feni conditions. The CO, W/C P.H. Baldwin,

Figure 33   Feni village scene (Howard).

Figure 34   A.J. Kappler with the technical ground crew of his favourite aircraft, 'P' for Peter at Feni, 1943 (J.D. Marquis).

Figure 35 W/C P.H. Baldwin with his Adjutant F/L W.J. Westwood* on the edge of the airstrip at Feni (J.D. Marquis).

and his Adjutant, F/L W.J. Westwood, are shown in Figure 35 on the edge of the strip in the early days at Feni.

The camp buildings at Feni consisted entirely of bashas (bamboo and palm-thatch huts). The Officers' Mess was fairly pleasantly situated around two tanks (rectangular dug drainage and water-storage ponds) on the edge of open woods with scattered mango, grapefruit, breadfruit and palm trees but with rice paddies and some fields of pineapples surrounding it. The fruits provided a supplement to our diet when in season, mostly before the monsoon. The camp latrines were smelly floored pits with foot plates in the oriental fashion.

There was a surprising amount of wildlife in the vicinity, from civet cats and boars to rats, mongooses, scorpions and a few krites (small venomous snakes). There were also many birds of which our favourites were the small green-winged pigeons that sometimes graced our table and black drongos for their aerobatic flight. When the fruit was ripe we would also be inundated with flying foxes (fruit bats). The Officers' Mess kitchen and lounge burned down in March 1944, after which we made do with a small basha with a terrace beside the tank where we used to sit out on the hot evenings having a convivial time, as there was scarcely room for us all inside. This was fine until the rains came and in the hot period immediately before when the evening was alive with flying beetles two inches long and other unknown horrors flying into our hurricane lamps. It was a fairly typical camp in the humid tropical Bengal setting.

Attacking River Shipping, Airstrips and Transport

The targets of offensive patrols in the early days were principally major river boats on the Irrawaddy and Chindwin, followed by trains and forward airstrips. The rivers still had numerous large propeller-driven and paddle-wheel steamers which were a principal means of transporting Japanese soldiers and material to the reserve areas of northwestern Burma. The steamers were commonly heavily camouflaged with nets and tree branches which served them not at all in midstream or when they were moored at river banks in agricultural areas. These shallow-draught steamers were up to 326 feet long and were mostly destroyed in the first month of 177 Squadron's operations. Also, at this time, train traffic was still moving by daylight so there was an abundance of available targets. In addition the Hurricanes based in the southern Arakan did not have the range to attack the forward strips at Magwe and Prome just east of the Irrawaddy, so the Beaufighters were soon pressed into this dangerous role.

The first sorties to have significant results were flown by a Section of two Beaus led by P/O T.C. Clayton with P/O J. Logan and F/O H.W. Street with Sgt J. Walsh. On 14 September on an offensive patrol of the Irrawaddy from Magwe to Prome they encountered and attacked two river steamers, one 200 feet long and a second of 75 feet which were left in flames. By 14 October, a month later, most of the steamers of the upper rivers had been attacked and destroyed, although the Japanese tried to protect them by mounting light flak aboard them. Ten different crews were responsible for this rapid destruction of the upper Irrawaddy fleet, all in bad monsoon weather and with several strikes carried out at night. In all eleven steamers were attacked; seven were left in flames and all the others were damaged.

The interdicting of river traffic was described by W/C Baldwin (1943) as follows:

> While patrolling the waterways of Burma both Squadrons (27 and 177) found plenty of targets... Attacking a variety of rivercraft between Magwe and Chauk on 13 September W/C Baldwin with

82

F/O Matthews and F/Lt Hunt with Sgt. Gibson reported that they knocked pieces off a 200 foot screw-type steamer and 100 foot covered [barge] in addition to numerous [large country craft]. These two aircraft encountered light AA fire receiving bullets in wings and fuselage without causing serious damage...

Steamers and [country craft] were left on fire [after attack] by Sgt. Waddell with Sgt. Mearne and Sgt. Crossing with Sgt. Hall between Monywa and Myingan on 24th September. One 150 foot double deck steamer, one 80 foot, one 50 foot as well as a 35 foot steam launch were attacked repeatedly from the beam and raked from bow to stern. Such was the weight of the attacks that all except the launch were left in flames. A country craft sailing across the river south of Monywa gave proof of its cargo when incendiary bullets started red flames and much heavy black smoke, oil no doubt. These activities attracted some AA opposition, but all that resulted was that one bullet hit the windscreen of one aircraft...

[September] was rounded off with a hunt for a large double-decked paddle steamer which was found and disabled on 1st of October. Although at first this vessel was thought to be the *Shwelan*, a representative of the second largest class of steamers now operating in Burma, later it was proved to be the *Maha*, a third line steamer with a cargo capacity of 250 tons and capable of carrying 2,000 troops.

As a result of photographs taken on the 29th of September the hunt was started on the 30th and ended the next afternoon when three Beaufighters found the vessel on the Chindwin at Alon, a few miles upstream from Monywa where the photographs had picked it up. In all nine sorties were flown in search of the vessel and up to the actual finding of it, other steamers, barges and oil tanks were attacked.

[W/C Baldwin with F/O Buckley] took off at 12:02 hours in JL505 from Feni to start the operation. They searched the Chindwin south of Monywa and the Irrawaddy down to Pakokku and Chauk where they set fire to a 60 foot steamer and attacked an oil tank as well as several rivercraft. [They attacked a 170 foot river steamer at Magwe and strikes were seen. On a second attack intense flak was encountered and the aircraft was hit in the port engine so they broke off, feathered the engine but used it again to climb over the hills even though it was vibrating excessively. As a result the Beau was forced to belly land on the beach south of Cox's Bazar and the crew then walked to Allied lines. The aircraft was a write-off, (ORB)].

Continuing the search the next morning one section of Beaus sighted a 120 foot steamer below Alon and a smaller one south of Monywa but [they were not attacked at that time although others were during the hunt for the *Maha* which was not found until the

1st of October]. Finally two aircraft of 177 Squadron [F/O Van Nes with F/O Matthews and F/O Bayard with P/O Seary] and one from 27 located the *Maha* camoufaged with brushwood at Alon.

Joe Van Nes recalls, 'During the operation we were to pick up top cover of Hurricanes at Chittagong. We met them as scheduled and commenced a normal climb over the hills but the Hurries rapidly fell behind and apparently returned to base.'

Baldwin (1943) continued:

> The 177 aircraft made between them eight attacks with cannons from the beam and quarter with the result that the vessel was left a mass of flames from stem to stern with smoke reaching to 2,000 foot... Photographs (Figure 16) taken during these attacks showed the vessel was burning well and emitting clouds of black, grey and white smoke. Subsequent sorties by both Beaufighters and Photo Reconnaissance Unit (PRU) aircraft have revealed the *Maha* with its upper deck burnt out and the bridge missing lying derelict on a mud bank 17 miles from the scene of attack...

The next day S/L H. Gandy, DFC with Sgt F. Jungawalla and F/L D. Nicholl with Sgt A.H. Bunn sighted the paddle-steamer *Assam* anchored at Myingyan, bows to the bank. This vessel, the largest paddle-wheeler in the world, had also been sought along with the *Maha* and the *Shwelan*. The Beaus made eight attacks in five minutes from abeam and threequarters astern. Blue-grey smoke poured out along the full length of the deck on the starboard side immediately after the last attack and some strikes were seen at the waterline where the engine room should be. The ship was covered with awnings but no camouflage. Flak was seen rising from the ship amidships and also from the nearby bank. One shell holed the port wing of Nicholl's plane and also a large explosion occurred under the fuselage but without causing damage.

S/L Gandy with F/O D.J. Houston and F/O R.K. Weston with Sgt G.D. Pirie also attacked the *Shwelan* at midnight of 14 September, eight miles south of Monywa. Damage was not observed and the attacks could not properly be pressed home because the reflector gunsights of both aircraft failed.

In its first seven weeks of operations 177 Squadron had successfully interdicted the traffic of troops and freight up the rivers by sinking all the large river steamers. Other targets also received sharp attacks during this early phase of operations, including locomotives and trains, MT, oil installations and airfields. These operations resulted in considerable success. The airfield at Magwe was supposed to be attacked at dawn on 19 October but the four Beaus lost contact during the night-time approach and did not carry out a significant strike; however no aircraft were lost. In total the squadron flew 126 sorties during the three weeks of September plus October and, besides the damage to shipping, destroyed 7 locos, damaged 26, damaged a score of railway freight cars, set on fire or damaged 16 oil barges and destroyed or damaged 20 vehicles. During these operations two Beaus went missing. On 8 October F/O R.L. Bayard, RCAF, with P/O L.A. Seary on were seen to enter a cumulo-nimbus storm over the Chin Hills en route to central Burma and did not appear at the target or return to base. Sgt M.H. Crossing, RAAF, with Sgt T.W. Hall disappeared on 10 October on a patrol between the Chindwin and the Irrawaddy. One Beau flown by F/O H.W. Street with P/O J. Logan was ditched after it had been damaged by flak, and there were two crash landings. Many aircraft received damage from light flak or machine guns. Sgt A.J. Kappler with Sgt C. Hennell were the only crew known to be attacked by Japanese fighters during this period. Kappler described the encounter as follows:

> On the 31st of October on a patrol started with F/S D. Rayner, RAAF, and Sgt G. Dinham, our plane was chased by a Zero or an Army 01 (Oscar). Flying east along the deck we were not able to keep ahead while taking evasive action and we were briefly attacked. My engines were overheating dangerously as I had gone through the throttle gate so I climbed towards the clouds at about 1,000 feet... The enemy followed us but we reached the cloud safely still climbing, turned north and after about 15 minutes we returned to an easterly course, coming out of the cloud above Chauk at 6,000 feet. As I came out of the clouds we were attacked again and our plane was hit repeatedly. The fighter followed us for a further 20 minutes making stern attacks as we took evasive action but we eventually reached cloud again and returned to base. Our starboard oil tank was perforated, our starboard tyre punctured and the rudder and underside of the fuselage were hit. Because of the punctured tyre the Beau swung violently on landing at Feni and the plane was pretty much a write-off.

The Burma Campaign in Late 1943

Rear-Admiral Lord Louis Mountbatten, as he was then, had been appointed Supreme Commander of South East Asia Command (SEAC) at the Quebec Conference in August 1943 and actually took command at the new HQ in Columbo in November 1943. His

Deputy was Air Chief Marshall Sir Richard Peirce, KCB, DSO, AFC. The RAF and USAAF were integrated under his command (Air Command South East Asia, ACSEA). American Major General Stratemeyer, second in command of the Air Forces of SEAC, was in charge of Eastern Air Command, in effect, the air effort in Burma, and he was in a parallel position to General William Slim, DSO, MC with the land forces. The Eastern Air Command consisted of:

1. The 3rd Tactical Air Force.
2. The Strategic Air Force.
3. Troop Carrier Command.
4. The Photographic Reconnaissance Force.

At this time about threequarters of the aircraft in the command were RAF (48 squadrons to 17) but the majority of the transport planes were American and the proportion of these was increasing. Many of them were dedicated to freighting over the Hump to China.

The Eastern Air Command HQ was set up in Barrackpore just north of Calcutta while the 14th Army, Tactical Air Force and Troop Carrier Command were all adjacent to each other in Comilla east of the delta and they worked together like a joint HQ (Slim, 1956, p.212).

The Third Tactical Air Force under Air Marshall Sir John Baldwin included:

1. The American Northern Air Sector Force to protect the air transport over the Hump.
2. 221 Group RAF with HQ at Imphal to support 4 Corps of the 14th Army on the central front.
3. 224 Group RAF with HQ in Chittagong to support 15 Corps on the Arakan front. Curiously this Group had never had Air Ministry authority (Saunders, 1954, p.299). Although the Beaufighter Wing, 901, was in 224 Group its operations ranged all over Burma south of Myitkyina and across to Siam and Indo-China.

The Wing consisted of four Beaufighter Squadrons, three on ground attack at the 'front' and a nightfighter unit, 176, at Dum Dum in Calcutta. The ground-attack squadrons were formed or reformed one after another and became operational between February 1943 and January 1944 as shown in the accompanying table. The air and groundcrew of the individual squadrons did not have a lot to do with each other, except that the original aircrew of

	27 Squadron	177 Squadron	211 Squadron
FORMED	1916	Jan. 1943	1917
Re-formed	Sept. 1942		Aug. 1943
BASE	Amarda Road	Amarda Road	Phaphamau
		Phaphamau	
		OPERATIONS	
BASE	Agartala	Feni	Bhatpara
Dates	Feb. 1943–Feb. 1944	Sept. 1943–May 1944	Jan.–May 1944
			Feni
			May–June 1944
REST	South India		
	Feb.–Sept. 1944		
TRAINING	Ranchi	Ranchi	
	Sept.–Oct. 1944	June–July 1944	
RE-GROUP	Dohozara		
	Oct. 1944		
		OPERATIONS	
BASE	Chiringa	Chiringa	Chiringa
Dates	Nov. 1944–Mar. 1945	Aug. 1944–June 1945	July 1944–May
			1945
	Akyab		
	Mar.–June 1945		
Disbanded	Mingladon	Hathazari	Bangkok
	Feb. 1946	July 1945	Feb. 1946

177 had a detachment with 27 to introduce them to operations in Burma. Otherwise it was not until November 1944 that we all shared the same base at Chiringa. Only a handful of operations were run on a wing basis. By the time the squadrons were all on the same base they were pretty set in their ways and there was a minimal of social contact except on the soccer field.

An extensive campaign planned by the high command was approved at the Cairo Conference in November 1943, and it was to be pressed home during the dry season of 1943–44. The plans called for numerous amphibious landings originating from Ceylon to the Andaman Islands and the Arakan, and a major air drop in northern Burma as well as advances into Burma on four fronts. However the resources allocated to support these initiatives were withdrawn as a result of Churchill and Roosevelt trying to placate Marshall Stalin at the Tehran Summit a week later, and to lend priority to the opening of the Second Front. An effective combined operations offensive campaign in Burma was thus eliminated. What was left was for the present forces of the 14th Army to attempt the long march into southern Burma from Imphal, and down the Arakan. Brigadier Wingate's second long-range penetration operation was to proceed and General Stilwell's Chinese Army was to advance on Myitkyina from the north (Slim, 1956, pp.212–222).

The Imperial Japanese Army was being steadily reinforced by major deployments from the Pacific and New Guinea theatres, so that early in 1944 there were three armies in Burma: the 28th in the Arakan, the 33rd on the border of Assam and the 15th in northern and northeastern Burma. Many of the new forces came via the Bangkok railway even though its capacity was only about a third to a quarter of what was planned (Kinvig, 1992, p.176). The shortfall in freight and troop movements was caused as much or more by Beaufighter attacks on the engines and rolling stock and the bombing of the bridges by Liberators as by poor design and construction. Also the Japanese made extensive use of new wooden coasters built in Burma for freight from the Pacific and these also came under sharp attack by the Beaufighter squadrons. The resulting supply difficulties had a melancholy and generally unrecognised impact on the Japanese offensive and retreat.

The Japanese also had allies in Burma that they scarcely trusted to fight but hoped to use in India — the Indian National Army (INA), which was composed of turned Indian troops. The INA had headquarters at Pyinmana and were nominally under the command of the Indian puppet government of Subhas Chanda Bose. Also originally on the Japanese side was the Burma Defence Army (BDA), which was formed to fight for freedom from British rule but soon established clandestine relations with the Allies to act against the Japanese, the more so as time proceeded (Thakin Nu, 1954).

The Japanese Air Force had a basic disadvantage in that it was entirely under army control. In the order of battle it was the 5th Air Division reporting to General Kawabe in Rangoon. It had no truly strategic component or thinking. As of mid-1943 the Japanese had about 740 aircraft in Southeast Asia, of which 370 were in Burma and north Siam (Saunders, 1954, p.311) and about 200 of these were Nakajima 01 single radial engined fighters (Oscars) based at Aungban, Chiengmai, Heho, Meiktila, and Mingaladon.

The Allies planned operations had varied results, but for the Beaufighter squadrons the broad objectives remained the same: interdict the supply routes throughout Burma and Siam, aid in the domination of the air by airfield attacks and provide detailed photo intelligence at low levels. The emphasis in interdiction changed as the war progressed and intelligence revealed the patterns of Japanese aggression and movement. First, the large river steamships were attacked and destroyed; then the roads and railways of central Burma received primary attention; and as the picture of Japanese advance into the Arakan became clear, attention was directed to motor transport through the Taungup Pass. This was followed by severe attacks on the new railway from Bangkok to Moulmein as it was completed and military traffic started to flow, because the range of the Beaufighters was increased with installation of wing tanks. However the whole gamut of targets were watched and attacked and the Burmese and Siamese airfields were swept as PRU revealed activity on them.

Interdicting the Roads and Railways of Central Burma

Once the rivers of Burma had been stripped of significant shipping, 177 Squadron's priority turned to making rail and road traffic as difficult as possible for the enemy. The intensity of the attack drove the Japanese to build loco shelters, to disperse railway freight cars during the day and to operate trains at night. They also sharply increased their light flak and machine-gun defences along the railways. In addition, motor transport began to move in convoys at night protected by flak nests and truck-mounted 50-calibre machine guns. The Beaufighter squadrons countered such measures by mounting strikes against the main enemy airstrips of central Burma: Magwe and Prome east of the Irrawaddy and Heho in the western Shan Plateau. They also increased their night operations, particularly in the two-week moon window.

In late 1943 the Beaufighter squadrons in Burma began experimenting with large fixed cameras in the nose-housing of the aircraft, and also in the flare chute in the belly with a 45-degree mirror facing aft which was not successful (Baldwin, 1943). The intentions were to aid PRU by low-level photos of hidden and camouflaged targets, to record the damage of Beaufighter attacks and to produce photos for propaganda purposes. The recording of damage was spectacularly successful and soon became the principal use of the cameras. A Fairchild F24 camera with a five-inch lens mounted in the nose, produced sharp 5x5 inch images. Initially there was a serious problem with condensation resulting from the descent from the cold conditions of 10,000 feet to the hot and humid conditions of the plains. This was rectified by simply removing the glass register plate. Also the camera shutter tended to run away until it was geared down to about 50 shots per minute. Shutter release was controlled by a lever operated by the right index finger separately from the cannons which were fired by an adjacent thumb button on the control stick. By November most 177 Beaufighters were fitted with these cameras and were taking operational photos. Naturally the successful camera adaptation in Burma was soon applied in the UK Beau and Mosquito squadrons.

During the last two months of 1943 the squadron flew 159 sorties of which 42 were at least partially at night. The most difficult operations were the two low-level airfield attacks: first on Heho and then on Magwe. Four Beaus were led to Heho on 25 November by W/C Baldwin with Sgt J.H. Gibson, W/O G. Herr with Sgt F.H. Burton, F/S W. Watson with Sgt J. McKenzie and F/O H.W. Street with F/O J. Logan. The attack was supposed to take place at dawn coming from the east out of the rising sun. However departure was delayed because one of the selected Beaus was unserviceable and consequently the sun was well up before the attack began. Worse still there was no surprise. The Japanese clearly had early warning of the impending strike for they had all their fighters in the air as the Beaus approached. The number of Oscars in the air was estimated from more than six to thirty. The flak was intense even among the enemy planes. There were no aircraft on the ground and the only targets were MT and fuel facilities. Only one attack was made under these circumstances and as the Beaus departed they were followed for some distance by the Oscars. No-one saw an attack on Street's aircraft but it did not return to base so it is presumed he and Logan were shot down.

The attack on Magwe two days later on 27 November was led by F/L Hunt with F/O L.A. Clark, F/O J.C. Van Nes with F/O J.T. Matthews, F/O M. Adamson with F/O D.J. Houston and F/S D. Rayner with Sgt G. Dinham. The four aircraft attacked line-abreast in the early afternoon. The attack was more successful than Heho because surprise was achieved and four aircraft were damaged on the ground as well as some MT, buildings and a possible flak position (Figure 36). The Beaus left the strip and patrolled the nearby roads and river and damaged four more lorries. No aircraft were lost.

These attacks provoked the Japanese to retaliate. On the morning of the next day, 28 November, a formation of 12 Army 97 bombers with fighter escort attempted to attack Feni (ORB, p.84). Warning was received about an hour before the attack and four Beaufighters were scrambled to intercept. Two Japanese bombers and four fighters detached themselves from the main formation and bombed from the south at 09:00 hours, undershooting the main strip and hitting Feni village with 10 bombs. The rest of the formation made a sweep to the

90

Figure 36 Strike against Magwe airfield on 27 November 1943. Although nothing much seems to be happening, four enemy aircraft were damaged on the ground as well as installations and the air is full of light flak (J.C. Van Nes).

west, turned east to bomb the strip north of its centre. Ten sticks were released and all undershot by 2–300 yards; more than 40 bombs were dropped (of which 10 were large). The two formations joined and flew away in an easterly direction. Cannon and machine-gun fire were heard overhead. Two radial-engined fighters, presumably Oscars, detached themselves from the main formation and dived towards the strip but broke away when Bofors opened fire. Casualties inflicted against the enemy are not known but three villagers were killed and three Indian troops were slightly injured.

About this time a Japanese reconnaissance plane was shot down by Spits near Feni. When the dead pilot was laid out in sick quarters, his penis was found to be tied with string to prevent leakage. An army officer examining the corpse said, 'Do fighter pilots always fly like that?' The Japanese aircraft were very light, without many of the safety features or armour we had, but this seemed excessive. We at least had neoprene bladders to urinate into in an emergency, but with our general copious perspiring we seldom needed them.

Attacks on Heho and Magwe continued in December but the tactics were changed to attacks by two aircraft at night. Some damage was caused to buildings and fires were started but no aircraft were seen on the ground. The Beaus continued after these attacks with offensive patrols of roads, railways or river, causing some additional damage.

The offensive patrols against locos, trains and motor transport continued successfully. During these last two months of the year, 32 locos were damaged and two trains destroyed with an enveloping fire while many freight cars were damaged. Rivercraft were rarely seen as they had mostly been destroyed but the S.S. *Assam* was eventually found and damaged so it could be destroyed the following day by USAAF bombers. Two small steamers were also set on fire. The traffic of lorries over the Taungup Pass to the west coast, the main supply route to the Arakan front, was attacked repeatedly and a great many vehicles were damaged or destroyed in night attacks, but only those that burned could definitely be claimed. For the first time the squadron experimented with using 40 lb bombs but the results were not impressive. The well-defended installations in the oilfield along the Irrawaddy north of Magwe were hit repeatedly with mixed results. The crews of F/L A.P. Wills with F/S J.H. Gibson and F/O J.C. Van Nes with F/O J.T. Matthews are pictured (Figure 37) at the Feni Officers' Mess with the CO after returning from the first night attack on the oil tank farm at Myaungla of the Yenangyaung oil field. The squadron also took part in air–sea rescue operations and convoy escort duty.

In addition to the incident during the first Heho airfield attack, enemy fighters attacked squadron aircraft on five separate occasions. One Beaufighter flown by F/S W. Watson with Sgt J. McKenzie hit a tree during evasive action from two Oscars and damaged a wing but was able to return to base. Another aircraft flown by F/O J. Lottimer with F/O R.A. Watson also hit a tree while pressing home an attack and lost much of its starboard wing tip and jammed the aileron (Figure 6). It too returned to base with the help of the observer to counter the strain generated by the jammed aileron.

Five aircrews were lost in these two months and another Beau was

Figure 37 Aircrew are shown at the Feni Mess after a successful night attack against the oil tank farm at Myaungla of Yenanyaung oil field on 13 November 1943; from the left, F/O J.C. Van Nes, F/O T. Matthews, the CO, W/C P.H. Baldwin, F/L A.P. Wills and F/S J.H. Gibson (J.C. Van Nes).

ditched but the crew recovered. Luck played its devious role in some of these losses. F/O W. Roberts with F/L Hickie crashed early in November on a night take-off in bad weather and were both killed — F/L Hickie died in hospital of his injuries. Wally Robert's regular navigator, Joe Marquis, was in hospital at the time with a septic lesion from a jungle sore and had to listen to the cries of his dying replacement. Also F/O Street with F/O Logan did not return from the Heho raid later in the month. In December two crews went missing near Ramree Island; one flown by Sgt C.A. Grant with Sgt C.S. Morgan separated from their leader and then disappeared. No trace was found of it and one of the search planes piloted by F/S K.J. Barwick with F/S P. Mead also went missing but ditched near Cox's Bazar. Both got ashore by dingy and walked into contact with the army. F/O M.W. Adamson with F/O D.J. Houston were seen to crash after being hit by flak near the Meiktila airfields on the last day of the year.

The first four months of operations by 177 Squadron got it well and truly initiated into all facets of its role in the air war in Burma. W/C P.H. Baldwin (Figure 35) had arrived at the squadron when things were fairly chaotic, he had brought it to order and launched it into successful operations. Officers of the squadron were photographed in early November (Figure 38) but five present would not make it to the New Year. Although casualties were severe on the squadron it had performed exceptionally well during its baptism in the novel conditions of ground attack against a well-armed enemy in a tropical country of diverse topography. The standards of courage, skill and perseverance shown in these first four months were those set for the rest of the life of the unit.

Figure 38 The squadron officers in November 1943. Top row left to right; F/O Street*, F/O Taylor, F/O Lottimer, P/O Houston*, P/O E. Lovett, F/L Hickie*, F/O Watson; middle row, F/O Van Nes, P/O Buckley*, F/O Kay, Sigs, F/L Rutter, MO, F/O Clarke, F/O Marquis, F/O Matthews; bottom row, F/L Wills, F/L Nicholls, S/L Gandy, W/C Baldwin, F/L Hunt, F/L Westwood*, Adj., F/O Scilley, EO (J.D. Marquis).

10

Operations From Feni, 1944

Taungup Pass and the Arakan Waterways

January 1944 was not a very successful month for the squadron, in part because of surprisingly poor weather at this time of year so that only 67 sorties were mounted. In addition two crews were lost. On 2 January F/O H.S. Botell with the Adjutant F/L W.J. Westwood as a passenger were killed in an accident flying from Feni to Comilla, and on 29 January F/S H.I. Highfield with F/S F.N. Jungalwalla went missing on return from a successful operation as number two to F/O G.R.Taylor in which three MT were destroyed between Magwe and Prome. On the return the flight leader lost contact with the second Beau and was not aware they were in difficulty, or that they had sent an SOS which was received at base. A search the next day turned up no information. Actually the pilot was killed in the crash but F/S Jungalwalla was captured and was eventually released from the Rangoon gaol at the end of the Burma war.

F/L W.J. Westwood (Figure 35) had been with the squadron since Amarda Road days as Adjutant. He was a likeable individual, called Wizzy by one and all, quiet, companionable and efficient. His loss seemed in many ways worse than operational losses, and he was missed greatly. F/S F.N. Jungalwalla, called Jumbo, was unique in that he was an Indian (Goan) Parsee in the RAF. He was originally S/L Gandy's navigator but teamed up with F/S Highfield after F/L Hickie was killed with F/O Wally Roberts and F/O Marquis went with Gandy. Jumbo was fairly tubby before he was captured and incarcerated in the Rangoon gaol but emerged lucky to be alive and very much thinner.

During January and February the majority of the operations were directed to attempts to interdict the Taungup Pass and the eastern coastal road and waterways. The target selection was geared to intelligence of the build-up of Japanese forces in the Arakan in preparation for their offensive feint there late in the February, before their main thrust later in Manipur. However the

95

Taungup Pass road was very difficult to attack day or night because it wound through the jungle-covered, complexly dissected terrain of the pass and was rarely exposed for much more than 50 yards. Also the steep hills close to the road allowed few effective angles of attack. Furthermore, at night it was frequently veiled in mist and truck convoys quickly doused their lights upon attack. To be successful, a strike had to be initiated immediately on sighting without much manoeuvring for line. Also the pass and its termini were stoutly defended by LMG and light flak. The waterways were scarcely easier to attack as the shores were overhung with trees along the indented and island-studded coast. It was not only difficult to attack in these areas but the results were seldom confirmed. Only a handful of MT appeared to be damaged in all these patrols.

Even though January was not an effective month, the squadron still damaged five locomotives and numerous railway cars, destroyed six MT, a steam roller, a 30-foot steamer and a covered barge as well as some native craft.

Commanding Personalities in 1944

The command of the squadron changed on 17 January when W/C Baldwin went to 231 Group in Calcutta as SASO and was replaced by W/C J.E.S. Hallas-Hill, known informally as Long John Hill for his lanky frame and anything but piratical nature. He quickly established himself as a good CO who, though rather aristocratic, was neither autocratic nor aloof and, like Baldwin, took his regular turn on ops leading the most demanding sorties. In his first couple of months he led the first four attacks against targets in Siam, three against the new railway and one against Chiengmai airport as well as a sweep of Augban airfield. Hill had a slight resemblance in form to a tall P/O Prune (Figure 39) but had neither Prune's vacant look nor his accident-prone nature. In contrast he had a relaxed appearance but focused on the job at hand and responded well to commitment from his troops.

The CO was helped in the effective running of the squadron by the arrival of F/L William Stewart Ferguson, a laconic Australian, who became the new Adjutant and one of the squadron ikons (Figure 40). Fergie was a survivor from the disaster of Singapore and his approach was fatalistic, informal and supportive but he tolerated no nonsense. He had a Hilter-like mustache which gave him

Figure 39 The CO, W/C J.E.S. Hill on the day the squadron left for Ranchi; G/C Lynch on his right (A. Sutherland Brown).

a rather gruff exterior and an abrupt manner of speaking but he was actually a friendly person. He was not an overtly fatherly figure but was able to give sensible advice to the young turks of the aircrew without raising resentment. He also knew the King's Regulations and the way to operate within and without them.

F/O E.G.T. Lovett as Intelligence Officer completed the effective administration of the squadron. Eric was a gentle, scholarly but probing person who performed his duties well and fitted in with the other two, and also the aircrew. Eric had a handsome bald head

Figure 40 A group outside the Officers' Mess, Chiringa, October 1944; from the left S/L H.B. (Mike) Hunt, DSO and Bar, DFC; F/L Eric G.T. Lovett, IO; F/L A. Sutherland (Soggy) Brown, DFC; F/L W.S (Fergie) Ferguson, MBE, Adj.; P/O Don M.Anderson, DFC (A. Sutherland Brown).

(Figure 40) and an elder-brother approach to the young aircrew. He was also good at ferreting out the facts of their missions and telling them what they should know about the enemy's defences. He was a non-drinker but was not a wet blanket in the mess.

Another change in February was that S/L H. Gandy, DFC, an experienced original squadron member and Flight Commander (Figure 41), was posted. Jim Marquis (F/L, DFC) said of Gandy, 'He was a bit older than most of us and was entitled to wear the metal winged bullet, the original insignia of an air gunner. He had flown in the old Westland Wapiti biplanes on the Northwest frontier dropping hand held bombs over the side onto recalcitrant tribesmen. He got his DFC flying Blenheims on shipping strikes in the UK early in the war. Being an old India hand he came equipped with his own shotguns and on numerous occasions graced the mess tables with boar and birds.' We also got a new Engineering officer, F/Lt Peter Hallas, so the complexion of 177 changed somewhat at the beginning of the year.

Figure 41 A group outside the Feni mess in 1943; from the left, F/O Joe D. Marquis, DFC; F/O G.R. Taylor, DFC, S/L H. Gandy, DFC, F/O T.C. Clayton (J.D. Marquis).

Still with the squadron was S/L H.B. Hunt, DFC, Mike to all his colleagues, and another ikon of the unit. Mike had a good-looking but rather bland face (Figure 40) and a typical 'good show chaps' response to most things. He was not a superb pilot nor a superior shot but he was a dedicated tactician and a consummate 'press on' type. He had a humorous demeanour and a ready laugh. He was a fairly boozy member of the mess but he slept it off and normally did not fly in what would now be called an impaired state. His real strength was an undemonstrative leadership. Every aircrew member considered him a friend and wished to do their best for him. In spite of his popularity he did not challenge the CO but supported and followed him. He was the character of the Squadron. Jim Marquis recalls:

> Mike, like most of us, drank fairly heavily, he also seemed prone to putting up blacks. Several of us were on leave in Naini Tal in March 1944 when Mike suddenly hopped up and leapt from table to table across the crowded dining room before launching himself upwards to swing on the chandelier, both he and it shortly afterwards crashed to the ground.
>
> His other side is revealed by his concern in September 1944 when so many experienced crews were leaving tour expired. I am sure Mike did all he could to stay on the Squadron, not leaving until

December. I had volunteered for a three months extension from 26th September and it was during the extension that I crewed up with Mike. From 21st of October to the 21st of November we flew on eight operations, six of them to Siam flying five and a half hours or more. It was on one of these sorties that, having completed our allotted task and being hit in the port wing by light flak, Mike decided he would like to take a look at the aerodrome at Meiktila on the way home where we found a warm welcome but no targets.

Attacking the Bangkok Railway

February was also not a great month with unusually poor weather, loss of another two crews and a continuing absorption with the Taungup pass. More than half of the 85 sorties carried out during the month involved offensive patrols to search and destroy motor transport and coastal craft used to carry the enemy to the front across the Taungup Pass and up the indented east coastline. It was not until late in the month that the new PoW-built Bangkok railway came under intensive attack.

Some of the sorties into central Burma early in the month were also very effective. On 5 February the CO with F/O G.W. Broughton, Hunt with F/O L.A. Clark, W/O D.R. Rayner, RAAF, with F/S G. Dinham and W/O D.M. Anderson, RAAF, with F/S R. White conducted an early-morning sweep across Aungban airfield near Heho and probably damaged one aircraft and shot up two flak positions without loss. Another successful operation on the 23rd by four aircraft led by F/L A.P. Wills with F/S J.H. Gibson, W/O W.S. Watson, RAAF, with F/O R.A. Watson, W/O D.R. Rayner with F/S G. Dinham and F/O R.K. Weston with F/S F.P. Smith was an attack on oil pipeline and installations between Magwe and Prome, a known dangerous patrol because of the flak protection adjacent to oilfield installations and the two airstrips. One of our squadron songs reflected in a sanguine way this danger: *Magwe to Prome, Magwe to Prome, You'll be bloody lucky if you get back home.* The pipeline in several locations was set on fire, as were tanks and pumping stations and a bus encountered was also destroyed. Unfortunately one Beau, true to the song, did not return; Rayner and Dinham were last seen over the southern end of the target area attacking an oil tank and pumping station.

There were only a few offensive patrols along railways but these were very successful. South of Mandalay F/O T.C. Clayton with F/S J. Welsh and F/S P.G. Bloom with F/S W.U. Humphries caused a small locomotive to explode and also damaged many rail cars. Unfortunately the second crew (Bloom and Humphries) were lost only a few days later on the 24th while on a patrol down the coast, when they were seen to hit the sea. Neither survived.

Long-range operations started late in the month. On 27 February the CO with G/C J.B. Lynch, station commander of Feni as navigator and F/L Hunt with F/L Clark made the first attack along the new PoW-built Bangkok railway. This was possible because the new Beau Xs and XIs were stripped of their machine guns and instead had long-range fuel tanks in the wings. These patrols, which spent six and a half hours in the air, monitored the railway south of Moulmein. The weather was excellent and the Beaus flew over the sea to the target area. They patrolled south from Mudon and saw immediately about 40 empty railway trucks but did not waste ammunition. However they did attack and set on fire a small factory beside the tracks at Tawku. At Kalwthut a train of at least 40 trucks was seen moving north with five or six flat cars loaded with guns and a staff car. Each aircraft made two attacks on the loco, with hits seen, clouds of steam emitted and water pouring from the tender. On the last attack the firebox gave way and the fire spread. Hits were also registered on the flat car with the guns and staff car. A number of enemy personnel were seen abandoning some of the carriages. At Thanbyuzayat another factory was set on fire. Farther south near Lutshan two more locos were attacked. The first was on the main track coupled to two or three trucks. After two attacks from each Beau the loco was enveloped in steam. A number of Japanese soldiers were seen to leave the trucks and take up firing positions. The second loco was a small shunter off the main line and Hunt's attack caused it too to emit steam. He then turned his attention to an open lorry full of enemy troops and forced it to run into a ditch before he ran out of ammunition. Hill had enough ammo left to attack a two-masted ship of about 200 tons near the shore as they set course for base.

The effectiveness of 177 and 211's attacks of the Burma–Siam railway were commented on by Probert (1995) mainly quoting from Kinvig (1992, pp.175–177). The latter states, 'Once the railway began to be raided regularly by the air forces, traffic came to a complete halt during the day and operated only at night. However in the early stages the main effect of the attacks was less the actual physical damage caused but rather the extent of the disorganization produced.' He goes on to say that the bombing by Liberators was not particularly accurate initially and that it was the strafing of rolling stock and engines done by the Beaufighters that proved particularly effective. 'From March 1944 Beaufighters of 27 and 177

101

[actually 177 and 211, as 27 left for southern India in February] were also able to get to targets along the line and to the main termini at Bangkok [no] and Chiengmai. [These heavily-armed] aircraft proved ideal for attacking rolling stock and locomotives which were costly for the Japanese to replace and time-consuming to repair. The railway engineers responded by building a system of bullet-proof pens and shelters for their locomotives. However in January 1944 [211 Squadron] ... equipped with rockets proved quite successful in dealing with even the protected engines. The Beaufighters were a very effective element in the war against the railway, and were nicknamed "Whispering Death" by the Japanese.' (Kinvig, 1992, p. 179).

March was a much more successful month for the squadron during which 102 sorties were flown, the most to that date; of these 27 were at night. Also, only one crew was lost. Sorties were also extended to attack the major airfields in Siam and the Bangkok railway again. Finally the enemy hardware damaged and destroyed rose to new levels; 3 aircraft were damaged on the ground and 2 more possibly damaged; 19 locos were damaged, 5 at night, as well as many rail cars and carriages; 15 MT destroyed, 23 damaged and others possibly damaged as well as many small rivercraft. In addition the squadron continued the patrols of Taungup and the coastal waterways, and conducted more defensive patrols of ship convoys and a number of low-level photo reconnaissance flights. Not surprisingly there was a noticeable build-up of flak, machine gun, light and heavy AA, especially along the railroads and airfields.

The second attack on the Siam railway on 6 March was practically a carbon-copy of the first one. Four Beaus were led by W/C Hill with F/O G.W. Broughton, F/L A.P. Wills with F/S G.D. Pirie, F/L D. Nicholls with P/O M.H. Bunn and Sgt A.J. Kappler with F/O J.D. Marquis. They followed similar operational procedures and had similar results. Ten locos were attacked, six were badly damaged and one left on fire, also two MT were damaged and several rivercraft.

Jim Marquis writing of this operation gives us a personal view:

> My first operation to the Burma-Siam railway, and my first with Sgt. Kappler as pilot, was on March 6th, 1944. The four aircraft flew down to the Advanced Landing Ground (ALG) at Hove the afternoon before.
>
> Take-off was at 06:30 hours; the brief to attack rail communications Moulmein and south to Siam. We were routed over the sea to cross the coast well south at Ngayok Bay and then east across the Gulf of Martaban to reach the target area on the railway south of Thanbyuzayat two hours after take-off. At Lutshan two of the Beaus attacked a small motor driven boat towing two barges and

102

Figure 42 Bangkok railway at Anankwin—four locos and three trains under attack by four Beaufighters on 25 March 1944. Heavy flak at the base of the hill put an 80 mm shell that did not explode through the fuselage of JM243 (J.C. Van Nes).

left the former burning. Two motor lorries, a number of closed rail trucks and a building were strafed.

At Anankwin there was considerable railway activity, it appeared to be a refuelling junction with four or five sets of railway lines and two or three additional lines branching off at each side (Figure 42). At least six locomotives were seen. The four aircraft attacked in line astern with wide gaps between them, Kap and I were number four. As the first Beau went in the flak opened up, getting more accurate with each successive attack. Each aircraft went in twice and by the time Kap and I dove in the second time (eighth attack) things were getting rather hot, both in the air and on the ground; the whole area was being obscured by smoke, steam and burning fires. Going on south a group of buildings and a pontoon bridge were strafed. At Taungzun one aircraft turned for base due to fuel shortage. Two of the remaining Beaus attacked two locos with fifteen to twenty closed freight and flat cars before turning back just north of Tadein. Kap and I continued to follow the line towards the Siam

103

border and made four damaging attacks on a large loco with two empty flat cars before steeply turning west to terminate the patrol.

Crossing the coast near Kaleguak Island we attacked two forty foot junks, knocking pieces out of them and bringing one mast down. Two more junks and four smaller boats were attacked and damaged as we crossed the delta near Bassein.

We landed back at the ALG at 13:30, taking off again at 14:35 after refuelling to return to Feni. All four Beaufighters returned safely after having caused severe damage to transport and installations along the main supply route of the enemy to Burma.

On 14 March one of the most notable squadron attacks took place when John Hill with Broughton, W/O R.K. Cameron, RAAF, with P/O H.S. Marshall, Mike Hunt with Clark, and F/S A. Beanlands with F/O A.F. Crebbin led the four Beaus to Chiengmai (Chiang Mai) aerodrome in northern Siam. It was not a flawless operation because the area was very hazy from smoke and they lost the surprise factor by milling around looking for the field. During the attack the CO's cannons had an electrical failure and would not fire, and Mike lost his port engine to LMG (light machine gun) fire on his second attack. Nevertheless the mission was a success. It showed that the RAF Beaufighters could even hit well-defended and important targets like Chiengmei deep in Siam; at the same time it pinned down Japanese aircraft on the eve of major American landings in the Pacific and it damaged up to five aircraft on the ground.

When the field was located the Beaus swept in line-abreast to mounting flak. In the west dispersal area five twin-engined aircraft were seen in revetments with camouflage nets and one was seen on the runway. As well a bowser (fuel truck), an MT and flak positions were seen in this area. Cameron made an attack on a single-engined aircraft in the west dispersal — his first burst from 600 yards missed but his corrected second burst severly damaged it. On crossing the runway and pulling up, his navigator, Marshall, put a burst into a twin-engined aircraft. Passing over the northeast dispersal the navigator again put a burst in another twin. Both were claimed damaged. Beanlands on the extreme starboard of the sweep flew over empty pens but sprayed them with cannon fire and his navigator fired his gun into them hoping to hit fuel or ammunition installations. Hunt made an attack on two twins in the west dispersal and claimed both damaged. On crossing the runway his navigator fired on the aircraft on the runway. Hunt then attacked the northeast dispersal but was hit in the port engine with oil leaks and flame developing behind the gills. He immediately climbed away to 6000 feet and was able after some difficulty to feather his propellor but by then had dropped to

5000 feet. He and Clark then set course to the west to pass south of Toungoo and Prome and cross the Arakan Yoma where it was relatively low. He then flew north to land at Hove, the southernmost friendly airstrip, virtually out of fuel after a 500-mile flight on one engine, which in itself gave cause for alarm with intense vibration under the long strain. Hunt was awarded the DSO for this remarkable feat and Clarke the DFC for the expert navigation on such a test.

Hill, not content with leading these successful and difficult sweeps, led another on 25 March taking five Beaus to the Siam railway again: Hill, Hunt, F/O J.C. Van Nes with F/O J.T. Matthews, F/O R.K. Weston with F/S F.P. Smith and F/S J.C. Forbes with F/S L.F. Reynolds (Figure 42). Combined they damaged 4 locos, over 20 railway cars and carriages; 7 MT were destroyed and others damaged including one motorised rail car and several small coastal craft.

On 29 March F/O Lottimer with F/O R.A. Watson and F/O A. Sutherland Brown, RCAF, with F/S P. Mead patrolling the Irrawaddy in the area of the oilfields came under heavy flak at Chauk without damage, but further south Lottimer was hit by two LMG bullets, one of which exploded his gunsight in his face and hit his right arm. With his navigator's assistance he was able to control the aircraft and fly it to Chittagong, land safely and be removed directly to hospital.

The one loss of the month was on a night patrol of the road and the main-line railway near Toungoo when W/O W.S. Watson, RAAF, with F/O G.H.E. Buckley took off on a single sortie and did not return.

The Japanese Offensives in Arakan and Assam Beaten Back

The Japanese and the Allies both planned offensives to be launched in the Arakan and Assam early in 1944. The Allies were aware of Japanese plans to some degree from code-breaking, V Force (a clandestine intelligence-gathering force behind enemy lines) and photo-reconnaissance. The enemy presumably knew something of the build-up of Allied forces by spy observation. The battles of the Arakan Yoma and the Chin Hills were to become one of the major campaigns of the Second World War, the largest land battles against the Japanese, a campaign that had many novel aspects and surprises, but is little known or appreciated in Europe or America. The Allied efforts were modest compared to the original design before the Tehran Conference and had to rely on the forces at hand and a

105

somewhat diminished *materiel*. Nevertheless, when the campaign was over later in the year, two Japanese Armies had been soundly defeated and driven from Chin Hills and the Arakan (Slim,1956, pp.223–336). This outcome was not obvious to many during much of the campaign, especially the Japanese. They were probably overconfident of their abilities to prosecute a war in the steep, almost trackless, jungly terrain of the Chin Hills. The Allies on the other hand, gained confidence as the fierce fighting ensued, and they were able to counter the Japanese encircling movements, stand firmly at the critical points of Imphal and Kohima, and to apply air power in a way, and with an intensity, that had never been used before in any theatre.

In the Arakan the enemy doubled the force of their 28th Army in January and February, moving it up from Prome, hence the constant effort to interdict this single supply corridor through the Taungup Pass by the Beaufighter Wing in January and February. The Japanese reinforcements had been withdrawn from the Pacific war so the Burma campaign had a beneficial effect for the American and Australian efforts there. The Arakan encounter started in the beginning of February with a whole Japanese Division passing through the 7th Indian Division unobserved in a typical bold move. However the Allied forces stood and fought and were able to do so because of complete mastery of the air and the ability to supply beleaguered ground positions by air drops. Two Divisions were completely supplied from the air during the height of the battle. The parachutes for this effort were made out of jute, a commodity abundant in Bengal, and were prepared for the 14th Army in anticipation, when it became apparent just a few months before the expected clash that regular nylon ones would not be available in sufficient numbers in India. The delivery of supplies was possible because the Spitfire squadrons shot the Oscars out of the air, enabling the Hurricanes to give superb direct ground support to the Indian Divisions. These Divisions regained the offensive in fierce hand-to-hand jungle fighting and, with tank support even in this terrain, destroyed the Japanese bunkers and drove the enemy back. The mopping-up was largely completed by the end of March.

It was evident before the Arakan was secure that the next blow would fall to the north in Assam. The Arakan campaign was in fact a feint designed to absorb the Allied reserves; the main show was to be an attempt to thrust into India, which was expected to rise in revolt, and to cut the railway bringing supplies to the airfields of upper Assam for China. The Japanese plans were both bold and risky. They counted on their own view of their superiority in jungle warfare and their ability to move unobserved through trackless

106

forested hills against the topographic grain and to capture the abundant stockpiles of Imphal. They needed to do the latter because their own supply lines were only able to deliver two thirds of the supplies they required. The plan that included a need to capture the Imphal dumps was severly criticised by HQ in Singapore with General Inada reported to have said that it was like 'skinning a racoon before you caught him' (Kinvig,1992, p.176) but the operation went ahead anyway. Japanese tactics made them less susceptible to air attack and they did move to attack with great speed and tactical surprise. However, they must not have considered the possibility of complete air supply, or the movement of whole divisions into reserve by air transport. They also probably did not expect their Air Division to be shot out of the sky and to be denied the use of its own bases. Japanese intelligence of Allied forces may have been good but their arrogance led them to underestimate the capabilities and resolve of the Allied forces, and they probably expected too much from a potential Indian fifth column.

There were three Indian Divisions deployed along the Assam 'front' in anticipation of starting their own offensive. As the Japanese initial moves became apparent, Slim decided to withdraw them to Imphal to secure his base. The Japanese moved even more rapidly and stealthily to cut off major elements before they could be completely withdrawn. The enemy also moved quickly to intersect the one surfaced road to Imphal, all in the first weeks of March. The Japanese advanced with minimum observation or encounter by patrols with mule-borne artillery and even some elephants and light tanks, but they had few supplies for they intended to capture the Allies' stockpiles. Slim and Baldwin convinced the high command of the need to dedicate more air transport to the battle to move complete divisions from the Arakan to the Assam battle as well as reserves from India.

The enemy laid seige to Kohima, an important small ridge village on the road with an Allied hospital and a small garrison. A battle of attrition took place at Kohima but it never fell. Also the Japanese laid siege to the Manipur valley and Imphal, sent major sorties into the valley, mainly at night because of the strong Allied air support, but they never achieved permanent occupation of any important part of the valley. The Japanese maintained positions from which they could shell the airfields at Palel and Imphal and sent patrols towards these fields to attempt to destroy aircraft on the ground. The pilots flew by day and many nights were spent in slit trenches defending their aircraft and airfield. Two Indian Divisions from the Arakan were flown into place at Imphal by 27

March and the reserves from India were in place and fighting at the beginning of April. Japanese patrols appeared at the railway line in the Brahmaputra valley at Dimapur but, with uncharacteristic lack of dash, continued to invest Kohima, engaging in fierce close-quarter fighting instead of bypassing it for the poorly defended railhead. By 18 April the British 2nd Division relieved Kohima and moved steadily towards Imphal. The Allies then passed to the offensive and relieved Imphal by 22 June. In General Slim's words, 'The battle was not over but it was won.'

During this time, the northern front became just a side-show in spite of fierce fighting, the rhetoric of Wingate in Quebec and Cairo and the efforts of Stilwell and the Chinese Divisions of the NCAC and Yunnan Army. The tactics of long-range penetration and the Chinese-American advance down the Ledo Road as it was built could not, in themselves, secure supply to China. It is even probable, as increasing evidence indicates, that the air efforts needed to supply Wingate's Chindits detracted from the main battle although the northern forces did pin down the 15th Japanese Army.

The campaigns for the Arakan and Assam were the first in which air superiority enabled complete air supply and transport of whole divisions by air. The American and British Dakota squadrons and 14th Army supply units worked around the clock for the whole campaign to make victory possible. The direct air support of front-line troops by the Hurricane squadrons was also a major factor in victory. A flight of eight Beaus of 177 Squadron was based at Tulihul airfield at Imphal during the latter part of the relief and played a part in the final battles. But the tough part of the victory was the resolute fighting of the Indian, Gurkha and British troops.

Two Hot Months in Feni

Although probably no-one, not even the CO, knew it, the squadron was only to spend two more months in Feni. The weather and operations started heating up in April. As the month proceeded the heat increased markedly and the thunder-heads built up over the Chin Hills. You could not climb into the cockpit and touch the controls or take the locks off them with your bare hands. Happily the pilots were issued with thin chamois gloves that provided insulation and sopped up sweat so one's hands would not slip on the controls. Once the 'fans' were started and the vent windows opened, the crew could breathe and the temperature dropped from burning to hot. It was time to get the Beau into the air as quickly as possible although

Hercules sleeve-valve engines were among the least likely to overheat with all the attendant risks.

Unfortunately the Operational Record Book from April to August includes only summary descriptions of operations and not the details of crews, aircraft and actual results. If it was ever written it must have been lost well before the squadron's disbandment as the stamped page numbering is unbroken. However, there are a number of personal narratives dealing with this period so that the actual record is reasonably continuous and reliable.

The squadron carried out 105 sorties during April of which 25 were at night. The main effort again was on the supply lines closest to the active front — the Taungup Pass and waterways (20 sorties) and the north-central roads and railways (26 sorties). The entry ways to Burma also received considerable attention with Pegu to Moulmein (18 sorties) and Mandalay to Lashio (8 sorties). Also the major aerodrome of northern Siam, Chiengmai, was attacked. The squadron always put in a major effort to recover downed crews in the Bay of Bengal and so eight sorties were flown to find and cover the rescue of Sgt Smith and F/S Wills who ditched after being hit by flak on their first operation. They were rescued two days later by a Catalina flying boat, suffering from severe exposure. Four sorties were flown to attack searchlights in Rangoon while Liberators were bombing the docks and other targets. A scattering of other targets were also attacked. For most of the long-range flights the planes refuelled at Ramu at the southern end of Allied-held territory. Commonly some of the Beaus were left at that strip and serviced there, so there was a lot of commuting to Ramu with two crews aboard.

During this period the squadron, together with 211, received signals of congratulation from Lord Mountbatten and from General Stratemeyer for their incisive attacks of the Siam Railway and Chiengmai aerodrome. Also S/L Hunt received the DSO and his navigator F/L Clarke the DFC for their effort of returning on one engine 500 miles from Chiengmai after being hit by flak during their attack in March. Damage to the enemy was the highest yet caused: 30 locomotives were attacked, most under steam; 50 to 60 MT were damaged or destroyed, 60 small freighting rivercraft damaged; as well as steam rollers, oil and railway installations.

The reverse of the coin was that the squadron lost two crews and two additional aircraft. On 5 April 1944, F/O Lindsell with F/S Willis were lost on their first operation which was one of the successful attacks of the Moulmein railway. On 22 April, F/O M.S. Gurski, RCAF, with F/O Hacker were lost after an attack on the main railway and a supply depot. They were intercepted by an Oscar and presumably shot down while the other aircraft successfully evaded the fighter. One other interception by an Oscar occurred during the month but the pilot successfully evaded.

These summary accounts of the month's activities are fleshed out by narratives of a representative group of different types of action. F/ L J.C. Van Nes recounts that:

> One of the most hair-raising operations to come to mind was a railway strike along the Burma–Siam railway on 5th April. We started at Moulmein and patrolled to the Siam border, requiring flying to Ramu on the previous day as the sortie was at extreme range. Using the advanced landing ground provided a margin of safety. The plan was for a single sortie to arrive at the target at last light. Intelligence reported 160 Japanese aircraft at Moulmein so we were briefed to stay clear. The target at Tadein was swarming with rolling stock including 11 locomotives [Figure 43 shows shells starting to hit a loco in the left middle distance]. Ground fire was accurate as usual which resulted in the starboard outer fuel tank being holed. On our fourth attack the front entry hatch in the belly flew

Figure 43 Marshalling yard at Tadein (Tardén) on the Bangkok railway on 5 April 1944. Eleven locos were present and five trains. One loco isolated on the left in the middle distance has just been hit. Van Nes's Beau was hit repeatedly by LMG and his front entry hatch flew open but he returned safely (J.C. Van Nes).

110

open so we broke off the attack and headed for the Gulf of Martaban and home. It might not sound like much of a hazard but we were operating at extreme range, had a holed fuel tank and were concerned that the added resistance of the open hatch could force us to ditch short of friendly shores to say nothing of tipping us up bow first in the drink and sinking like a stone with an open hatch. Ramu was about 600 worrying miles distant.

A few minutes later we were over the sea at 900 feet. I asked Matt to come forward and try to close the hatch. He tried with all his might, even using the starting handle as a pry. All his efforts failed even when I reduced speed to 90 knots, close to stalling. When Matt nearly fell out of the Beau we gave up. At this time a three masted schooner appeared heading to Moulmein or Rangoon. This was too good a target to pass up so we set it alight and then headed in the general direction of home skimming along the top of a welcome layer of cloud. Eventually we saw Ramree Island, a familiar point of the Japanese-held Burmese coast, and soon came in to land at Ramu. The slow trip with intense noise and anxiety about our fuel supplies was eventually over.

Jim Marquis (F/L, DFC) as observer describes a very different sortie, one of the searchlight capers at Rangoon, which was the most heavily defended area in the whole of South East Asia (Kinvig, 1992 p.175). This operation was a success but was followed by a crash at Ramu. Marquis described the events as follows:

Kap (Sgt. A.J. Kappler, DFM) and I were flown back to Ramu as passengers, standing in the entry well behind Joe Van Nes. That night we carried out an operation lasting over 5 hours to shoot out searchlights north of Rangoon, while another Beau was doing the same to the south. Apparently Liberators of the Strategic Air Force had been suffering losses and it was thought that the Japs had developed some system involving the searchlights.

We were briefed to arrive before the bombers and not to leave until after they had finished. We duly shot at any searchlight that came on and tracer spewed up in return. We weren't hit by either bombs or flak so far as we knew and, when the light and sound show was over, we patroled part of the Irrawaddy on the way back to Ramu as briefed.

Over this period any crew flying to or from Ramu ferried another crew, viz. our trip with Van and Trevor (Matt). I am sure Kap and I flew a crew down to Ramu on the 6th and another back on the 7th. We had flown "E" down on the 6th, flown "X" on ops that night and "Y" back on the 7th. Joe had flown us down in "B" on the 9th and we had taken "Z" to Rangoon.

On the 10th we were flying "Z" back from Ramu to Feni with a

111

Figure 44 'Z' in disarray—crash caused on take-off at full power at Ramu returning to Feni after refuelling with unrecognised engine damage from enemy action. Pilot Kap Kappler with Joe Marquis and passengers Robin Cameron and Bert Marshall all escaped unhurt just as it ignited (J.D. Marquis).

second crew, Robin Cameron (W/O, RAAF) with Bert Marshall (Sgt H.C.) as passengers. On take-off things started to go wrong quickly. We were heading for a couple of Mosquitoes parked on the edge of the runway and so Kap decided the only thing to do was to retract his undercarriage, which he did. The remnants of the paddy bunds started tearing the bottom of the aircraft and the rear gun broke loose and clouted me on the side of my head. When we came to a stop Robin and Bert made their exit over Kap's shoulders. I was half unconscious and was having difficulty opening the rear cupola so Robin came back and helped me. We hit the deck running as the aircraft was burning, dived into the nearest gun pit and crouched there while the Beau burnt out with cannon shells and .303 bullets exploding and whizzing all over the place. Figure 44 shows all that was left after the crash. We spent the rest of the night at Ramu and were flown back the next day by F/O R.K. Weston, MBE in "B". Investigation of the crash at Ramu revealed that we had been hit by a machine gun bullet over Rangoon on the 9th which later caused the failure with the engine at full bore on take-off.

A typical successful railway operation also involved Joe and Matt and it was reported in the South East Asia Command newspaper (SEAC) printed in Calcutta. The author, War Correspondent Bill Duff, flew in the well on a lively sortie on 19 April 1944 and reported his experiences as follows:

The pale blue spinners of our Beaufighter seemed to revolve almost lazily as we climbed to 10,000 feet to clear the desolate and savage mountain peaks that barred us from our target of the day in the heart of Burma. Below there was much haze, and Matt in his navigator's cabin behind was not finding pinpoint navigation too easy. Van in his pilot's seat was not too concerned. He knew that Matt would get us where we had to be with minimum of fuss. I stood behind Van in the well wondering whether I was frightened; decided that I wasn't yet, but very shortly would be.

My presence in "Y" for Yorkie as a "useless mouth" needs a little explaining. The previous day I had sought permission from Air Marshall Sir John Baldwin, Commander of the Third Tactical Air Force, to do an operational trip with one of his squadrons, either RAF or USAAF. He consented at once, suggesting a trip in a Beaufighter provided the squadron commander did not consider his aircraft would be imperilled thereby. So off I went to HQ of a very famous Beaufighter squadron indeed (about which much remains to be written).

Over the mountains

In less than five minutes after my arrival I was scheduled to go on a strafe next morning at 06:30 hours — which meant rising at 05:00 hours. I decided the squadron was being, if anything, just a shade too willing to help.

So there we were Van, Matt and I boring through the early morning mountain air. I thought over what I had heard of my companions, as a chilly breeze plucked at my shirt through the open door to the rear cabin. Van — full name F/O J.C. Van Nes: "Motor-Cycle Van", you remember, the man who frightens Japs over precipices (SEAC, 19 April) — is 27, Canadian, quick of speech and action, passionately keen on his job of discouraging the Jap. Matt (F/O J.T. Matthews), from Sale, Manchester is five years older and more deliberate but no less keen.

Ideal Team

They seemed to me an ideal team — pilot all fire and dash, navigator patient, careful, controlled. Just how ideal the team was I was to learn within the hour, and to marvel at throughout the remainder of our 900 mile, four hour trip. We were steadily dropping down until the tree tops were a bare 200 feet below us. In front lay the silver ribbon of the Irrawaddy. I looked idly round and the bullet-proof doors between the two cabins, which had silently closed a second or two before reminded me sharply that we were not out for pleasure. Suddenly through the intercomm came Matt's voice: "This is it", he said and Van swung the huge machine into a tight right-hand turn at 200 mph, when you are not expecting it, is quite a thing...

113

This is It

Below us now was paddy and scrub, sparse stunted trees. Not much cover and no sign of life. The cross lines on Vans' reflector sight glowed blood red as I gazed over his shoulder. This was business and the hunt was up. At that moment — for the last time that trip — I was not sure whether I was really grateful to Sir John or not. Thereafter I was too excited to care, and as you will see, too ignorant. Over another bend of the river the country was changing. Cover was becoming denser, trees still sparse in trunk and foliage, more closely ranked. Again, "This is it", over the intercomm, another sharp swing and we were following the single track railway that leads north to Swebo and Myitkyina, life line for the Japs in northern Burma.

The main purpose of our patrol was a photo recce of certain features along the line, with, of course secondary intention to shoot up anything Jap that moved. But said Van apologetically before we started, "I'm afraid this will be a rather dull party. The Japs know we have this line taped and they are moving on it only at night. We may not see a thing or fire a shot."

Just how dull the party was is shown by the facts — and the photographs that establish them. We — I mean Van and Matt — destroyed 4 Jap locos, 3 of them under steam, and damaged 2 more, exploded an oil tanker and turned a perfectly good and amazingly well camouflaged, water-tower into a gigantic colander. A dull party indeed! And we used 1,000 rounds of 20mm ammo and 3,000 rounds of .303 in doing it, so you can take it that the property that was busted was well and truly busted.

The Jap is an industrious and crafty blighter. He builds little bashas for his locos and hides them among the trees so you need an eagle eye to find them. Unfortunately for the Jap, both Van and Matt have just that kind of eye. For me, I could have stooged up and down the line for a month and seen nothing, except of course, the grand big loco obligingly left with its coaches uncoupled and dispersed smack on the track. Even I saw that, but its makers never will again. We gave it three attacks and it vomited forth everything it had in the way of steam, water and oil (Figure 45). As we pulled out of the third attack more steeply than ever before Van turned his head and asked: "Are you all right?" Thinking he meant had the steep dive to 50 feet minus and the sharp pull-out unnerved me, I called back, "Yes thanks."

Star-Shaped Scar

Then he pointed to the centre of the windscreen. A beautiful star-shaped scar marked the spot where a Jap machine-gunner with incredible accuracy had scored a bull. Van patted the perspex lovingly with his gloved hand and laughed, "I like that stuff a lot," he said. And that goes for me too.

114

Figure 45 Loco under attack by F/O J.C. Van Nes with F/O T. Matthews and reporter Bill Duff as passenger in LX905 on 19 April 1944 on the line north from Mandalay near Wuntho (J.C. Van Nes).

The oil tanker had been earlier in the proceedings — our first strike in fact, and a satisfying one. By some miracle Van had spotted it under a roof of thatch, and down we went. From my stance in the well the view was a grandstand one, practically through the gun sight. Beneath my feet there sounded the staccato, angry rumble of the cannon. Through the cockpit floor came the acrid but stimulating fumes of cordite. A brilliant flash of flame marked the end of the tanker as its gas content ignited blew it to no good at all.

As we stooged on along the line Matt was busy in his office with map and camera. Every strike we made was recorded by the big camera in the nose. Every feature that had to be reconnoitred, and everything new and likely to interest the Intelligence Officer, was recorded. Matt and Van were old stagers on the run. A large patch of scorched earth was pointed out by Van. Two months before they caught a party of Japs unloading rail trucks filled with 25 gallon drums of petrol. The Japs ran when they saw "Y" for Yorkie screaming down on them. But they could not run as quickly as the blast from the exploding drums. That had been a very good strike indeed.

We've Been Hit

Not that anybody was complaining about ours. Van had found a newly-laid railway spur over which the Jap had actually placed

115

sandbags as it crept between the tall trees. At the end of the spur what should there be but another loco with its little summer house. It is an ex-loco now.

It was about this time that a heavy clang shook the aircraft. "We've been hit," I thought though there was no sign of flak (the Jap had given up using tracer in the daytime; it gives away the gun position). "A vulture," said Van after a moment, as nothing appeared amiss. Back at the base we found the vulture was a .303 bullet that had penetrated the cannon panel, pierced an ammo chute (causing a stoppage), missing everything vital, and done little damage. This was not the Japs lucky day.

Another wide sweep and the sun settled down to shine on our port side instead of the starboard. Our outward patrol was over and course was set for base. Back along the line we flew, always at fighting height, always on the alert for targets.

"You might as well have a rest now," said Van. "There's nothing more to see." And I found my legs were glad to let me down on the step into the navigator's cabin. As we climbed to meet the hills I felt the fresh breeze again behind me. The bullet-proof doors were open and Matt, whom I had not seen it seemed for ages, was grinning at me over his reports and maps.

Honour These Men

Van was slumped, relaxed in his seat. "Y" for Yorkie was climbing leisurely and unhurried back to 10,000 feet. What a machine is "Y" for Yorkie. I felt then as I feel now tremendous affection for her. She drove like a luxury train all that morning. Everything she was asked to do she did perfectly. Jap flak she took in her stride.

As I gazed contentedly at those pale blue spinners I thought of the men responsible for the Beau's perfection, the ground crew who mended her. Not for them the joys of Jap-strafing; not for them the serene beauty of the heavens at 10,000 feet, nor the throat-catching thrill of tree tops at 50 feet. Never for them the headlines, but always for them the honour and the glory. Don't forget these men ever. Their pilots honour them and so must we; "Y" for Yorkie was doing them proud, as they had done her.

Base was chattering away to Matt over the radio giving a "fix". Van grinned, turned up a thumb as we heard a bearing. We were precisely where we should have been as we came down from the mountains. Just another ordinary everyday miracle of precise navigation. "This," said Van, "is a piece of cake."

Ahead of us 20 miles lay the home strip. We announced ourselves politely, and "May we come in?" we asked. Yes indeed we might, they told us, and with a final majestic sweep the Beau circled down to a perfect landing. I looked around the cockpit for the last time as we were touching down. There in a rack beside me lay my parachute. I remember sharply the mixed feelings with which I con-

116

templated it four hours before. "Can you give me twenty minutes notice before I have to jump?" I had asked Van. It would take me all that time to put it on.

Van Just Grinned

But Van just grinned and said 'You won't really need it at 50 feet.' That seemingly cynical remark was just the assurance my early morning nerves needed. A pilot who jests about a crash at 220 mph — and more — from 50 feet is a pilot who will have no such part in any such nonsense.

And Van was that pilot.

I climbed out clutching a battered map that Matt had politely lent me. The implication that I could map read my way around the target, a very nice compliment indeed. In point of fact, it was only the total absence of snow that confirmed my view that we were not over the South Pole. That is the kind of aerial map reader I am.

Still, if Matt should read this I would be awfully glad if he would let me have that map when he has done with it. It will remind me down to my extreme old age of two very grand chaps and a superb machine. And of course I shall be able to shoot a horrid line down Fleet Street on the strength of it.

Unfortunately Bill Duff, a courageous reporter, didn't get to do that. He was lost in a Mitchell bomber on his next operational trip.

During May, the last month the squadron was at Feni another record was set for the number of sorties — 126, of which 22 were at night. Despite this not many of the operations were highly successful, mainly because of the deteriorating weather and attendant poor visibility. Fourteen sorties were aborted, all but one because of weather. The true monsoon did not strike until the end of the month but large cumulo-nimbus storms were everywhere and became more numerous and larger as the month progressed. The summits of the Chin Hills were constantly buried in these storms and avoiding the turbulence in their core which could rip off the wings of an aircraft, became increasingly difficult because the thunderheads were embedded in a sea of stratified cloud. When aircraft did get through to central Burma the target area(s) could well be covered by a large storm with sheets of rain and ragged low clouds making the patrol dangerous and ineffective.

Despite the difficulties several very successful attacks were made against railways and a total of 16 locos were damaged. Attacks against MT continued to be frustrating because of increasing difficulty of access in poor visibility and because most of the encounters with convoys were at night when only vehicles set alight could be claimed. Nevertheless, 12 MT were burned out, 13 others were claimed damaged and 11 probably so. Other targets attacked included oil pipelines, some small rivercraft and factories.

One benefit of the poor weather was that ground fire was less intense and accurate. Two Oscar MKIIs intercepted two Beaus near Mandalay on the 17 May but one Beau evaded by climbing into low cloud; the other was followed for five minutes along the deck while taking evasive action and the enemy fighter was only able to make one attack which failed to strike the Beau.

The most successful sorties during May were on the 12th by two aircraft patrolling the roads and railway from Kyaukse south of Mandalay northward then climbing to the northeast into the Shan Plateau along the Lashio line. Led by S/L Wills with F/S J.H. Gibson and F/O A. Sutherland Brown with F/S F.J. Lumley they attacked three trains with locos under steam near Maymyo, three more stationary ones and seven MT of which four were set on fire. Both aircraft exhausted their ammo by Hsipaw so broke off and returned to base. Later in the month Willy was able to celebrate receiving the DFC.

The most successful attack against motor transport was made by a Beau on 13 May which encountered 50 lorries showing headlights in the Taungup Pass; the aircraft attacked 14 times causing significant but not readily assessable damage.

The price in May was two aircraft lost. On the 7th two Beaufighters patrolled the southwestern railway throughout its length from Kyangin near Prome south to Bassein. One loco and two MT were damaged before one Beau flown by F/S Beanlands with F/S A.F. Crebbin was hit and the pilot badly wounded. Beanlands managed to bring the aircraft within sight of the ALS at Ramu before he lost control. His navigator, who was standing in the well, attempted to bring the Beau in to land, virtually impossible even for a pilot. Presumably he was trying to save his wounded pilot or he could have climbed to 3000 feet and bailed out. His approach was fast and erratic, so resulted in a crash and fire. Beanlands died before medical help arrived and Crebbin died of injuries the next day. Crebbin's gallant attempt may not have been recognised officially but it was by the squadron aircrew.

The other loss occurred on 9 May during a patrol of roads west of the Lashio line. Near Mogok a Beau piloted by F/O R.N. Peever, RCAF, with F/O R.A. Watson was presumed to have hit a hillside while pulling out of a diving attack. This was not seen by the other crew but the Beau was immediately missed and, on circling the site, a crash on fire was observed on the wooded hillside.

177 was withdrawn from the line at the end of the month to Ranchi in Bihar, 200 miles west of Calcutta. The squadron had had a tough go since it started operations and it needed to equip the aircraft with rocket rails and to train the crews for rocket attacks at the Special Low Attack Instructional School (SLAIS). Also the monsoon was not the most productive time for low-level and night attacks. Beaufighters started flying out on 29 May and all the aircraft were in Ranchi by the end of the month. Most Beaus made more than one flight in abominal weather to an unknown base as they assisted the move by freighting minor equipment, records, aircrew and critical groundcrew. Air Marshall Sir John E.A. Baldwin, KBE, CB, DSO, the commander of the 3rd Tactical Air Force came to Feni to congratulate the squadron on its fine record while in the line. An informal photo (Figure 46) of most of the aircrew and many of the groundcrew was taken on the same day with the CO, Long John Hill, and the Station Commander, Feni, G/C Lynch front and centre.

Figure 46 The squadron on departure for Ranchi, 31 May 1944. The group about the starboard engine includes Alf Aldhan, the head above the kneeling corporal, Gee Herr holding Gurkha hat, Soggy Brown, Mike Hunt, Mac Mackay*, Arthur Platt*, T.C. Clayton and Pete Hallas, EO, successively to Gee's left. The group around the nose includes the CO, John Hill and on his right over his shoulder Willy Wills, ?, Joe Walsh, G/C Lynch, Station Commander, Feni, and Kap Kappler at the back. To the CO's left are Joe Van Nes, two unrecognised groundcrew, Fergie Ferguson, Adj., Don Anderson, Rupe Horwood. Beyond the engine and above the kneeling airman is Eric Lovett and to his right F.J. Lumley*. At the far right with his arms akimbo is the army liaison officer, Major Hughes, and beside him G.R. Taylor (A. Sutherland Brown).

120

11

Ranchi: Rocket Refit, Training and Rest

Ranchi was a change from Feni in every way. It was a relatively pleasant second-order hill station that was an old summer capital of Bihar. It is situated at the eastern end of the Chota Nagpur hills, really a plateau with small conical hills projecting above the common height of about 2000 feet. The town had some substantial buildings including a Government House, a few attractive inns where you could get a good meal and a few restaurants where the meals were OK but the chance was high of intestinal troubles to follow. The accommodation for all ranks was a cut above what we were used to. The officers' mess was a commodious Victorian villa of brick and stone with high ceilings and large rooms. Furniture was sparse but adequate in the lounge and, although we shared four or more mosquito-net-draped beds to a room, it was luxury to which we were not accustomed. The countryside was composed of rolling agricultural fields with some woodlands and dotted with temples and villages. Although the weather was intensely rainy it was a cool and pleasant break from steamy Bengal.

It took twelve days for the main party of groundcrew and equipment to arrive by train with only one derailment en route. Setting up shop, conducting major aircraft maintenance, fitting the rocket rails under the wings together with just plain bad weather meant there was not much flying or training until 12 June. In addition most crews had leave in June, so serious flying did not start until about the 20th and rocket firing on the range not until a fair number of conversions had been completed by the end of the month. We did have a 'spirited' mess life, played organised sports and had a dance for all ranks that was held under the auspices of the Governor of Bihar, His Excellency, Sir Thomas and his chatelaine, Lady Rutherford, at old Government House. Many cricket and soccer matches were played by squadron teams against military units and local sports clubs. There was a large Indian Army Hospital staffed mainly with British nurses in Ranchi and we were entertained in more ways than one by a visiting ENSA troop, so that there was a social life for all ranks. Joe Van Nes met his future wife Jean, a British Army Nursing Sister, in

Ranchi and many less permanent friendships developed. Sutherland Brown (1992) described one aspect of these brief encouters:

> The ENSA troupe included the sister of Ronald Frankau, who because of her advanced age of thirty something, was a sort of den mother to the troupe. It also included an attractive actress who showed a passing interest in me. I can remember little about her except she was a pretty and sophisticated young Englishwoman not of the Memsahib type. I do remember she had a remarkable retractable silver toothpick she was fond of wielding after dinner for its shock effect or possibly for her pearly white teeth.

Ranchi was nothing like Feni or Chiringa to follow. It was a welcome idyll.

Not all was hibiscus. The CO had a battle with dysentery and was in hospital for three weeks during which Mike Hunt took over. There was constant rain with a solid low cloud-deck trailing ragged fringes just above the irregular plateau and the windscreen made opaque by sheets of driven rain. The crews, especially the pilots, had to quickly learn the local geography, roads, railway tracks from tree-top height to avoid smashing into one of the many low, beehive-shaped hills projecting above the plateau when carrying out the training exercises and rocket attacks on the range. Landing under such conditions was often difficult. Alf Aldham remembers an incident his pilot (A. Sutherland Brown) has forgotten:

> Our aircraft swung violently on landing, but a remarkable bit of steering took us through the parked Beaus and just past the Control Tower before coming to a halt and taxiing in to dispersal. When we got to Flights, Soggy (ASB) took a lot of stick from his fellow pilots, who had heard the scream of brakes and roar of a correcting engine. However, all were silenced when a phone call came through from the Tower 'Praising the skill of the pilot in avoiding a serious accident.'

Towards the end of July two old hands were tour expired and posted. F/L L.A. Clark, DFC, Mike Hunt's navigator who originally served with 27 Squadron, and F/L J. Lottimer, DFC were among the first to reach this milestone on the squadron. They received a send-off as befitted their good service and likeable personalities.

Serious rocket training — lectures, dummy and live attacks on the range — began on 1 July. We flew several flights almost every day regardless of constant bad weather. The latter experience was as valuable as the rocket training. Most pilots had an initial prejudice against rockets because the fixed rails of the early Beau Xs certainly slowed the aircraft some 15 knots, not a welcome fact when one considered the near parity of the VIs and the Oscars. The pilots soon learned the rockets were effective weapons and the style of attack was little different from that with cannons. The rockets initially seemed to fly in close formation with you but suddenly accelerated towards the target. Their trajectory was not as flat as cannons (Figure 59) and took a little getting used to. The rockets could be fired as singles, in pairs or as salvos of eight. A well-aimed salvo of 60-pound high explosive (HE) rockets could be devastating. The 20-pound armour-piercing rockets could be as deadly to tanks or ships that were hit just below the waterline. The squadron went on to use these weapons effectively.

During all this low flying in abysmal weather we suffered no accidents. Some local villagers were not so lucky. They made a habit of gleaning the metal from the range almost as you were firing even though serious attempts were made to keep them away. Some of them tried to smelt the iron and steel and one unfortunate destroyed part of his village working with a live 60-pound HE rocket.

Apparently there was some debate at AHQ about our next move. Possibly we were headed for the south of India, but on 23 July it became official we were to return to 224 Group at a more forward airstrip, Chiringa, between Chittagong and Cox's Bazar. The squadron was to move entirely by air. The date was not confirmed in the signal but was indicated to be after the 26th. The squadron became aware of the actual date on the morning of the 26th when six USAAF Dakotas arrived to load. Remarkably these Dakotas were loaded and took off by noon with an advance party under F/L Van Nes. The next day three Beaus departed with equipment and passengers and three more transport planes arrived, loaded and left. However the pace then slowed because the Chiringa facilities were inadequate at that time, the site dirty and the weather foul. The bashas had been used by cattle during the monsoon, there was only one water well and the latrines had not been completed. Nevertheless the site, No 2 camp, (Figure 50) was otherwise quite pleasing and home to the squadron for most of the rest of its existence. The move had not been completed by 3 August when a flap occurred to send a detachment of eight Beaus to Imphal post-haste. They were in the air the next morning for the three-hour flight to Imphal in relatively benign weather and flew five sorties out of Tulihul the next day patrolling the roads between the Chindwin and Irrawaddy Rivers for enemy transport. The squadron was pretty good at moving, flexible and able to mount offensive operations at almost any time.

123

12

The Siege of Imphal

The respite was over. After leaving Ranchi the detachment did not waste much time getting operational. The first sortie was off the ground by 10:00 hours on 5 August, the day after arrival, the first of five flown that day. The brief sojourn in Imphal was as intensive and difficult as the stay in Ranchi had been relaxed.

Technically the siege of Imphal was lifted very late in June when the British 2nd Division met the Indian 5th Division on the road between Kohima and the Manipur valley. However, no retreat had started. The perimeter of the valley was still invested by the Japanese in strong defensive positions with field artillery in the hills, and sharp attacks into the valley were still a nightly occurrence. When we arrived a group of Japanese bodies lay in a drainage tank near our mess where they had been counted but not yet buried. The airfields still needed stout defence against incursions.

Manipur was an isolated, verdant and tranquil valley before the Japanese offensive. It had a floor at an elevation of about 2500 feet and the peaks of the surrounding hills reached 8 to 9000 feet. The Manipuriis are a handsome people and the surrounding hills are the home of the fierce Naga tribe who, happily, were our allies against the Japanese. The valley had been supplied entirely from stockpiled stores and by air supply since March. Our food ration was Spartan. We occupied a small quadrangle of bashas north of the strip and near the town. There was no common mess life because of our intense and staggered operations.

The squadron detachment at Imphal was led at first by S/L Hunt and then by W/C Hill until the last few days. We had no Adjutant, IO or EO and only a corporal's guard of fitters and riggers. The IO of the Hurricane squadron at Tulihul served us, the CO was Adjutant and a senior NCO acted as EO. Tulihul was a relatively short airstrip near the western valley wall and the valley floor had a number of projecting hills. The strip had few navigational aids and minimal number of paraffin flares to mark the runway for night flying as it was within range of Japanese field guns. Understandably it was not an ideal site for night operations in the worst of the monsoon. Although the moon period was at hand and the moon may have been bright at 30,000 feet, it was not much of a help to the 177 crews as they attempted to run operations in the intense rain with ragged low clouds and ground mist. Imphal received more than 200 inches of rain that season. In spite of the conditions in the twelve days of the detachment, two of which were wiped out by the fierce intensity of the rain, the Flight of eight aircraft put up 57 sorties, of which 12 were at night. Most crews put in about six to eight sorties during their stay.

It was not a triumphal operational series because of the difficulties cited and relatively poor maintenance resulting from the short-staffed groundcrew: their work carried out in the drenching rain with inadequate spare parts. However the Beaufighter pilots did have an advantage with their confidence in night ground attack and their capability to stay aloft on patrols four hours or more, far longer than the Spits or Hurricanes. The Beaus generally went up and down the target areas both ways rather than being launched to specific targets and returning like the single-engined fighters. Operations were all by single aircraft and were staggered so there was a continuing sequence of patrols. The prime targets were the roads to the Chindwin River, the river itself, and the roads and railways in the area between the Chindwin and the Irrawaddy. The prime purpose was to intercept and destroy reinforcements and supplies for the now beleaguered enemy forces. Commonly our offensive patrols started a few minutes after take-off as we reached the south end of the Manipur valley at Tamu or Tiddim to follow the roads through the hills to Kalemyo and on to the ferry site at Kalewa. Across the Chindwin we patrolled the road to Ye-u and on down the railway to Monywa and back by some variation thereof. The roads were scarcely visible in much of the area because of overhanging trees; jungle on the hills and teak forests east of it. Only beyond the Ye-u railway line were there open paddy fields where enemy transport was exposed. Also, during the monsoon there was no indicative dust-cloud raised by the vehicles. Still MT were seen at night by their masked headlights and were located during the day by observant patrolling.

During the detachment 16 MT vehicles were destroyed by fire, 22 damaged and as many more probably damaged. Two small steamers were destroyed, and 30 or so barges, pontoons and rivercraft. Two locos under steam were damaged and their trains raked. Also two rail coasters were damaged. Probably the most destructive sortie was on 10 August when Sutherland Brown with Alf Aldham took off at 03:20 into light rain but occasional bits of moonlight to intercept the Chindwin at Paungbyin east of Imphal and follow the river down to

Alon near Monywa then back up the railway to Ye-u, returning along the road to Kalewa — a flight of just over four hours. Two 50 to 60-foot motor launches were destroyed on the river and a moving train with six carriages, presumably full of troops, was attacked — the loco erupted like a geyser while the carriages were raked with cannon fire. On return a previously damaged larger riverboat received more attention.

The price paid for the success at Imphal was the loss of one Beaufighter. On 14 August F/O Arthur J. Platt with F/O C.A. Kidd did not return from a sortie that took off at 11:29 to patrol Kalewa–Ye-u–Monywa. No evidence of what happened came until after the capture of Rangoon where F/O Kidd was released as one of the prisoners. They had been shot down by ground fire and after the crash were handed over by hostile or fearful villagers to the Japanese. Arthur Platt was a cocky and courageous pilot and may have been shot by them for not showing sufficient humility.

W/C Hill left for Chiringa on 14 August and three days later the rest of the detachment left by Beaufighter and Dakota for their new base. The operations of the squadron at Manipur contributed in some measure to the defeat of the Japanese by being able successfully to attack their transport by night as well as by day.

13

Operations From Chiringa, 1944

Another Base — The Same Songs

The move to Chiringa, which was started before the departure of the
Flight to Imphal, was accomplished mainly by air in Dakotas. Two
small ground parties with the remaining personnel left Ranchi on 11
and 12 August. The detachment at Imphal came in by Beau and
Dakota on 18 August 1944. The Squadron was together once again
and ready — ready to celebrate our reunion but more particularly
Joe Van Nes's and Matt Matthews's DFCs and S/L Wills's navigator, P/O J.H. Gibson's DFM. All are shown in Figure 37 at the start
of their tours. On 20 August we celebrated another DFC, this one to
F/O G.R.Taylor (Figure 41).

Chiringa was situated on the flood plain of the Ganges–Brahmaputra delta but just west of the first long linear ridges of the Chin Hills
formed of young sandstones and shales which had been crumpled
into sharp geological folds. The small native village of Chiringa
(Figure 47) was composed of a couple of dozen bashas along the
road from Chittagong south to the equally small villages at Ramu,
Cox's Bazar, Ukhia and the head of the tidal inlet of the Naf. The
airfield (Figure 48), close to the village between a major bend of the
Matamuhari River, was a single long runway oriented north. The
runway was highly cambered and the earth covered with thick canvas
impregnated with bitumen. As a quick way of building all-weather
airfields this was effective but took quite a bit of maintenance. The
hard standings for the aircraft were made of interlocking steel plates,
noisy to taxi over but also effective. The Squadron's dispersal area is
shown in Figure 49, and Figure 48 shows the lower left (southwest)
of the runway with the briefing room etc. in the nearby woods. There
were no blast shelters, as attacks from the air were not considered a
serious problem when the field was built. However, there was good
airfield anti-aircraft defence. Initially the drive from the field to the
camp went through the village with its randomly dispersed children,
chickens and dogs and was an excruciating ride because the road was
formed of a single layer of bricks laid over clay which heaved under

Figure 47 Chiringa village on the Arakan road. Note the sign with Ramu and Cox's Bazar (C.R. Fox).

Figure 48 Chiringa airfield looking north across the Matamuhari River. 177's dispersal is on the southwest and the Ops room adjacent on the edge of the wood (N. Boyd).

128

Figure 49   177 aircraft at dispersal, Chiringa (N. Boyd).

Figure 50   Chiringa Camp from the south, Officers' Mess in the road loop (D.M. Anderson).

129

Figure 51 Airmen off to Flights in the morning, Chiringa; notice all wearing Gurkha or bush hats now; compare with Figures 9 and 27 (W.E. Bellingham).

Figure 52 Line up for dinner at the Airmen's Mess, note the kite hawks in the air and compare with Figure 27 (W.E. Bellingham).

heavy loads during the rains. Later a direct road was built of similar construction to the runway to avoid these hazards. The groundcrew left early in the morning standing up in trucks (Figure 51) for the airfield.

The camp (Figure 50) was situated to the southwest in open fields and was fairly breezy, hence relatively free of mosquitoes, but otherwise it was less attractive than Feni. The Officers' Mess and living quarters were in bashas within and just outside the road loop, the Sergeants' nearby to the south were similar. The Airmen's Mess was much larger with lots of room for evening recreation, but the men lined up for their food (Figure 52). The bashas were pretty basic but really quite comfortable housing in the climate. The airmen's quarters were similar but undivided — really bamboo barracks. Neither the aircrew nor the groundcrew could imagine what it was like being bivouacked in the monsoon in the jungle with the 14th Army and scarcely wanted to.

The first operational flights out of Chiringa were flown on 14 August when four Beaus took part in convoy escort and the next week most of the sorties were from Taungup Pass to Prome or the reverse. The following week, sorties became more diverse with a number of missions to the Mandalay–Katha–Maymyo area of east central Burma and one long-range operation to the Siam railway on the 27th. In all 45 sorties were flown from Chiringa in August but 15 were abortive because of weather, engine or fuel trouble. Three sorties were long air–sea search flights in very bad weather looking for the downed crew of P/O Horwood, RAAF, with W/O Bateman.

Operations were not as successful as in some months, even allowing that operations were for only part of a month and mostly with only half a squadron. Only two locos under steam were attacked and damaged; two MT destroyed and eight damaged; eight country craft that were shot up burned with copious black smoke, so were probably carrying oil drums; many more were attacked. Oil tanks, installations and the pipeline were attacked and severely damaged twice.

One Beau was lost for unknown reasons on a local flight to Chittagong. That of F/S E. Hall with F/S K. Haigh and passenger Cpl Morris, photographer, crashed and caught fire just after take-off on 28 August. All were killed. Another Beau was ditched but the crew returned after a harrowing ordeal described by Chas Bateman later.

F/O Keith Reid describes the first return to the Siam railway since the respite at Ranchi. This operation encountered intense and accurate flak. Three of the four Beaus were hit and Horwood's had to be ditched. Reid recalls:

Figure 53 Two Australians, Royce Rayner*, and Rupe Horwood, DFC (J.D. Marquis).

On August 27th, 1944, the usual pattern of operations was followed — up early, breakfast, briefing by the CO and IO, Eric Lovett. Our aircraft were allotted and we began our departure preparation and checks.

Four Beaus with the following crews were designated: Robin Cameron, RAAF, with Bert Marshall, Rupe Horwood, RAAF, with Charles Bateman, Kap Kappler with Joe Marquis [Figures 53 and 54] and myself with Norman Anderson. My starboard engine showed excessive drop in revs on run up when the magneto switches were tested so we had to change aircraft, to the disappointment of the groundcrew and ourselves. The others were off the ground at 11:00 and out of sight when we got in the air. In order to catch up I found it necessary to increase boost and revs, which concerned me because of the extra fuel we would burn on this long range operation. However, when I caught sight of them

132

Figure 54 Another crew on the 27 August 1944 rhubarb to the Bangkok railway when Horewood ditched and was missing for a week; Kap Kappler, DFM and navigator Joe Marquis, DFC (J.D.Marquis).

hours later over the Gulf of Martaban, I was able to throttle back to normal cruising speed.

After the initial attack we divided into two pairs — Robin and Rupe in one and Kap and me in the other. We shot up one loco and train while the Aussies attacked others. Rupe sustained severe damage to one engine from flak. Kap's plane must have been hit about the same time and we lost sight of him as we continued east along the line. The countryside was really rough, with sharp forested hills with occasional projecting very high trees. There must have been a well camouflaged gun emplacement as I could hear the bullets cracking past; fortunately we were not hit. We had come to the limit of the plane's endurance so we turned over the hills and proceeded west to the Gulf again heading for Chiringa without any knowledge of what had happened to the others.

Nearing home a close watch was kept on the fuel gauges with the thought of the possible need to land at Cox's Bazar, which was on track. At last Chiringa was in sight and we landed with perhaps only fuel in the carburettors. The trip had taken just over seven hours, where the theoretical endurance was only six and a half.

Andy and I were first to land and were met by the CO in his jeep just as Robin and Bert were sighted. They ran out of petrol on entering the airfield circuit on their approach. Beaufighters glide like bricks. They were on the eastern side of the strip but attempted a wheels up landing across the runway and continued on into a 'chaung' (slough) covered with water hyacinth. This looked shallow and quite solid but it wasn't. When the CO tried to walk to the 'ditched' Beau he sank up to his waist through the hyacinth. Robin and Bert by this time had emerged from the upper hatches and were standing on the wing as he attempted to approach. They broke into hilarious laughter probably partly from relief at surviving the crash landing. Hill was not a small minded or humourless man but he couldn't see the funny part of this.

Kap also landed safely but somewhat shot up by flak. Both were lucky not to be hit. Rupe and Chas Bateman did not arrive back. Over the next few days three long patrols down the coast were flown in appalling monsoon to look for them without success. However they arrived back on their own five days later.

Horwood and Bateman's story, which is one of skill, fortitude and luck, is related by Chas Bateman:

Rupe and I were crewed in H Harry. We flew in loose formation at sea level on a course which would keep us out to sea to the southwestern tip of Burma. From there we headed eastwards across the Gulf of Martaban straight to the target area which we reached at 14:00 hours.

The four Beaus went into strafe in line astern, our Harry bringing up the rear. The railway passed through a wooded cutting and Horwood spotted locos hidden here and opened fire hitting two engines and raising billows of steam.

At this point, between Thanbyuzayat and Anankwin we were hit by flak, a large jagged hole appeared in the nacelle of the starboard engine and I alerted Rupe. He immediately decided to climb out of the gully because we were at about 50 feet and he wanted height in case the engine cut. We had reached 1,500 feet on a westerly heading across the Gulf by about 14:30 when the engine packed up and with it the R/T and wireless which were both powered by the engine-driven generator.

We discussed whether to ditch at Elephant Point, south of Rangoon, where there was a hidden cache of supplies but rejected this action and pressed on. Horwood was successfully maintaining course and height on one motor so we crossed the estuary of the Irrawaddy. On reaching the Bay of Bengal I gave him a course to steer for the Oyster Island Lighthouse near Akyab, a good 250 nautical miles northwest.

When we eventually sighted Ramree Island, Horwood reminded me that there was a cache of supplies on its northern coast near Kykaukpau but still in enemy territory. We again decided to stay on course hoping we had sufficient fuel to get beyond Oyster Island. The weather soon deteriorated to 10/10ths cloud with squally conditions. By now it had become obvious to Horwood that the fuel was extremely low and he said he could no longer rely on the gauges as they neared the empty mark. So we made provision for ditching, e.g. took off our parachute harness, loosened catches on upper hatch and rear cupola. We ditched just after 18:00 hours in a position I estimated to be 15 nautical miles southwest of Oyster Island. The aircraft submerged in a sheet of spray as we hit the sea but porpoised quickly to the surface. We jumped overboard and scrambled into the dingy which had self inflated thanks to the immersion switch. The dingy was anchored to the port wing by a cord and one of us found the knife strapped to the side and quickly cut it. We used the paddles to move us away from H Harry as it was sinking rapidly. We next paid out the drogue anchor and a line attached to a packet of fluorescent dye for marking the sea.

Taking stock of our situation, Horwood's forehead had struck the reflector gunsight and I had bumped my head and bruised my shoulder. We were wearing one-piece (so called) escape suites and our .38 revolvers. I had brought the navigator's bag with maps, a Very pistol plus two or three signal cartridges. The rations in the dingy consisted of a small tin of Horlick's tablets and two cans of water which we subsequently found to be unfit for consumption. It was now dark and the weather appalling, heavy rain and waves crashing over the waterproof cover from which our heads and shoulders protruded: paddling was impossible.

The next day was no improvement; we had not seen the light-house but believed we were in the approaches to Akyab harbour. As the dingy rose to the tops of the waves we could see land and for a short period there was a small warship in view. Later on we realised that we were drifting closer to land but towards dusk of the second day a heavy squall from shore changed our direction of drift.

During that night for some time, there was scraping and scratch-ing along the bottom of the dingy; we were drifting across shoals of submerged rocks, possibly those guarded by the lighthouse.

Dawn of the 29th found us in similar monsoonal weather but we were less sheltered so that waves filled the dingy. We took turns bailing with the canvas bucket. Our faces had turned yellow through being splashed by fluoesein-stained water. During that morning there were two occasions when we heard aircraft but could not see them owing to the low clouds and poor light. Horwood judged when they were overhead and fired the Very pistol. Late that afternoon a Beaufighter passed over us but our remaining car-tridge was a dud through being soaked with seawater. On the 30th, the fourth day and final day as it turned out, the weather improved but I don't recollect much of it. We were both exhausted through lack of sleep and food, and because the sea was calmer, we prob-ably slept through most of the day.

Towards midnight the skies had cleared and there was a bright moon overhead. We drifted onto a beach; the dingy touched bottom in a stretch of shallow water. Our first reaction was that if this was Jap-held territory we had better get ashore pronto and find some cover. So we got out and, though stiff in all our muscles, we dragged the dingy up the beach and into some sand-dunes. We found a deepish hollow and pulled the dingy over us for shelter.

We were awakened early in the morning by three excited natives wearing dhotis, and in Bengali they were saying, "Sahib, sahib — Japaniwallahs" pointing inland. Quickly we deflated the dingy and buried it with our Mae Wests which were so conspicuous. The natives were beach fishermen and must have come across our foot-prints in the sand. They helped us to find a more suitable hiding place.

Their village was called Alethangyaw they said, indicating it was north up the beach. I knew the name from map reading on pre-vious missions, and that it was on the southeast shore at the entrance to the estuary of the River Naf. This inlet forms a natural and political boundary between India and Burma. The dingy had drifted some 60 miles north from the place of ditching, driven by the southwest monsoon. The fishermen made us understand that we should stay in hiding and they would return that night. We had to trust them but we also feared that they might reveal us to the Japs. However they did come back at dusk with rice and fruit and, more importantly, water.

We set off with them northwards along the beach in our stock-inged feet; we had discarded our jungle boots soon after getting in the dingy to avoid damaging it. The night was bright with moon-light so we felt very exposed. After about two miles the natives turned inland; soon we were crossing paddy fields till we eventually arrived at their village. Here they led us to the hut of the headman who soon made it clear that we were not welcome. We assumed he feared for the safety of his village if he gave us shelter. It was dawn as we set off along a track we guessed would lead us to the Naf. We had only gone a few hundred yards when two Gurkhas stepped out of the bushes and challenged us with weapons at the ready. As we tried to identify ourselves to them a British corporal arrived and we gave him our names, rank, etc. He led us to the river where a camouflaged rowing boat was anchored. We got in and he rowed us out to midstream towards a large island where he tied up to a small wooden jetty. On stepping ashore we could see that it was an army encampment.

The corporal took us to his CO, a captain, to whom we again told our story. He provided us with K-rations, all they had, plus a welcome peg of rum. Now what we needed was a bath, clean clothes and footwear. We soon had these; khaki drill shirts and trousers plus pairs of plimsolls. The captain had contacted his base at Maungdaw and arranged for a boat to take us up the inlet.

The three fishermen had been waiting on the river bank and the captain arranged for them to be brought over for a little ceremony of the British Raj. We had given the captain the Burmese silver coins from our money belts, he sat at a little table outside his tent and divided the coins into three equal piles. We shook hands with each one as they received their money and left the camp. Soon a small landing craft arrived to collect us and take us to Maungdaw and comparative safety at last.

Full Bore From Chiringa

In September the squadron was operating flat-out again; flying 103 sorties in mixed but mostly poor weather. Six sorties were aborted because of weather and one through engine trouble. The chief focus of operational activity was the main railway line from Mandalay to Rangoon against which 30 sorties were flown with great success. Other railways — Mandalay to Lashio, Rangoon to Prome and the Bangkok line — were all attacked repeatedly with a total of 25 sorties. The effort was rewarded by severe damage to 30 locomotives and many freight cars some of which were burned. Nevertheless, the most noteworthy strike during September was against Japanese shipping in the Gulf of Martaban in conjunction with 211 Squadron. This was followed by several reconnaissances to find more ships in the Gulf.

Operations for the month of September included a variety of other targets and reconnaissances. The roads, rivers and railroads in central Burma between Ye-u and Chauk were repeatedly patrolled as were the roads in the Shan Plateau. These sorties destroyed 28 MT and damaged a further 30. The patrols of the coast and rivers included several oil barges set on fire as well as some large country craft. The shipping strike against coastal freighters in the Gulf of Martaban resulted in considerable damage that was the result of 211's attacks as well as 177's. Several air–sea rescue missions and one photo reconnaissance sortie were also flown. Clearly the effort was directed to limit re-supply of the enemy forces in severe difficulty in the Chin Hills from the pummelling of the 14th Army. The Arakan and the Taungup Pass were now less important.

Maintenance had been a problem during the whole monsoon. Heavy rain at squadron bases at Ranchi, Tulihul and now Chiringa had been the main cause of trouble because all work was done on the airstrips in the open. Despite double filtering, water in the fuel had been a serious cause of engine failure. Also the squadron moves, with attendant disorder, limited technical staff, and a poor situation regarding spare parts had exacerbated the problem. With a stable base and severe rain becoming less common, maintenance improved.

It was also a month of visits by the Brass. Air Commodore, the Earl of Bandon, DSO, the new AOC of 224 Group visited us for two days. His superior, the new Commander of 3rd TAF, replacing A/M Sir John Baldwin, Air Marshal W.A. Coryton, CB, MVO, DFC also visited and we received a congratulatory signal from Major General Stratemeyer regarding the success of the shipping strike with 211.

The squadron celebrated its first anniversary of operational flying on 10 September, the same day as the emergency resulting from discovery by 211 of a shipping convoy in the Gulf. It may have been a tense day for some of the aircrew but it was celebrated just as seriously by the airmen with free beer, a sing-song and a party in the Airmen's Mess. With a year of ops behind them, the survivors among the original aircrew were starting to be tour-expired. Joe Van Nes and Matt Matthews left the squadron for postings to Special Low Attack Instructional School (SLAIS) at Ranchi where Joe was Chief Pilot and soon engaged to Jean, the Nursing Sister he had met in our sojourn there previously. In September also the Operations Record Book reported fully on squadron activity for the first time since April, another result of a consolidated unit at a stable base.

Ground fire encountered during September was again intense after a minor respite during the worst of the monsoon. Many Beaus were hit and returned with various damage, some so critical that aircraft crashed and were written off. One pilot, W/O James Denny, was wounded in an arm and a leg but returned to base successfully and was quickly hospitalised in Chittagong.

Worse still — two crews were missing. On 15 September W/O J.C. Forbes with W/O L.F. Reynolds failed to return from a sortie briefed to patrol the main Rangoon line from Thazi south at dawn on a day of poor visibility. They were leading a section of two Beaus which arrived at the target, and south at Yamethin they were seen by their number two to attack a loco which then emitted a column of steam, but they warned the second Beau on the VHF not to attack. No flak was seen but Forbes said on the RT they were returning to base and they were seen flying west with a feathered propeller. The No.2, W/O R.A. Hawkins with W/O D.A.S. Hollay, followed them for a few minutes flying along the deck when they approached a bank of low cloud. Hawkins called that he was going to climb above it and this was acknowledged, but Forbes's Beau was not seen or heard from again.

The other loss was the crew of F/O J.A. McKay with F/O A.J. Ede about whose fate nothing is known. They were briefed for a 04:00 take-off for a railway patrol from Prome south towards Rangoon. They were not heard from again after their night take-off.

The operations in September are illuminated by narratives of four aircrew. W/O R. White, navigator to P/O D.M. Anderson, narrates *Adventure with Engines* about their experiences on the 4th–5th of the month:

Toungoo is a long ride from Chiringa in south Bengal: head south-east over the hills of the Arakan Yoma, across the Irrawaddy, hop over the little Pegu Yoma and there is a railway town of Toungoo sitting along a calm stretch of the Sittang in south Burma.

The river there looks good from 1,000 feet up; a picture of smooth water among the greenery of trees, shrubs and grass. Having succeeded with the aid of Mercator and drift recorded, in getting the pilot to point the Beaufighter in the right directions on the way across, I relaxed a relieved moment to savour the view. I wondered what it was like down there: what sort of birds would be living on the water, what animals were getting their teeth into what food they could find, whether there would be snakes slithering around the floor of the forest — but one thing's certain: there would be plenty of insects in that warm and wet monsoon environment. Half an hour amongst them and a multitude of lumps would be showing where the insects had found their meal for the day; and if they had left you any blood, the leeches would be looking for it.

No, 1,000 feet up is the best place to experience that sort of scenery. With the Beaufighter's wing pointing earthward as it banks steeply to the left over the water, there is a clear but distant view of the beauty of the place and time to feel sorry for the sods who have to battle Nature to live there.

Reports of railway activity on the Rangoon — Mandalay line had triggered our orders telling us to seek, find and destroy. Up along the railway, eyes skinned for targets, keeping track of where you are, I had no more time to appreciate the creativity of Nature. Anyway the Beau is not there to create any thing but with four cannons and 6 machine guns, to destroy whatever it can of Japanese communications.

Shadowed by an accompanying Beaufighter piloted by Paddy Taylor with Jimmy Rainbow looking out of the cupola, we see rolling stock in sidings here and there; make them useless with a few rounds and, hey, there's a lorry on the road — set it on fire and wonder whether the cloud of black smoke means it was loaded with oil. Continuing our destructive swath until — what's this? — Shweymo railway station and goods marshalling yard with all sorts of rolling stock; open goods wagons, barrel-shaped tank cars, closed carriages — and, yes, a steam engine! It is camouflaged with tree-branches, obviously parked ready for moving at night. We can hardly believe the luck. Down we go all guns blazing, flashes showing hits and steam billowing up. We wheel and make more runs to make sure we've hit everything in sight and then leave the Japs to sort out the mayhem while we go looking for more targets.

Ah, but as we pull away I see a long black stream pouring past me from the starboard motor. I shout a panicky warning to Don who has a quick look at his instruments and spots zero showing on the oil pressure gauge. We quickly climb to get a bit of height before shutting down the engine to prevent it catching fire, feather the prop, shove on left rudder, open the port engine, and there we are zooming along on that one alone.

Is it enough? We're losing height. Don recalls our CO had crash landed his Beaufighter after it lost one engine so he shouts to me, 'Prepare to ditch!' I look down and see 300 feet below the humpy terrain of the Pegu Yoma which, as it gets closer, looks more and more awkward. Not a pleasing prospect to imagine the aircraft getting to grips with at 100 miles an hour. All the same, you have to think that the belly landing will be successful so what are you going to do after you've got out? Hundreds of miles to plod back to base; don't know a single word of Burmese, so conversation with anyone but my pilot is out; eats could be a problem, though a good chew on a newt if you could catch one would keep you going, and there should be plenty of insects and caterpillars all full of nourishing protein. Wonder if I could get used to the flavours? The natives seem to find them palatable. Must avoid the Japanese.

When we were flying so low that I could tell what the trees were dotting those humps — and if humans were present I would have been able to see the whites of their eyes — Don says 'She's holding her height now; I'm going to try and follow the railway northwards towards Myitkyina.' I thought, 'I've heard of a wing and a prayer' but it seemed a good idea compared to the alternatives. [Myitkyina had just been captured by the Allies and a flight there did not involve climbing.] It was certainly better than a crash and a long walk; and better than heading southwest, skirting the Arakan Yoma and then heading northwards over the sea past Akyab to base with all the difficulties of coping with monsoon storms on one engine and the danger of encountering USAAF Lightnings which were prowling up and down that coast and shooting down everything in sight including the odd Beaufighter. No, good thinking Don, to follow the railway north in good weather to Myitkyina. Back over the railway line, a cheering improvement to our situation, my thoughts came off survival in the jungle; having got away from the Pegu Yoma, we're now at about 300 feet above the deck again. Marvellous. There goes Meiktila on the port side but, awful thought, all the airfields where the Japanese park their fighters must be just over on the left. Mustn't forget we're not only a lame duck, we're also a sitting duck if any Jap marksmen or aircraft have a go at us. Mind you, we are 'Silently into the midst' so by the time any marksman knows we're there, we're gone. Did the Japanese have radar in Burma, and if they did could they have picked us up at 300 feet? That doesn't stop marauding enemy fighters spotting us; I know we've still got our number two along side, but if an Oscar appears Paddy will scoot if he's got any sense.

No good worrying about that, and no need for me to worry about navigating either if Don had decided to follow the railway to Myitkyina. He let the railway wander off to the right as we neared Mandalay and then picked it up again north of the town, heading alongside the Irrawaddy, towards the railway terminus at Myitkyina. Nothing for me to do but make sure my Vickers gun was ready for use, keep an eye out for any Nips in the air and enjoy our bird's eye view of the forests of the rolling Burmese countryside at the same time.

Or that's what I thought until we were on the run up to Myitkyina when a US North American Mustang appeared and buzzed us. I thought, 'Good Lord, we haven't got this far to be shot down by our allies surely!' I fired off the Very lights of the day, flashed the Aldis lamp hoping the pilot would see it and know that we were on his side. He flew across the top of us, came up alongside, climbed, turned and came down behind us but there was no sign of tracer streams thank goodness. After half a dozen passes the Mustang galloped away. I looked astern to see whether our companion Beau was getting examined by the Mustang but all the looking failed to find it. It was then I realized Paddy wasn't with us — what had happened to him and Jimmy?

The American General Joe Stilwell had led a international force of Chinese, Americans, Kachin Burma Regiment, the Chindits and the 3rd Indian Divisision to attack the northern railhead of Myit-kyina. On the 4th of August 1944 his Army took the airfield. Exactly a month later Don and I were thankful for their presence there. Although there was still fighting going on in the town, the Japs didn't interfere with us; the welcome sight of a friendly landing strip after limping vulnerably over enemy held land for so long was beautiful.

Perfect landing on one engine. Landing with both isn't easy but with the power only on one side it must be extraordinarily tricky; remarkable judgement to get the right height, distance from the runway, rate of descent, and speed to glide all the way in. And it had to be right the first time — no hope of going round again. Yet for me in the back it all seemed to go off as smoothly as a normal landing. Lucky for me to have a pilot who could cope immediately with the emergency of having to adjust to flying on one engine, keep the machine in the air for 500 miles and then to have to land like a glider pilot.

Don seemed quite normal (I wouldn't have been) when we looked at the duff engine and saw the cause of all the trouble was a small bullet-hole in the oil cooling vent sticking out of the leading edge of the starboard wing. As the oil was pumped through the vent to cool it, it had come spraying out. No other damage at all — just one little bullet had done the engine in.

It was a comforting sight to see our fellow Beau parked alongside us. At Matlia, where the river turns south again after a westerly course and a big bend, we had taken the shorter course following the railway; Paddy thought we had followed the river and had not seen us leave. He had gone the longer way but got to the airstrip first and was telling the Americans that a crippled Beau he was accompanying must have gone down not far south. While he was telling them this, one of them pointed to the sky above the far end of the runway and said 'Hey fellers ain't that a Beaufighter approaching?' Paddy was as relieved to see us as we him.

In the mess afterwards I talked to the American pilot who had buzzed us. He said he hadn't seen the Very signal lights or the flashing Aldis lamp, (how could he not have? It looked like a fire-works display) but recognized us as a Beaufighter although he had not realised we were on one engine. It would be advisable to send him west to teach the Lightning pilots a bit of aircraft recognition. How can anyone miss the distinctive shape of a Beaufighter?

Paddy and Jimmy would carry us back to base next morning. They were short of fuel at Myitkyina and would only give us enough to get us home. Don and I stood in the well behind the pilot and enjoyed flying in a Beau with two engines working. Up we go heading westwards over the Chins; there's a huge storm in front, cumulo-nimbus reaching well over 20, 000 feet — skirt around that to find another one half an hour on. Very different scene below to the placid-looking Burmese countryside — craggy great mountains, and great white and slate-coloured clouds thousands of feet thick with turbulent upward thrusting currents which could destroy any aircraft trying to fly through them.

All this altering course avoiding storms is soaking up petrol; Myitkyina could only let us have 100 gallons, just enough with which to get back to base but the monsoon storms were making us use more. Before we were clear of the hills Paddy realised we would not have enough to make it to base. Possibly not even enough to clear the Chins.

Chittagong was the nearest airfield, so Chittagong it had to be. Don was leaning forward over Paddy's shoulder, frantically switching from one petrol tank to another to ensure that every last drop could be used, but those enormous jungle-covered mountains were still beneath us. Lucky the tanks held some reserve after the gauges showed empty; when the engines faltered, Don switched to another apparently empty tank. The engines picked up until another splutter triggered another switch-over. The mountains were still there, seemingly endless but at last the ridges got lower; Paddy reduced power and descended from 8,000 feet, half gliding over the foothills towards the Chittagong airfield.

Plains below us at last, the airfield in sight and then both motors stopped. All the switching was unable to find another drop of petrol. Down went the nose to get gliding speed. Daren't lower the undercarriage so as not to increase drag and in case we had to crash land before reaching the strip. Just enough height to glide there to scrape the aircraft's belly along the runway. Plenty of sparks but no fire — no petrol.

After clambering out of the top of a Beau for the second emergency in two days I felt it was good to get my feet on the ground that I never expected to reach gently and then reflected on what the four of us had done. The destruction of that steam engine and rolling stock had cost our war effort quite a bit: one crippled Beaufighter at Myitkyina which would need a visit from an RAF maintenance team, and a second Beau at Chittagong with a sore belly and bent props.

So what? We'd upset the Japanese by interfering with their communications, no doubt about that — your run of the mill Burmese railwaymen don't have rifles to fire at Beaufighters. And most importantly: four aircrew involved in the adventure survived to have a go at some more boats and trains and ships and planes.

The most important operation against the Japanese shipping on the approaches to Rangoon took place on 10 September. This is the only operation by Beaufighters in Burma that Saunders in his history of the Royal Air Force describes (1954, p.347). It started with a patrol on the 9th at last light by 211 Squadron Beaufighters which encountered a convoy of 13 small vessels, steel-hulled freighters and accompanying escorts. They attacked it immediately with cannons and rocket inflicting severe damage but as they were at extreme range they had to return and did not see all the results of their attack. Group HQ quickly ordered 177 Squadron to strike the same targets next morning and for 211 to follow with another attack towards evening. W/C Hill was on leave, S/L Hunt had just returned from a dawn attack along the Lashio line so S/L Wills briefed the Flight attack. It was led by F/O A. Sutherland Brown with F/S Aldham in 'L' (NE814), W/O R.E. Wiscombe with W/O Kelly in NE709, W/O F.J. King with F/S R.G. Harrison in NE661, and W/O T.C. Forbes with W/O L.F. Reynolds in NV127. The Flight was in the air at 10:30 hours. Sutherland Brown (1992) writes:

> On 10 September a flap developed when a sister squadron encountered and attacked a convoy of coastal freighters with naval escorts south of Moulmein near Kalegauk Island. Our squadron was ordered to press home the attack with armour-piercing rockets as the others rearmed for a third strike... We were quickly briefed and in the air by mid-morning. We flew in a loose formation [to save fuel] down the coast at wave tops to avoid radar and likewise across the Gulf of Martaban which was like glass. In such conditions flying into the sea is a hazard but running out of fuel was a more serious one as the operation was at extreme range. We arrived off the island to find one coastal freighter stationary at sea. Attacks were made *en passant* to try to sink it but we continued around the lee of the island where six or seven ships were moored or beached. They opened up with flak as we dove towards them [Figure 55] and the results were hard to confirm in the confusion of the melee except we had a number of direct hits. We had no time or inclination to linger so we again formed a loose gaggle and this time cut across the delta flying just above the trees. All our tanks were vir-

144

Figure 55 Advertisement by Bristol Aircraft Ltd. in *Flight* magazine, April 1945 referring to the strike of the convoy at Kalegauk Island. A bit unreal—ships too large, dive too steep, reflector gunsight not in position and no flak (A. Sutherland Brown).

tually empty as we landed safely at base after six hours and forty minutes in the air. If this was a Japanese experiment in reinforcement it was one they did not continue but it was scarcely the great victory in the Andaman Sea as reported in the *Calcutta Statesman* of 13th September.

The Squadron Operations Record Book reported further details:

... Two aircraft made cannon attacks on an MV probably about 500 tons. It appeared all metal construction and one crew reports it seemed to have been attacked previously. A balloon of flame came from the ship when it was attacked. Two vessels were seen lashed together 200 yards off shore. One was a MV about 700 tons and the other a motor boat with twin gun mountings but they were not manned. One aircraft made cannon attacks and claimed hits on both vessels. NV127 fired a salvo of eight RP's which fell just short and followed with two cannon attacks. On returning NE814 made two cannon attacks and sprayed the jetty on shore while NE661 made one cannon attack and reports that a quantity of oil was on the water around the ships. At the south end of Kalegauk Island seven ships were sighted, three about 500 tons and four smaller ones. NE814 made three cannon attacks and NE661 four cannon attacks on the three larger vessels and claimed hits amidships above the waterline. NE709 fired a salvo of 8 RPs at vessels farthest off shore but they fell 20 yards short. NE661, the last to leave the target, reports that one vessel was on fire. Smoke resulting from cannon attacks hung over all the vessels and flashes were also reported... NE709 experienced engine trouble on the way back and fired off its remaining ammunition over the sea. The engine cut but later recovered and the aircraft reached base safely.

On approaching Akyab, Sutherland Brown broke radio (RT) silence to discuss the individual fuel situations. All felt they had enough to land at Chiringa and did.

On 14 September the squadron received a congratulatory signal from General Stratemeyer:

My congratulations to the Commanders and aircrew of 177 and 211 Squadrons for the determined and courageous attacks made on shipping off the Tenasserim coast on the 9th and 10th of September. and the groundcrews who made this possible. The enemy is having the greatest difficulty in supplying his forces in Burma and these attacks carried out at extreme range of the aircraft in spite of intensive defensive fire, will by destroying or seriously damaging at least 8 ships, undoubtedly restrict him more still. I would like to add to my congratulations on this effort [also ones for] the consistently good work the Beaufighter Squadrons are doing in reducing the supplies and reinforcements which the Japs are getting in Burma.

W/O T.J. Denny reports on a sortie on the 22 September when he was briefed to patrol the coast and Taungup roads and photograph some bridges near the Irrawaddy. He took off at 09:15 in NE738 with W/O J. Yates as his navigator.

Joe and I had been detailed to make a low level patrol down the Arakan coast, skirt heavily defended Taungup, follow the road to Prome. This was the fourth mission of my second tour. Accurate navigation was vital on these tree top height patrols in order to surprise the enemy and avoid known highly defended positions. Joe

146

had little experience of this type of flying. Our first three trips together had consequently been very exciting and we had already collected several bullet holes in our plane.

We took off without incident. It was the tail end of the monsoon and was still very hot and humid. In these conditions potential over heating of the engines necessitated a fast taxi to the end of the strip and a quick take off. In spite of this we were usually completely soaked in sweat by the time we were airborne and would remain that way through the whole trip.

We headed out over the ocean from Chiringa and followed the coastline south cruising at 220 mph at 20 feet. As soon as we were abreast of enemy territory we flew in to land to pick up the coastal road along which the Japanese had to bring all their supplies. This long narrow coastal plain is covered by jungle and mangrove swamps, the road meanders and makes enormous detours, and I had great difficulty in following it at tree top height. There was no sign of life — even the few native villages seemed deserted and certainly there was no sign of Japanese activity. Their transport usually moved at night and holed up in the daytime under excellent camouflage. We flew on for 30 minutes and then, as our orders were to avoid Taungup, I asked Joe for an approximate position. He was confused by our erratic progress down the coast road but was sure we were not at Taungup yet although I could see a large village coming up ahead. I decided to fly over it and try to identify it on the map. We got to the outskirts of the place and all hell broke loose — it was of course Taungup. At that height I could hear the crack of machine guns and rifle fire above the noise of the engines; tracer bullets were coming at us from all angles, then I heard the thud of light anti-aircraft guns. Joe reported shells bursting above and behind. I put the Beaufighter down to about 10 feet, gave it full throttle and crossed the remainder of Taungup weaving to avoid huts, trees and telegraph poles. It seemed to take an age to cross that mile or so of scattered buildings and dumps as I crouched down in my seat. Somehow we got out of town and I could no longer hear gunfire although shells were still bursting above and behind us. I flew around a low hill to shield us and then looked for damage and immediately saw a row of four jagged holes in the port wing roughly in line with the cockpit with the last only five feet away. They had obviously been fired from almost directly beneath us. The one nearest the cockpit seemed to be right where the fuel tank was situated but Joe reported no sign of a leak. I assumed the self-sealing system had worked. No other damage was visible so I decided to press on after making a few caustic remarks about his low level navigational capabilities.

I flew along the north side of the road, climbing steadily with the terrain as we crossed the Arakan Yoma. As before there was no sign of life and at the pass I throttled back and put the nose down to follow the road with its numerous s-bends. My last task on the patrol was to photograph the bridge at Padaung where the road crossed a tributary near the Irrawaddy. I opened the throttles and hugged the tree-clad slopes, keeping out of sight of the defended bridge until the last second. I switched on the camera and shot across the bridge; a few stray tracers came up as we reached the far end and then we were out of their vision behind trees again. At that time I noticed the tops of large red and yellow sails on the river a mile or so to the right. I turned and approached the Irrawaddy and saw they were large junks with square sails. We were supposed to attack any form of transport for the Japs used all types. I climbed to 500 feet banked steeply and dove raking them with cannon fire. I then stayed low, turned northwest for base, putting on a little extra speed as this whole area between the end of the Taungup road and Prome was known to be dangerous. Soon I could see the Taungup–Prome road again white amongst the trees. At that moment there was a tremendous bang in the cockpit, a harsh brittle sound accompanied by smoke and dust. I felt strangely numb for a second or two then my brain started to work again and my first thought was that a cannon shell had exploded right in the cockpit and yet there seemed no obvious damage. Then I felt a numbness in my right forearm and on raising the arm saw three blackened holes in the fleshy part which at that moment started to bleed heavily. I called Joe on the intercom and as I did, noticed I was heading straight for three tall palm trees. Just in time I pulled hard on the control column with my left hand and cleared them with little to spare. I realized I was in no condition for a low level return to base and would have to take the risk of gaining some altitude. I trimmed the Beau in a steady climb and headed in the general direction of Bengal. By this time Joe had crawled up to the front and had the first aid box out. I held my arm up to him to bandage and a stream of blood ran off my elbow on to the instruments at the right hand side of the cockpit. Joe made a fairly sound job of bandaging and then I noticed blood was soaking through the left leg of my flying suit and I found several slight wounds there. However it was virtually impossible to put a bandage down there so I just had to leave it. The pain from my arm was intense now and I felt faint and sick with the heat and the loss of blood. I had a drink of water and splashed some on my face and held my head down as far as possible. The faintness eased off.

I turned in my seat and looked at Joe standing behind me — white and anxious. If I had passed out, even if he had managed to drag me out of my seat and get the controls, he had never handled a plane and could not have got it down in one piece. I pulled myself together and started to take a more intelligent interest in our return flight. I had a look around the cockpit and eventually found the cause of all the trouble was not a cannon shell at all but a rifle bullet which had entered through the bottom left side of the nose, smashed the top of the undercarriage lever and passed out through a neat hole in the perspex at the top right hand side of the cockpit close to my right ear. On lining up the two holes it was evident that the bullet had passed between my outstreched arms as I held the spectacle-type control wheel. My wounds must have been caused by splinters of metal.

We were at 10,000 feet by this time and almost over the centre of the mountains. At this height I was within radio range of Chiringa and called them to report the position and estimated time of arrival (ETA). After that there was nothing to do but keep on course and wait for the strip to appear on the horizon and hope there were no Jap fighters about as we were still a hundred miles inside Japanese occupied territory. Time dragged interminably, my right arm throbbed painfully, my hand was numb and I could only use my thumb and forefinger. I began to worry about how I was going to land the aircraft.

At long last the strip came in sight and, after a call to the control tower, I lowered the wheels and made a hasty pre-landing cockpit check. I made the final approach rather low and fast in order to do a wheel landing rather than a three-pointer. This would put less strain on my right hand and meant I would fly the plane under low power until the front wheels touched and then whip the throttles shut and wind back the trim tabs with my left hand.

Everything went smoothly until the wheels touched and began to take the full weight of the aircraft, then the left wing dropped and we began a dangerous swing to the left towards trees lining the strip. I realized I had a flat tyre on the port wheel, no doubt punctured by another bullet. There was nothing to do but apply full right brake. Unfortunately the brake lever on the control was designed to be operated by the right thumb but I managed to get my left hand on it and squeezed as hard as I could. The swing checked and our speed of about 80 began to drop. The good old Beau kept amazingly straight until about the last quarter of the landing run and then swung off the runway, shot between two lorries full of groundcrew waiting to cross the strip and skidded to a stop in a cloud of dust. I switched off and clambered wearily out of my seat and down the hatch. The MO was there in his jeep and took me directly to a nearby West African Rifles field hospital. On the 30th I was transferred to the RAF hospital at Chittagong where I spent the next five weeks. They successfully operated on my right arm to remove the worst of the fragments.

Sutherland Brown (1992) described another operation on 27 September 1944:

...we were briefed for an offensive patrol by ourselves along two branch railways in central Burma that met the main line at Thazi Junction. I was wrenched out of a sound sleep at about four in the morning. I quickly evacuated my bowels, a fairly automatic reaction; donned my light drill flying suit, tied my money belt full of silver Rupees around my waist, put my kukri (Gurkha) long curved knife on my belt, checked for my goulee (ball) chit and silk escape map and grabbed my leather helmet which I had for months laid aside in favour of earphones. The chit, money and map were aids for escape if you survived a crash landing in Burma; no one thought seriously about parachuting out of a Beau, flying like we did along the deck. We were picked up by a ³/₄ ton truck for a cool, jolting ride to the hard standing of our Beau, 'E' (NV260). I drank a sickly sweet cup of tea in a dirty mug given to me by a cheerful erk (mechanic) and took part in some light banter; strapped on my parachute and climbed the ladder behind the cockpit and swung like Tarzan into my seat. This was formed of a deflated dingy attached to the chute in which the gas bottle invariably cut into one's ass. When Alf [W/O A.J. Aldham] was ready I fired up the engines, did the cockpit check which was AOK, waved away the chocks and quickly taxied to the end of the strip. After the vital action check was completed we were charging down the runway, tail up in the darkness, lifted the wheels and climbed away.

Our route took us close to Mt Victoria (10,018 feet) so we climbed over it and let down towards the Irrawaddy as dawn cracked in the east. We passed close to the twelfth century temple city of Pagan, seeing the multitude of domed and pyramidal spires over the plain as silhouettes. Further on in increasing light the cone of Mt Popa was black against the brilliant dawn. It was a beautiful clear morning as we picked up the railway before Meiktila. This was a little dodgy as this town was the site of the largest group of airfields in Burma from which most of Japanese sorties were flown. We skirted the airfields, picked up the railway again and followed it to Thazi Junction and then up the branch line climbing into the Shan Plateau toward Taung-gyi. Although the weather was perfect in the plain, the plateau was enveloped in solid cloud so we went to our second target which was to stooge around Meiktila and Thazi before following the main line south. We caught two lorries climbing up the mountain road and set them alight, then a bowser (gasoline) truck and a staff car near Meiktila and did the same to them. We exhausted our ammunition (250 rounds per cannon) soon after we headed south and so I said to Alf, 'I'm turning on to 270 (west), give me a corrected course for base.' Alf said, 'I think you should go farther south, Skipper.' By then I had turned and was speeding above the scattered acacias and continued stubbornly. Alf was right: within seconds I flashed over an empty revetment (blast shelter) and saw a minor grass airstrip ahead which was well south of the main group. At the same time light flak started coming up at us so I began jinking among the trees, throwing maps and loose gear flying around the cockpit. We were hit by numerous bullets and exploding shells. One blew up Alf's radio in his face and another caused black oil to pour out of the left engine nacelle. Thinking it was engine oil I had to start climbing to give us a chance of getting home on one engine. As soon as I did black explosive puffs of heavy flak started bursting around us. The oil plume had stopped quickly and I realized it was hydraulic not engine oil so I dived to the deck again and flew an erratic course out of the area.

There were either no Oscars at Meiktila or they didn't find us for we continued with our battered craft over the mountains to Chiringa. It was difficult to assess the damage in the air; we had no radio and no hydraulics but both of us were unscathed. I made a pass down the runway to indicate I had no landing gear or flaps, came around again and approached as slowly as I could while still trying to grease her on to the grass. It went not too badly except we struck a plank roadway which caused more damage than necessary. My head crashed into the gunsight but it only hurt and did not break the skin. Thank goodness for the fluke of switching back to a helmet. We had thirty seven bullet and shell holes in "E" but she lived to fly again.

At the debriefing I was given hell by Willy for not avoiding the roadway, I gave myself hell for not paying more attention to Alf, but mostly I was thankful we survived. This became more poignant that same day as two of my better friends and basha neighbours, did not return from their sortie, F/O Mac Mackay and F/O A.J. Ede.

'The CO's Missing'

October was an unfortunate month for casualties. At the beginning, on the 5th, W/C John Hill and his navigator F/O G.W. Broughton did not return from a sortie. They left on a solo mission at 09:45 to patrol the communications networks in a quadrangle in central Burma from Magwe to Monywa in the west and Nantok to Maymyo in the east, a common patrol that gave great latitude for initiative to the crew. Nothing was known of their misfortune at the time but in May 1945 they were among the prisoners released by the Japanese when they retreated from Rangoon. Hill, who had health problems on the squadron, soon was suffering in gaol from severe beriberi. These prisoners received none of the treatment supposed to be accorded PoWs by the Geneva Convention, of which Japan was not

151

a signatory — they were not acknowleged to the Interational Red Cross, no information was issued to their relatives, they were subjected to starvation diets, deficiency and bacterial diseases and many were treated inhumanely. Although they did not suffer the brutal work and starvation regime of the prisoners building the Bangkok railway, they were treated as war criminals in prison and not PoWs like those in Siam (cf. Dunlop, 1990 and Hudson, 1987). Apparently Hill and Broughton were shot down by Oscars and quickly taken prisoner. At the time it was a downer for the squadron for, although we were hardened to casualties, the loss of a CO was difficult. The word quickly went around, 'The CO's missing.'

The ORB stated, 'The loss of the Commanding Officer is greatly felt by all members of the Squadron. He was a personality who was loved and respected by all members of the Squadron, and his "on-on" spirit had been of inestimable value to everyone.' S/L Hunt took over as Acting CO although he had just completed his second tour.

The Squadron suffered the loss of two other crews during the month; on 15 October P/O A.E. Stuart-Cox with F/S P.C. Woods disappeared on returning from a sortie with W/O R.F. Abel with F/S R. Loffill and F/O S.J. Emery, RCAF, with F/S R.G. James. They crashed into hills near the airfield on a night take-off and the aircraft was seen from the tower to explode. These losses are described further in the following narratives. One near thing involved F/S H.W.G. Hart with F/S R.H. Welsh on 2 October. Patrolling the roads and railway to Lashio they encountered intense flak and were hit in the inner port fuel tank. It did not seal, so they followed Anderson's route to Myitkyina but landed at the emergency landing ground at Taro, refuelled and got home the next day.

The southwest monsoon still had a grip on Burma and the weather for much of the month was as bad as any during the season. Consequently only 98 sorties were flown of which 10 were at night; three sorties were aborted for weather and others were truncated because of it. The main target day and night was once again the main railway line and roads from Mandalay to Rangoon with over 30 sorties, while the Lashio line and roads received 11 and the Bangkok line 4. However, the most important single operation was a sweep of the Rangoon airfields, Hmawbi and Mingladon, by six aircraft each from 177 and 211 plus a Flight of DeHavilland Mosquitoes. In addition, the southern Arakan and the Tenasserim coasts, the southern rivers, and central Burma all received some attention. In addition, three air-sea rescue missions and a number of reconnaissances were carried out to identify radar installations or to photograph bridges for PRU. These operations resulted in 10 locos severely damaged together with much rolling stock attacked, 7 MT destroyed and 32 damaged, 13 launches and barges as well as many large junks and schooners damaged or destroyed. Active targets were getting both harder to find and to attack.

October saw the start of the changing of the guard, which was completed before the end of the year. Although the squadron aircrew and staff were changed completely squadron spirit continued — apparently transferred from those leaving and those still staying on. S/L Wills, DFC, was tour-expired and left on the 31st posted to 224 Group. W/O A.J. Kappler, DFM, who had flown with F/L J. Marquis, DFC, (Figure 54) for much of the latter's tour, left in mid-October. W/O G. Herr, RCAF, with W/O F.H. Burton were also tour-expired and left. S/L Hunt, DSO and Bar, DFC, took over as CO and stayed on in operations until the new CO arrived and was comfortable. F/L J. Marquis, DFC, also extended his tour on the CO's request to continue as Squadron Navigation Officer. The Engineering Officer, F/L P.S. Hallas, left to be replaced by F/O K.G. Gardner, who then promptly broke a leg, although he was soon back with an uncomfortable walking cast. However, the dominant change was the arrival on 4 October of seven new crews, several of whom were starting second tours, others were experienced Beaufighter crews and some were novices. The slate included F/L O.E. Simpson with F/O N.F. Archer; F/L R.H. Wood with F/O J.W. Harper; F/O S.J. Emery, RCAF, with F/S R.F. James; F/S W.J. Hudson with F/S J.K. Smith; F/O A.H. Rieck with F/O T.N. Allen; P/O A.E. Stuart-Cox with F/S P.C. Woods; and W/O R.F. Abel with F/S R. Loffill. They arrived one day to find their new CO missing on ops the next. Unfortunately three of these crews were also lost within a month.

A positive factor on the squadron in transition and under stress of high losses was a large increase in sports and entertainment generated on the squadron. Almost every three days there was a soccer match between flights or with neighbouring military units such as the West African Rifles. There were also gramophone recitals, band practices, card games and sing-song evenings, and a very credible art exhibit and French classes.

Narratives related to October include a jungle search, a couple of first sorties, an aerodrome strafe and an operation with an unexplained loss. Reg Loffill (1989) described his first operation in his contemporary diary:

On Saturday October 7th we heard that we were 'on' the following day and would be briefed at 9 PM... We went over to the briefing room and got all the 'gen' — our section was to raid Thakon [no. 2

to Wiscome] — two more sections were to raid other small towns [on the main line railway yards and loco shelters by rocket attacks]. Take off 07.40 — seems quite a nice show — not as worried as I thought I should be — got all my kit together and went to bed... Got up at 6 and had a good breakfast — borrowed Bob's Bedon jungle [escape] suit but didn't wear it — caught the gharri [³/₄ ton truck] at 7 and went straight down to dispersal — felt nervous hanging around the kite before taking off — 211 had 8 kites to go and we had six — they were on the same job as us and took off at 7:30 — got airborne, formed up and set course — climbed to 9,000 feet over the hills and then streaked down the other side at about 220 knots — then on the deck across the Irrawaddy following old Wiscome [probably 21 or 22 years old] — could see Soggy Brown in front followed by Simpson — didn't bother so much about map reading as watched out for fighters but did keep a check — we went down to a hill position, then the sections broke up and made for their respective targets — 10 minutes later arrived at Tatkon — climbed to 1,200 feet and then Wiscome went in from the northwest and we followed — couldn't see any results from the back but bags of smoke in the target area down the railway line — right down on the deck and straight for home — never saw anything at all — took three hours — got debriefed by the IO — everybody back and the IO quite pleased with the show — I know they won't all be as quiet as this one!! — still — F/L Simpson flew straight through his own debris and damaged the main spar — kite to go to Repair and Salvage Unit...

Reg Loffill (1989) comments about this and other operations in his book manuscript:

There was nothing special about this operation; very run-of-the-mill in fact, except that it was our first. But it had all the ingredients in common with our future sorties. First the 'grip' on the stomach when the news came through that we were on; the first tremors of fear that stayed there until the job was over. Then the briefing in the operations room; details of the work to be done. Navigators were especially busy in the hours that followed briefing, getting routes planned on the maps.

There was none of the conventional navigator's charts on this type of work. Low flying required a special navigational approach centred entirely on map reading. Five minute intervals (15 nautical miles) were marked out along the projected track and pinpoint fixes were sought continually. One anticipated say, a road junction, a confluence of rivers, a railway line with its towns at intervals. When a fix showed a drift to port or starboard a snap correction was made by the pilot for a new track so calculated. None of the finesse of wind speed and direction here! The navigator sweated all the time, for an aircraft covers much ground in 60 seconds at 60 feet. We were most careful to mark on our maps beforehand any areas reported where flak had been experienced, and we tried to skirt these zones; no point in looking for trouble.

Meanwhile the pilots were busy with their chores. Aircraft had to be checked with the ground crews — engines, airframes, armaments; there were documents to be signed that the work had been done etc.

The period of waiting for take-off, with maybe a nights sleep first, was a period I disliked most... but I never remember having any trouble sleeping. Then the short journey by truck with our equipment to the aircraft dispersals. These were the moments I hated; the last cigarette — then into the aircraft. Strangely, all these sensations disappeared as soon as we moved down the runway, the butterflies in the stomach quietened and it was a relief to get busy with the many tasks that had to be done.

Tension returned as we crossed into enemy territory, but there was much to concentrate on — navigation, eyes skinned for fighters, the sortie to be carried out. The penultimate phase was the journey home and as we crossed back into safer areas we could climb to a relaxed 1,000 feet or so. The tension had largely disappeared; the job was nearly over and another entry could be added to the total of sorties in our log books. Finally the landing and the sensation which comes when danger [has been faced] but is no longer imminent, the feeling that it is wonderful to be alive; there is a perceptible feeling of well-being — that is until a day or so later the phone rings shrilly in the Sergeants' Mess that we were to report to the Ops Room.

On our second trip we had a different kind of experience. We were briefed to carry out a strike at dawn on the Prome–Taikkyi railway line. This stretch of line was constantly patrolled by Beaufighter squadrons. It was only a single track line but was of great importance to the Japanese as it linked the port of Rangoon with Prome on the Irrawaddy from whence supplies and troop reinforcements moved north on the river up to the confluence with the Chindwin and east to Mandalay. This was the main Burma supply route in the west.

We were to fly in 'O' (NV376), No.2 to P/O Stuart-Cox with F/S Woods. As this was their sixth trip they were considered senior and therefore flew as No.1. We took off at 04:30, picked up Stuart-Cox who was already airborne and flew with him in loose formation, there being just enough pre-dawn light to see each other. The diary reports... "climbed across the hills at 8,000 feet then down the Irrawaddy valley just as dawn broke — bags of low lying mist about and I was rather worried about the proximity of Prome.

However, Woody seemed to have got things taped, and stooged down alongside the river on the deck of the west bank — I was really het up as I thought we were further south than we actually were — we crossed over the river and soon struck the railway — I got a PP (pinpoint) and all was OK and we stooged on down the line weaving and going around the villages and small towns — hit Paungde a bit unexpectedly but didn't get fired at — nothing was on the railway...

We saw bags of bullock carts and never bothered them [although they certainly carried freight for the enemy] — at Ityma, Roy spotted a warehouse and gave it a burst, and as we passed over I heard the rattle of LMG having a go at us — Roy didn't know and as a result didn't weave — we found afterwards that we'd been hit near the starboard wing tip — knocked off patrol and headed for the sea — Stuart-Cox followed us and after a while we got separated — we saw him away to starboard going great guns, and that was the last anybody saw of them for when we got back we found that they hadn't arrived and they didn't turn up — later Ron Welsh went to have a look [follow their reciprocal track] — what happened is a great mystery..." The mystery is that the crew made no attempt to contact us on R/T which they surely would have done in an emergency. Was their transmitter hit? As they were never found it's likely they went down at sea.

Tony Rieck had a fair amount of experience ferrying Beaufighters to North Africa before he arrived with the group of seven at the squadron. He narrates his experiences with Tommy Allen on their first few operations:

We did our first operational trip on Friday the 13th. We flew No.2 to a crew with long experience on the Squadron. We were to patrol the railway in central Burma from Yamethin to Taungdingyi. Flying low level we came across the railway slightly before I expected it. The leading aircraft banked hard to starboard and to avoid him I was forced to turn inside him, which meant I found myself leading down the railway line instead of as planned the other way around. The consequence was that the other Beau received all the accurate flak from the Japanese gunners. I was not popular and the comment on return was I would not survive more than a few operations. I have never been superstitious about Friday the 13th since.

W/C Hunt had done more operational flights than anyone on the Squadron and took over as CO when W/C Hill went down. I did three trips to Siam as No.2 to Mike. I can still see him calling across the dining room table in the mess, 'Tony, let's hurry to Siam before breakfast tomorrow.' Two of these flights

156

were planned to arrive at Chiengrai at first light and were most successful. On one occasion we caught four lorries loaded with Japanese troops. All four were destroyed. At the beginning of November we attempted the same by moonlight. I lost sight of Mike in the dark, but continued and made an attack on lorries with headlights. On firing our cannons, the intercom went unserviceable so any communication between Tommy Allen and myself was accomplished by him clambering over the ammunition boxes — through the armour plate doors and shouting in my ear or handing me a piece of paper with the course for me to steer.

Cumulus clouds were building up over the mountains on the way back and we had to climb to 14,000 feet to clear them. This was about the maximum ceiling for the derated Beau X which was designed for low level operations. All that was below when we cleared the cloud was the blackness of thickly jungle clad hills. Our ETA over Chiringa came with nothing but black below, no lights or land marks. Fuel was getting low and I realized we were in real trouble. Tommy sent out a Mayday call on the radio and we were eventually given a course to fly. The fuel gauges were now reading zero and then below in moonlight I saw the airstrip. I made a quick circuit with a pass down the runway. There were no lights anywhere, but luckily the moon was bright and much to my amazement I did a smooth landing in the darkness.

I was relieved to see rows of friendly Dakotas parked on the perimeter. We taxied still in darkness to what looked like the control tower, switched off the engines and clambered down through the hatch onto the friendly earth, to be met by an Indian soldier with a fixed bayonet which he pointed at my throat and demanded an identity card. It turned out we had landed at Hathazari. We had been in the air 6 hours and 30 minutes. I had obviously been flying slightly north of our intended track all the way back. I will always remember watching those fuel gauges go steadily down with no idea of where we were and only dense jungle below.

F/O Emery's crash in the night of 16–17 October was followed by an intense effort by P/O Don Anderson, RAAF, and others to get to the crash site. Don led a party including the Group Padre, S/L G.N. McCulloch, early in the morning by canoe but they were unsuccessful. Don then borrowed a Harvard from 211 Squadron the next day and with F/S R.G. Harrison found the crash from the air and accurately pinpointed it. He then led a second party to the crash site. Jim Marquis accompanied Don on one of the trips. He describes it as follows:

157

Don was going back to have another go on the ground and I asked if I could tag along. Fairly early in the morning Don and I were dropped off on the bank of the Matamahari River which flows by Chiringa. It was a supply line for our forward troops and Don and I got a lift in two dugout canoes taking in supplies. We went up the river all day. It was a peaceful scene with abundant egrets fishing by the river but also West African infantrymen walking along the southern bank making their way individually back to their unit at the front.

In late afternoon we arrived at the Forestry Officer's bungalow, he unfortunately was down with fever but we set up our beds and mosquito nets on his verandah. Next morning we set out with an interpreter and a guide armed with a long-bladed machete. In that area there were white patches on the maps and other areas marked impenetrable bamboo forest. At times the only way we could make progress was to wade up the stream courses. We had to stop frequently to rid ourselves of the leeches we accumulated. We also encountered elephant tracks but fortunately did not catch up with them. Don and I had our service revolvers, .38 Smith and Wessons, and Don had a Sten gun and I a 12 gauge shot gun, good for most things but not elephants.

Eventually we arrived at a small village, a few huts angled out from the steep hillside with a verandah at the front supported by bamboo stilts. We sat on the headman's verandah smoking cheroots as Don questioned him through the interpreter.

On our way back we encountered a magnificent 'Flame of the Forest' tree in full bloom in a clearing with small deer, Black Buck, beneath it. We spent another night at the Forestry Officer's verandah and in the morning got a lift down river in an empty dugout. Don had shown as much determination in his quest as he did in his operational flying.

The ORB describes the successful search party led by Don on the 20th:

The crash was discovered partially embedded in the side of a hill near the village of Futyarjiri approximately 47 miles south south east of Chittagong... The aircraft had exploded and burnt at impact — there was nothing left to salvage. The bodies of F/O Emery and F/S James were removed and buried in separate graves dug some 20 yards from the aircraft. F/O Emery's grave was marked by a portion of the undercarriage and F/S James by the rear Browning gun barrel. P/O Anderson read the burial service and the party fired a volley over the graves... P/O Anderson and the rest of the party must be congratulated for their persistent effort in difficult country and conditions.

The major operation of the month was a joint one of 177, 211 and a Mosquito squadron in which they attacked the airfields of Rangoon. S/L Hunt with W/O Anderson led the six 177 Squadron Beaufighters, together with F/L R.H. Wood with F/O Harper, P/O Elliot with F/S W.J. Perry, W/O F.J. King with W/O J. Yates, P/O N.H. Boyd with F/S E.E. Ruddell and F/S J.I. Munday with F/S F.J. Lumley. Eric Ruddell describes the operation as follows:

On the 18th of October 1944 all flying had been suspended. 'Something big,' said the old hands, 'Probably an aerodrome strafe.' The rumour multiplied when six crews were called to preliminary briefing and sworn to secrecy. P/O Noel Boyd and his crew (me) were most interested in all this because we headed the standby crew list.

I was a member of the Sergeants' Mess at that time and it was during tiffin (lunch) on the 16th that the Mess phone rang. An eerie silence fell. A colleague answered the phone: 'Yes he's here.' I was handed the receiver and heard F/L Simpson: 'Eric, Paddy's gone sick. You're on the big do. Briefing in the Ops Room at 2:15, OK?'

It was indeed an aerodrome strafe. Six aircraft from 177 were to lead and six from 211 would follow. Nine Mosquitoes from another squadron would leave later and catch up to us. The rendezvous would be Lake Hlawga: we would turn north and strafe Hmawbi, 211 would turn south and hit Mingladon and the Mosquitoes would run through and strafe Yamethin some miles to the east. The conclusion of the briefing sticks in the memory: 'Mosquitoes, if you see a Beaufighter in trouble stick with it. Beaufighters, if you see a Mosquito limping home on one engine stay with it if you can keep up.'

S/L Hunt took off at 06:45 on the 18th followed by the rest of us and then 211's flight. The twelve Beaufighters formed two V formations over the airfield and set off south. We were stationed on the right of 177's formation and, as navigation would be more or less passive map reading for the next few hours, there was time to reflect on the trip. It was hoped that our attack would prompt the Japanese into putting up all their fighter aircraft and a force of US fighters would shoot them down. Later in the day Liberators would bomb all three airfields without fighter interference.

As always we were on strict W/T silence but on the way down the air was full of chatter. The US fighters were already on their way!

Crossing the Burmese coast at Gwa Bay we settled down to tree-top height, the planes gently rising and falling as we hurtled across the flat Bassein–Irrawaddy delta. Unfortunately the aircraft ahead of us were disturbing flocks of small birds and these were flying up and pelting the underside of our Beau as we brought up the rear.

Eventually Noel told me he could see Lake Hlawga and I turned to look forward. Perhaps eight or ten aircraft were circling over the lake at about 2,000 feet. 'I see the [Republic] Thunderbolts are here early, Noel.' I took another look. 'Good Lord, they're Oscars or Tojos.' The Japs were indeed waiting for us.

211's Beaus moved closer to us as if to push us further south and for a moment planes seemed to be everywhere but S/L Hunt and three others of us held formation and turned north to Hmawbi. At that moment 211's planes wheeled south and nine Mosquitoes swept east through the gap. Perfect timing!

I cannot say what ground fire opposition we encountered. Having been forbidden to make a second run over the target we merely flew in formation over the aerodrome firing continuously at anything that got in the way — there was too much smoke, dust and noise to see or hear any machine-gun fire. Certainly the bamboo hangers we saw and photographed were empty, probably the aircraft they sheltered were already in the air.

The journey home was uneventful and, still in formation, we crossed Chiringa at 11.45. We were delighted to learn that the two aircraft separated from us in the melee at Hlawga [they had been followed by the enemy fighters] had landed just before us but saddened to hear 211's leader had been lost.

The ORB adds that the enemy fighters followed the Beaus over the target but at no time approached closer than 1000 yards and no attacks were made. During the run over the airfield, hangerettes and two gun positions were strafed and a steam roller attacked and hit. Moderate light flak and slight LMG, both inaccurate, were encountered and the wreckage of an aircraft was seen on the north centre of the runway.

South by East

November was a good month for 177 at Chiringa. The weather improved, the number of sorties increased to the second highest total, successful attacks increased again and only one crew was lost. The changing of the guard was completed with a new CO, a new MO, and a new Adj in the offing; four new crews arrived while eleven veteran aircrew left. And yet 177 remained much the same in competence, vigour in attack, spirit and in its relaxed style of squadron life. Sporting, recreational and intellectual activities of the whole squadron, but particularly the groundcrew, continued unabated.

The new CO, W/C George R. Nottage, AFC, arrived on 7 November from what was originally to be our sister squadron, 176, a nightfighter Beau unit at Dum Dum. He did not wait long to fly his first sortie with us as, on the 11th he took part in a long-distance operation, patrolling the roads of northern Siam as No.2 to Mike Hunt, a good guide. He continued taking his turn on ops and quickly showed himself to be friendly and without hauteur but also a good administrator and judge of men. The squadron once again was lucky in its leader.

Operations included 113 sorties of which 9 were at night. None was aborted because of weather although several had difficulty with low-lying mist and a couple with engine malfunction. The emphasis once again was on the main line, particularly in the south, as well as the roads and railways in the Shan Plateau and northern Siam. Over half of the sorties were directed to these target areas. Figure 56 shows a bowser exploding during an attack in the southern Shan Plateau near Bawlake. A further eleven sorties were directed to the Moulmein–Bangkok railway or the southern Gulf of Martaban. Other southern targets included 20 sorties of roads, rivers and railways in the Taungup–Prome–Bassein southwestern quadrant of Burma. A relatively small number of sorties were flown in central Burma. A few special recces were carried out for air–sea rescue, army intelligence and photo reconnaissance.

Figure 56 A bowser exploding during attack by F/L A. Sutherland Brown on 11 November 1944 south of Taung-gyi in southern Shan Plateau (A. Sutherland Brown).

161

Figure 57 A train attacked after pulling out of Pegu at last light 27 November 1944. The loco was hit in the first bursts and emitted copious steam while rolling three miles to a stop (A. Sutherland Brown).

Locomotives became harder to find although ten were attacked and damaged. Figure 57 shows what was usually necessary during this period — attacks at last light or at night. Sutherland Brown describes this sortie:

> As part of the strategy of dusk and night attacks Alf Aldham and I on 27th November carried out a rhubarb by ourselves in N.E. 807 (A for Apples) patrolling from Toungoo to Pegu, two fair sized towns about 130 miles apart on the main railway line north of Rangoon. The operation was typical of many successful missions. We were briefed by the CO and Intelligence Officer about lunch time and prepared our maps and equipment for take-off at 14:55 hours to arrive at the start of our patrol in the late afternoon. The weather was good and we flew obliquely across the southern Chin Hills where these were only about 5,000 feet high. We let down to treetop height east of the hills to cross the Burmese plains and low dissected bad lands of the Pegu Yoma out of radar view. We avoided the hotly defended town of Prome on the Irrawaddy River and Toungoo on the railway to intersect the latter at the small town of Octwin just to the south. So far so good. The main north road roughly paralleled the railway so our patrol covered both. We had no sooner turned south than we saw a staff car and ignited it on our first attack. A Japanese truck was seen pulling into Pye further south but it quickly got under cover of the large spreading banyan

162

and mango trees in the village and we could not see or attack it. Another 25 miles south at Penwegon, another small, well-treed town, we flashed across a stationary locomotive that did not seem to have steam up but was just outside a loco shelter. We pulled up sharply into a steep turn to attack across the railway line and were surprised to find that upon our first burst of cannon fire it emitted clouds of steam. We pressed home four more attacks and in the end a fire started by collapse of the fire-box. A little further south the train for the loco was dispersed in groups of two and three box cars which were raked without dramatic effect. By then defensive 50 calibre machine gun fire was heating up so we turned south again. By now we were into the short dusk but we continued on to be rewarded by the sight of a loaded train in open country pulling out of Pyinbongyi, a village just north of Pegu. Our first attack caused the loco to emit clouds of steam (Figure 57) and the train then coasted to a stop in about three miles, sufficiently far from the station that there was no flak from it and none on the train. We continued to attack the box cars until we were out of cannon ammunition. The loco was severely damaged, out of steam and pouring water on the tracks from the boiler. The sun had set and night descended quickly as we set course for home and flew at a comfortable 200 feet above the deck returning to our base at Chiringa where we arrived at 20:00 hours. Not all rhubarbs were actually pieces of cake.

The Japanese-operated railways were now in a shambles with patched-up locos, damaged rolling stock and more and more destroyed bridges. The latter resulted chiefly from low-level bombing by US and RAF Mitchells and other light bombers, although the Beaufighter squadrons repeatedly struck them with rockets. Our photos aided in assessing the damage. The enemy became adept at quickly building temporary bridges and started using converted trucks with both tyres and rail wheels on the railways to bypass bridges and haul loads on the lines. The interdiction of the railways was really starting to bite. Nevertheless, motor transport received the brunt of squadron attacks this month with 36 MT destroyed and 31 damaged. Also nine steamers and powered barges were destroyed or damaged as well as many lesser targets.

The increased level of sport, recreation and intellectual activity that came with the move to Chiringa continued to the benefit of all.

The Allied Air Commander-in-Chief, Air Chief Marshal Sir Richard Peirce, KCB, DSO, AFC, together with the new commander of 3rd Tactical Air Force, Air Marshall W.A. Coryton, CB, MVO, DFC, met the aircrew on 8 November and addressed and congratulated the squadron on his leaving the Command.

163

The squadron continued its change of personnel with the expiry of tours for all the remainder of the original group: Australians, P/O Donald M. Anderson, DFC, F/O Robin K. Cameron and P/O Rupert Horwood, DFC; Canadian W. Gordon Herr; and Britons, W/O Charles M. Bateman, W/O Fred H. Burton, P/O J.H. Gibson, DFM, W/O Alec J. Kappler, DFM, F/O H.S. Marshall, F/L Jim D. Marquis, DFC, and W/O Dick White all were posted. The long time MO, F/L L.D. Rutter, who had been suffering from amoebic dysentery, was repatriated on medical grounds and was replaced by F/L Eric G. Saint. The new crews who arrived were F/O B.N. Jacobsen, RNZAF, with Sgt D.W. Buckman; F/O F. MacIntosh, RCAF, with F/O F.N. Royle; F/O S. Sinibaldi, RCAF, with F/O J.R. Hews; F/S G.S. Taylor with F/S C.B. Rainbow.

The squadron also lost a relatively new crew when F/S W.J. Hudson with F/S J.K. Smith went missing on an operation briefed to patrol roads in northern Siam. They were flying No.2 to Mike Hunt when his engine controls malfunctioned and he had to turn back but they continued to an uncertain fate.

Change of the Guard Completed

The squadron was composed of diverse personalities with diverse backgrounds and nationalities, yet it functioned as a cohesive unit with little but self-discipline and genuine motivation to prosecute the war. It did this with the old guard, now left, and it continued with the new. It is hard to imagine such diverse personalities as gentle pipe-smoking, non-drinking, thinker Eric Lovett; the boyish, boozy, press-on type Mike Hunt and laconic pragmatist Fergie Ferguson, who all functioned at the top of the squadron with mutual respect and allowances for each others' idiosyncrasies. The aircrew got along the same way; most of us were drinkers, some verged on wild; others were teetotal but were tolerant of the majority and joined our celebrations. The Canadians, Australians and New Zealanders were not treated like colonials as they were in a few units. There were no fights or even strident controversies among the colleagues even when some were much the worse for wear. A person who valued privacy was allowed it. The aircrew changed but the squadron remained the same. Only Mike Hunt and Eric Lovett are both in Figure 38 taken in November 1943 and in Figure 58 taken a year later.

Among the survivors of the old guard leaving the squadron at the end of the first year there were many with distinct personalities whose

Figure 58 Officers of the new guard in front of the Chiringa Mess in November 1944; top row from the left; J.R. Hews, Eric Saint, MO, J.W. Harper, Fergie Ferguson, Adj, Soggy Brown, M.F.C. Elliot, J. Stoney, Gummy Archer; second row, Mac MacIntosh, Noel Boyd, F.N. Royle, L. Green, new IO; third row; Z.A. Aziz, Sigs, Tony Rieck, Sinbad Sinabaldi, Simmy Simpson, Mike Hunt, George Nottage, CO, Timber Wood, Eric Lovett, IO, Blondie Newcombe; front row, A.C. MacDonald, Peggy Gardner, EO, Ken Waldie, Tommy Allen (A. Sutherland Brown).

character developed under fire. Others functioned as efficiently but stood out less. Comments may be odious but some are necessary.

Doc Rutter was with the squadron from the beginning and eventually suffered from the complaint we all dreaded, amoebic dysentery. He was a bit of a bulldog and a medical pragmatist. It was said if you went to see him he started with a random medication and if that did not work proceeded serially along his shelf of notions. His replacement, F/L Eric G. Saint was a different type, a bit of a boy scout who went as an observer on a long operational flight, an enthusiastic medical practitioner and cheerful soul. The original Engineering Officer, F/O Scilley, who had come out on the trooper with the groundcrew, was of the old school, fairly severe, and had come up through the ranks in the Apprentice programme. He was one of the few permanent force RAF. He was replaced by F/L Peter Hallas a clean-cut, quiet, efficient engineer, and who was replaced in turn by

F/L K.G. Gardener who was equally effective but a bit more boister- ous and was called Peggy for unknown reasons.

The aircrew leaving included Willy Wills, DFC, who was a bit stand-offish and shy but had a whimsical turn of mind evident in the mess (Figure 37). He was an effective Flight Commander and had a good operational history. George Taylor, DFC, was a dour Scot, a veterinarian before joining the RAF so a bit older than most, also a good Flight Commander (Figure 41). Joe Van Nes, DFC, (Figure 37) was a straight arrow, a natural pilot and a superb shot probably stemming from his youth in the 'wilds' of northern Manitoba. He was posted as Chief Pilot of SLAIS in Ranchi. Lottie, or even Auntie Lottie, Lottimer, DFC, was a humorous guy who had a gift for handling the difficult positions he got himself into: flying his Beau back with a third of his wing missing (Figure 6) from hitting a tree (Mentioned in Dispatches); wounded by light flak near Chauk and getting back again; and falling out of a window in Calcutta after going in search of a bathroom after a heavy night — luckily he landed on his head. Chas, Charlie or Bubbles Bateman, a quiet man, showed his stuff with Rupe Horwood in surviving in a dingy in a stormy sea for a five days. Pinky (T.C.M.) Marshall was itinerant navigator to various COs and Flight Commanders, surely one of the toughest jobs. He was invariably cheerful and pink as a result of facial burns on ops on another squadron and always chose the pink ball in the game of Slosh (a snooker variant). Robin Cameron, an unusual Australian, looked like a diplomat, with starched bush shirt and regulation shorts, clipped moustache and manner. He had a ready laugh — too ready when the CO sank up to his armpits while trying to get to Robin's crash-landed Beau. He ended the war in an appropriate role as an ADC to HE, the Governor of Bihar. Rupe Horwood, DFC, was a clean-cut Australian youth (Figure 53) but tough survivor whose favourite expression was, 'Finer than a fairy's fart.' Don Anderson, DFC, was intrepid as a pilot and in his attempts to rescue fellow aircrew, a staunch friend and fun in the mess (Figure 40). Why were all our Aussies such gentlemen, unlike the common perception? And why, as gentlemen, were they not com- missioned until they were on the squadron? Gee Herr, another Canadian from Manitoba, was like Van, dapper and moustached. He was also a good shot, an easy-going member of his mess. Gee was pilot to Freddie Burton whose memoirs, and especially his post-war trips to Burma, form such an important part of the history of the squadron and its downed aircrew. Dickie White, Don Anderson's navigator, was a tall leprechaun with a London accent who took life easy as his narratives show (Figure 31). T.C. Clayton (Figure 41) was

166

a classic Brylcream boy who even wore his sunglasses to bed! Kap Kappler (Figure 64) was a rugged individual who was held at Sergeant for a long time because while in training in South Africa he beat up a beach at which, unfortunately, a senior RAF officer happened to be sunbathing. His court martial barred him from further promotion; ironic considering his operational flying was mostly at 50 feet or less. He was still a sergeant when he was awarded the DFM in June 1944. The CO and Adjutant worked at erasing the stigma and he ended up a W/O by the time he left the squadron and soon a P/O. Joe (or Jim) Marquis was one of the longest-serving aircrew on the squadron. He was a fine navigator and a good observer, vouched for by being appointed Squadron Navigation Officer. He flew with a host of excellent pilots, joining the squadron with Wally Roberts, a Canadian who was killed on a night take-off. He then crewed with S/L Gandy until the latter was posted, later with W/O Kap Kappler until he was tour-expired and finally with Mike Hunt. Both Hunt and Marquis were asked by Fergie to extend their tours to aid in the transition of the squadron. Both did and were effective in their roles.

And what of the more than 50 who did not survive, one third of all the aircrew who served? Some were with the squadron such a short time they were not known well except by those who trained with them. Many others served much of their tour before they were lost. The squadron had no time to mourn them then, beyond the individual responses. The survivors today, however, remember them jointly and individually more as time goes by. All are listed in Appendix 4b.

Farewell to Forty-Four

The end of the year saw an intensive effort by the renewed squadron with 115 sorties flown of which 37 were at night, but also more stand-downs than we were used to. Effort was concentrated in the south and east again as the bomb line started to inch out onto the plain as a result of the advance of the 14th Army across the Chindwin at the end of the year. Most sorties (34) were flown on the Taungup–Prome–Bassein southwest quadrant of Burma to catch movement both to the Arakan front and the start of a retreat. Another 12 were aimed at the southern Irrawaddy, the oilfields and roads of southern Burma. The main line also was attacked 17 times and volume of traffic seemed to be considerably lower because of accumulated damage to locos, rolling stock and bridges. The east was not neglected (27 sorties) but more emphasis was placed on covering the minor roads and tracks of the southern Shan Plateau and also some in the Lashio area and Siam roads and railways. There also were some searches, recces and intruder operations, and an attack of the Rangoon power station.

The new CO, W/C Nottage, had his period of familiarisation and then started to experiment with tactics, partly because targets were getting harder to find. A larger percentage of sorties (one third) were flown at night to catch the enemy moving. Intruder operations about airfields were initiated. Some patrols were tried at higher elevation to achieve a longer lead-time for sighting. More sorties were flown to follow up on earlier successes or sightings. Rocket attacks of mountain roads, to cause landslides, and road and rail bridges to increase the harassment of enemy transport were tried. The CO himself led in these tactics, attacking the Rangoon power station and leading off an evening of four intruder operations at Meiktila. Not all the new tactics were rewarding and some, such as high patrols, were abandoned. Also rocket attacks of roads on steep hillsides did not have much effect. The weather during December was mostly good but low mist during night patrols was an impediment.

Losses and casualties were severe; two crews were lost at the start and three aircrew were wounded. F/O B.N. Jacobsen, RNZAF, with Sgt D.W. Buckman, a new crew, were lost on 1 December in the Prome area in what may have been a trap. W/C Nottage met such a device in the same general area where a U/S (unserviceable) truck was set in prominent view with attendant abundant flak. His navigator F/O T.C.M. Marshall was wounded in the foot on this sortie and immediately flown to base and then to hospital where he spent about a month. The following night W/O R.A. Hawkins with W/O D.A.S. Hollay, an experienced crew, were lost in the same general area. No distress signal was received from them.

Two pilots were wounded by explosion of their own shells in the Beaufighter blast tubes. The regular ammunition was in short supply and another type (Dura), which had caused trouble before, was used and resulted in accidents on two days at the end of the month. F/L A. Sutherland Brown was wounded in both legs on the 28th and F/O K.S. Waldie was wounded in his right leg on the 31st. Both were in hospital for more than two weeks and, as it was Sutherland Brown's 48th trip, it was his last.

The final stages of re-staffing occurred with Mike Hunt leaving for Ranchi, Eric Lovett for HQ of 224 Group and Fergie Ferguson for Australia around the end of the year. Two new crews arrived; F/L R.J. Newcombe, RCAF, with F/O J. Stoney and Sgt A.B. Wilson whose navigator was in hospital in Chittagong. Blondie Newcombe had been assigned to the squadron earlier but was subsequently seconded to the Chindits for an experience of a lifetime, slogging through the jungles with Wingate's Long Range Penetration Group. F/O L.D. Green assumed the duties of Intelligence Officer.

The results from the month's operation were 7 locos damaged, 11 MT destroyed and 22 damaged, 1 powercraft destroyed and another damaged, and the oil pipeline was set on fire once.

Lord Louis Mountbatten visited the Wing on 18 December and gave an informal address to all ranks (Figure 26) after a brief parade of the squadron clad in working garb. The day before, Air Chief Marshall Sir Richard Garrod had a discussion with the aircrew and spoke later to the groundcrew, congratulating all.

The month had its celebration centred on Christmas. The CO tossed a coin with the CO of 211 Squadron for who got a two-day stand-down over Christmas and won, to set the stage. F/O Z.A. Aziz shot a wild boar as a starter and those in charge of supply and catering outdid themselves as the menu, Figure 28, shows. The Officers served the Other Ranks in the traditional manner and there was mutual entertaining between the Officers' and Sergeants' Messes. A nice touch was that those on Intruder operations on the night of 24 December were met on their return at their dispersal with *burra pegs* of their choice. The celebration continued through Boxing Day with a concert party and band recital on the evening. The daily inspections of aircraft did not take long on either day. It was generally agreed to be a great occasion, considering where we were and what we were doing. The obverse of the coin was that 177 did 211's ops over the New Year period with 21 sorties in the last two days.

Narratives of December 1944 operations flesh out the bones of statistics and the summary history with tales by three aircrew who spent some time in No.61 RAF Mobile Field Hospital in Chittagong. James Denny describes a sortie soon after he returned to the squadron after his sojourn recovering from wounds at Chittagong:

> We checked into the Continental Hotel [in Calcutta] but after two nights being savaged by bed bugs we managed to get into the Aircrew Club for the rest of our sick leave. On November the 22nd I reported back to the hospital for a check-up and medical board... I was pronounced fit to rejoin 177 but they made the proviso that if I had difficulty controlling a Beaufighter with my weakened right hand, I was to report back to hospital. So on November 26th I was back on the Squadron. During my two month absence six crews had been lost including W/C Hill. I was crewed up with a new navigator, W/O Andy Anderson and after we flew a familiarization

flight and cannon firing practice I found I could still cope. Soon after arriving back two more crews were lost.

On December 10th I went on a daylight patrol of the Lashio–Laikha road in mountainous eastern Burma. We had an uneventful low level flight across central Burma, passing a few miles north of Mandalay. The only interesting thing I had seen so far was in the foothills where we flew past a beautiful pagoda surrounded by a forest of sharp pointed columns rather like an English church surrounded by high tombstones. I was stimulated to take a few phoographs with the nose camera.

The road was soon in amongst the mountains, winding up hairpin bends and over passes. I was flying about 100 feet above it on the right-hand side but saw no activity. Somewhat too casually I followed it around the shoulder of a mountain on my left and then to my alarm, found I was in a closed valley not wide enough to turn around in. Intent on watching the road on my left, I had not noticed the mountain slopes on my right closing in. Ahead was a high pass which seemed much too close for me to gain enough altitude to clear it and on either side were craggy mountains rising two or three thousand feet above me. The pass was our only chance and I put on full power and lowered the flaps slightly for maximum lift. I called Andy on the intercom and told him to tighten his straps as we might not clear the ridge ahead and have to belly land on the 45 degree slope. All he said was 'Christ it's a 400 mile walk back.' Then I sat there for what seemed ages while the Beaufighter strained upwards and the top of the ridge loomed closer and closer. By this time I thought we might just make it but it would be a near thing. I decided to take a gamble; at that point I could have made a fairly safe belly landing whereas if I tried to clear the top and failed, we would hit the mountain hard. Up we staggered with the plane not much above stalling speed by now. Our fate came nearer and nearer and just as it seemed we were going to crash there was a scraping of some stunted scrub under the belly and the next instant we were over. Fortunately there was a steep drop on the other side which enabled me to put the nose down and gain a safer flying speed immediately. The whole incident took only two or three minutes, but for weeks I had nightmares of flying into what the Americans call a blind canyon with no way out and too high to climb over. I was still learning the hard way.

Good old 'L' for London saved us that day and it was the same plane I was flying when I was wounded near Prome and got me home and also the Beau in which I did my first barrel roll.

Norman Bolitho had returned to 211 Squadron after another bout of dysentery in the Chittagong hospital when he was asked to go to see W/C George Nottage at 177 because his navigator, Pinky Marshall, had been quite badly wounded in the foot. He reports:

So the next day I reported to him and he explained about the wounding and said he would like me to fly with him. At the time I was a Flight Sergeant so could hardly argue although I did not want to leave 211. In any case the posting was arranged and I moved my kit to a new Mess and billet.

Our first flight was to Barrackpore (Calcutta) and back. The CO had some administrative business [and also wanted to pick up some short nose cones for our TFXs so we could mount cameras]. It also gave him a chance to see if I was any good before it was critical...

We flew several missions to Siam and one along the main line without many problems or results. On Christmas Eve there was a sudden panic that the Japs had brought aircraft in to Meiktila and we laid on a series of intruder patrols of the airfields there. We were first off at 20:30 and flew there directly, we saw little except searchlight activity but while we were returning to base the aircraft replacing us [Soggy Brown] flew directly over us only missing by 20 or 30 feet. The whole operation had been laid on so urgently that no one thought of going to and fro on different tracks or elevations. Our flight lasted 2:45 hours and as soon as we got back we arranged different routes to save further near misses or worse.

On the 26th W/O Roy Abel and I flew down to Ramu to attend commission interviews with Air Commodore, the Earl of Bandon. He asked me if I enjoyed the Christmas festivities and chuckled when I said, 'Yes but it was a very abstemious day.' — then a clap on the shoulder and his best wishes. I saluted and withdrew wondering whether I was acceptable or not.

At 17.08 on the 27th we took off to find and attack Rangoon Power Station with eight 60 pound explosive rockets. The sortie lasted just over five hours. It was moonlight and we found the power station by following the chimney smoke to its source. We were flying at 4,000 feet as the CO said this was a difficult height for nightfighters to find us because of ground returns on their radar. There was some searchlight and tracer activity but with a shallow dive off went the rockets in two attacks. I was amazed at how the rockets illuminated our aircraft. I was also disappointed that the power station did not blow up in spectacular fashion; I hope the Japs were at least upset.

Sutherland Brown's last op, like so many, was exciting (A.S.B., 1992):

[This sortie] was similar to mine on the 27th of November [Figure 57] except it was entirely at night. We saw a train pulling out of Pegu and attacked it repeatedly by moonlight while tracers from heavy machine guns sprayed towards us from the train. Suddenly there was an explosion under my feet and I banked away knowing I had been wounded in the legs. At the time I thought it was enemy fire, but it was a prematurely exploded shell from one of our own cannons. We immediately set course for home with me unable to tell how bad it was and Alf unable to get in position to help. My left knee and right calf were hit and my trousers soaked with blood. I removed my feet from the rudder pedals and flew on the stick all the way home with a clear sense that the bleeding had stopped and it could not be too bad. On approaching base I tried gingerly to raise my feet to the pedals to land but initially could not move the right one. Actually my boot had filled with blood, overflowed and congealed around the sole. A small additional effort freed it and I felt foolish at my fright. The landing went all right and I was quickly attended to. Initially the MO thought the fragments could be left in my legs but after several days I could not walk or properly straighten one leg without considerable pain so I was flown to hospital in Chittagong. It turned out both legs had small ragged chunks of shrapnel in the fleshy part of them and these were removed the next day. I then lay in a hospital that had once been the Bishop's Palace and the days passed pleasantly enough as we were wheeled out on the terrace overlooking the broad meanders of the river below. My colleagues had provided me with a little medicine to ward off tigers and so, when tired of things in the evening one just rolled down the mosquito net and went to sleep. There was no stumbling home in the dark.

14

Chiringa in 1945

The New Year's Change

The New Year brought with it a new situation for the Beaufighter squadrons as well as for the SEAC forces in general. The 14th Army was on the offensive having mauled the Imperial Japanese Army in the Chin Hills and started an advance down the coast and a breakout into the north central Burma plains. All of a sudden there was a meaningful but moving bomb line, north and west of which we could not attack without endangering Allied troops. 177 Squadron's reaction to the new situation was to mount a record number of sorties; 154, of which 42 were at night. The sorties by day and by night blanketed the coastal approaches to Akyab, the Kaladan valley and the Taungup Pass. Ninety-one sorties were launched against these targets to limit movement and disrupt the enemy retreat. In addition nine sorties were flown in direct army co-operation. As always the coastal waterways and the Taungup Pass road were frustrating target areas because of the nature of the jungle cover, lack of open shots and restricted visibility resulting in an apparently disappointing number of successful attacks. Nevertheless, the chain of sorties was considered a success by the SEAC HQ, as Lt General Sir Oliver Leese commended the Wing for their sustained and successful efforts and particularly praised the groundcrew for maintaining the aircraft in the face of such intensity of effort. The ORB in particular praised F/S Hodgson, Sgt Iddon, Sgt Armstrong, Sgt Hay and Sgt Flower for directing and encouraging the work of the flights in keeping the Beaufighters at a high level of serviceability during this intense effort. All leave had been cancelled for the squadron during this period which included the occupation of Akyab and landings at Ramree and Cheduba Islands. 177 covered both landings and had been able to mount sorties at night without a moon and when the weather was too bad for the Spits and Hurricanes to fly.

Returning from a coastal flight, F/O F.M. MacIntosh, RCAF, with F/O Royle observed a column of smoke near the bomb line and then an Aldis lamp signal, *SOS Rations 400 men Recce Regt*, and had the presence of mind to signal, *Maintain smoke signals. Am in touch with HQ. Wait.* The crew then contacted HQ by VHF and were ordered to land at Cox's Bazar to pinpoint the area without talk on R/T. Only a Beaufighter crew on army co-op with an observer who was a trained signaller could have handled this mission so adroitly.

Other targets received plenty of attention as the main line was attacked on 17 sorties. The southern Irrawaddy, where small country craft were being assembled to evacuate the Japanese across the broad river, also received 14 patrols; the Gulf of Martaban 9; northern Siam 4; roads of the Shan States 4; the Prome-Rangoon railway 3; search for downed aircraft 3 sorties, and a few other types of operations. The two longest sorties yet flown by the squadron, or by Beaufighters without belly tanks, were carried out by the CO with F/S N.A. Bolitho and F/O A.H. Rieck with F/O T.N. Allen to Tavoy on 29 January, a total of 675 miles from base. The following account is a synthesis of Tony Rieck's and Norman Bolitho's short narratives with additions from the ORB:

> We took off together in the dark at 03:30 hours to attack shipping off Tavoy the following dawn. Tony managed to keep formation with George Nottage flying with his navigation lights on and without expending too much extra fuel. Together we flew over Rangoon without mishap to make the outward leg as direct as possible and arrived off the coast near Tavoy at 06:30. We quickly found four coasters in close proximity and immediately attacked them with cannon fire. At one time they attacked the same coaster simultaneously from opposite sides and both ended up with cannon shells that had obviously ricocheted into their wings off the deck of the coaster. In Tony's case it was an incendiary shell which ended up lying beside one of the fuel tanks. Luckily on hitting the deck of the coaster, the fuse had been damaged. He still has this shell, less its explosive, as a lucky charm. The shell had unfortunately caused a large rent in the wing and damaged the pitch control so that the propeller was stuck in fine pitch at 1950 rpm. The two planes communicated by VHF and George Nottage flew close to Tony's Beau to look at the damage to his wing and recommended he returned to base. Normally Tony would have cruised in course pitch at low revs for maximum fuel efficiency. However, although he was unable to do this, they still made it back to Chiringa although their tanks were almost dry. Before Tony had turned for home the two Beaus had left two coasters burning and the other two damaged.
>
> George Nottage continued northward up the road from Tavoy and was rewarded by sighting a number of MT heading the same direction loaded with oil drums. Each one when attacked burst into flames. They then broke off for base arriving back at 09:50 having

completed the longest flights undertaken by Beaufighters in the Command; a total of 1350 miles or the equivalent of a flight from London to Venice and back. Both crews received a congratulatory telegram from the AOC 224 Group for this operation.

Sorties for this month damaged 5 locos, destroyed 13 MT and damaged 25. In addition 32 barges, sea-going coasters and native craft were damaged or destroyed as well as 400 small rivercraft which were increasingly being used by the enemy. An important factor in the coastal and army co-op sorties was the disruption caused to the retreating enemy. The most important strikes, however, were those against two river steamers in the delta. Sgt G.I. Hook with F/S G.D. Robb near the end of a patrol of the delta distributary rivers on 29 January found two camouflaged steamers at Maubin, 40 miles west of Rangoon. One was a passenger ship of about 200 feet and the freighter slightly smaller. Hook made four attacks on the passenger steamer and one on the freighter before his ammunition was exhausted. They left the first one smouldering. The next day W/O J.I. Munday with F/S F.J. Lumley with a new squadron crew as No.2, F/L K.J. Gibbons with F/O J.B. Acton, attacked the ships again with 60 and 25 pound rockets and cannons (Figures 59

Figure 59   Rocket attack by W/O Munday with F/S Lumley of two steamers at Maurbin in the delta. These were found the previous day, 28 January 1945 by Sgt G.I. Hook with Sgt G.D. Robb at the end of a patrol when they were nearly out of ammunition (A.H. Rieck).

Figure 60   Cannon attack on a new steamer in February in the delta (A.H. Rieck).

and 60) and completed their destruction. Both ships were shown to be sunk by a recce photo taken by a squadron aircraft days later.

During this intense operational activity no aircraft were lost — a unique month indeed.

The parade of awards, promotions and departures continued as F/L W.S. Ferguson received the MBE for his sterling service and, probably better, repatriation to Australia. F/O D.M. Anderson and P/O R.S. Horwood were both awarded DFCs but were not so lucky as to get the order of the boat. S/L Hunt finally left the squadron for SLAIS in Ranchi. F/L Eric Saint showed keen spirit in not only flying on one of the last operational sorties of W/O R.E. Wiscombe and W/O N. Kelly, known to be as dicey as any first trip, but he also took over the duties of Adjutant temporarily as well. F/O L.D. Green, the new IO, also flew on a night sortie with Rieck and Allen. Wiscombe and Kelly became tour-expired on 12 January and F/L A. Sutherland Brown when he returned from 61 MF Hospital on the 22nd. Hence even the early re-reinforcement crews were now leaving the squadron. F/O K.S. Waldie returned to duty after recovering from his wound. Promotions included Timber Wood's rise to Squadron Leader and the EO, K.D. Gardener, to Flight Lieutenant.

The squadron strength at the beginning of the year was: 20 aircrew officers (6 RCAF and 1 RNZAF); 37 NCO aircrew; 4 ground staff officers and 261 other ranks.

176

Recreation was a little restricted under this heavy workload but one unusual event occurred. Cpl Bender was rewarded for his efforts by seeing the airmen's magazine *The Gen* returned from the printers in Calcutta (*see* Figure 27 and Appendix 7), a work that reflects well on its authors and cartoonist.

The squadron pilots together with some critical groundcrew left on 30 January 1945 for a ten-day refresher course on rocket attacks at SLAIS in Ranchi. The move was accomplished with a minimum of fuss by eight Beaufighters with spare crews, the Harvard and a Dakota load.

14th Army Breakout and Advance to Meiktila

The Japanese 28th and 33rd Armies had been soundly beaten in the Chin Hills of the Arakan and Assam and the 15th Army was backing away from Stilwell's Chinese–American–Indian Army Force (Northern Area Central Command) and the Yunnan Chinese Armies. The enemy strength in the vicinity of Imphal was 115,000 at the height of the battle in Assam but when it was over they had been reduced to 50,000, and many of these in deplorable health. Their casualties included few wounded for, with typical savagery, they tended to shoot those not able to join the retreat (Slim, 1956, p.351). Other heads fell too as many of the Japanese Generals, and their staff returned to Japan in disgrace including the Commander-in-Chief of Burmese Area Armies, General Kawabe. General Kimura came directly from HQ in Tokyo as a favourite of militarist Prime Minister Tojo to replace Kawabe. The Japanese did not take defeat lightly.

On the Allied side there was not much celebrating. The 14th Army was exhausted even if its casualties had been much lighter (15,000 battle casualties) but there were many sick and even greatly under-nourished soldiers. The army needed rest and re-grouping so it entered a phase in September of slow pursuit while many units were rested. The army had had the rough go but what they did would have been impossible without the close tactical air support and supply they received. General Slim (ibid., p.368) acknowledges this as follows:

> Air supply and close support by fighters and bombers had been carried out with precision and effect in full view of the army, but far beyond the range of its sight the enemy's lines of communication and administrative installations had been kept under almost constant attack by Allied bombers [sic]. The cumulative effect of this was immense; his river craft, his motor transport and railway trains slunk along haltingly only at night.

177

He talks only of bombers, not knowing of, or not separating, the impact of the cannon and rocket attacks of the Beaufighter Wing of 224 Group with which he was less familiar than 221 Group whose HQ was based with him and which had no Beaufighters that could range over the whole of Burma and Siam.

And so it was December before the real advance began with the objective of reaching Rangoon before the monsoon — a tall order. Earlier dreams of taking the Andaman Islands and then a seaborne landing along the delta evaporated for lack of sinews. It was left to the 14th Army to advance through central Burma (Map 5). Several other unpleasant surprises were in store for General Slim and his army. General Gifford at SEAC HQ was replaced by General Leese with a staff from the 8th Army, knowledgeable about desert warfare. There had to be an inevitable delay to become comfortable with Burmese conditions. When General Slim moved his HQ to Imphal direct control of the forces in the Arakan (15 Corps) was removed. Worst of all, without notice after the plans for the offensive were completed, 75 US Dakotas were withdrawn to China as part of the fallout from Generalissimo Chiang Kai-shek's feud with General Stilwell whom he had dismissed (ibid. pp.383–396). Quick recalculations led General Slim and his planners to go ahead even with these setbacks but there was no margin for error. The Japanese had been expected to fight on the Shwebo plain but it was soon evident that they were withdrawing to defend on the south and east of the wide Irrawaddy (the Irrawaddy shore). The 14th Army plan then consisted of initial, broadly distributed crossings of the Irrawaddy north and west of Mandalay followed by a surprise move east of the Chindwin to cross in force at Pakokku and advance quickly with tanks to Meiktila.

In the Arakan the 15th Corps started advancing at the same time down the Mayo peninsula opposite Akyab and, more importantly, down the Kaladan valley which would cut off the enemy forces in Akyab. The advance went swiftly and the Japanese, realising their peril, withdrew from Akyab. It was indeed captured by a Hurricane pilot who, on flying low over the island on 2 January 1945, saw residents waving their arms indicating the Japanese had left. The pilot was a New Zealander who had been a Judge on the island before the war. He returned later in a light plane to be greeted by the local doctor and took Akyab (Saunders, 1954, p.349). This was a precursor of the fall of Rangoon!

The advance continued swiftly but was hobbled by a lack of air supply and had to rely on rusty old naval landing craft for much of the landings and supply. One of the principal objectives was to

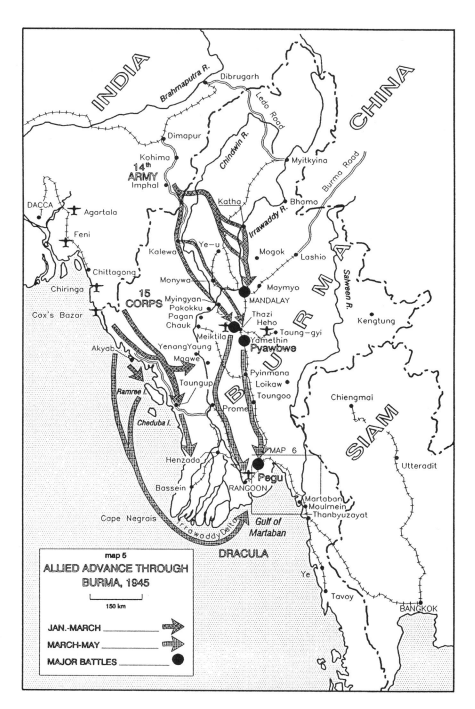

INDIA

CHINA

Brahmaputra R.

Dibrugarh

Ledo Road

Dimapur

Chindwin R.

Kohima

Myitkyina

14th ARMY
Imphal

Katha

Irrawaddy R.

Bhamo

Burma Road

DACCA

Agartala

Ye-u

Feni

Kalewa

Mogok

Lashio

BURMA

Chiringa

Chittagong

Monywa

MANDALAY

Maymyo

Salween R.

15 CORPS

Myingyan
Pakokku

Cox's Bazar

Pagan
Chauk

Thazi
Heho

Taung-gyi

Kengtung

Meiktila

Yamethin
Pyawbwe

Akyab

YenangYaung

Magwe

Pyinmana

Taungup

Loikaw

Ramree I.

Toungoo

Chiengmai

Prome

Cheduba I.

MAP 6

Henzada

Pegu

SIAM

Utteradit

Bassein

RANGOON

Martaban
Moulmein
Thanbyuzayat

Cape Negrais

Irrawaddy Delta

Gulf of Martaban

DRACULA

Ye

Tavoy

BANGKOK

map 5
ALLIED ADVANCE THROUGH BURMA, 1945

150 km

JAN.-MARCH _____

MARCH-MAY _____

MAJOR BATTLES _____ ●

capture Ramree and Cheduba Islands to build airfields for more direct support for the 14th Army. This was accomplished before the end of January 1945. The other principal objective, to advance across the Taungup Pass to Prome, could not be met because of withdrawal of some air support to facilitate the battle of Meiktila. The Corps did arrive at Japanese defences at Taungup and at the pass on the An track leading to Magwe early in March, but there it stalled.

Monywa was captured on 22 January and Slim moved his HQ there together with 221 Group's on 8 February. One of the surprises after the defeat of the enemy at Monywa, and seen several times afterwards, was that the defenders marched into the water with full battle equipment to drown rather than surrender. The 14th Army was in position along the Irrawaddy by the end of January and the first crossing in strength occurred on 13 February well north of Mandalay. Other crossings went well, even some against stiff opposition, and the Japanese fell for the deception that these were the main thrusts. As a result they moved their reserves piecemeal to meet this challenge. The main crossing to the south near Pakokku did not go as well, but in late February IV Corps of the 14th Army was across in strength and did not wait to regroup before advancing rapidly on Meiktila to the surprise of the Japanese High Command. The town and main airfield were captured on 5 March but immediately had to survive fierce counter-attacks. The railhead at Myingyan was secured on 18 March, providing a port on the Irrawaddy for supply of the army at Meiktila and its advance towards Rangoon. A few battered old locos were patched up to provide this service. In the last week of March the Battle of Meiktila was won and mopping up around Mandalay proceeded swiftly.

The scene for the Beaufighters was thus changing rapidly during the first quarter of 1945 with the focus more and more to the south, on the Japanese lines of retreat and in army co-operation.

Practice Helps

The squadron pilots had an intensive ten days at SLAIS in Ranchi in which all flew about five hours firing rockets with increasing accuracy at targets. The squadron movement was expeditious both ways with no days lost. However, the sojourn took a big bite out of the month so that only 84 sorties, 13 at night, could be flown in February. The principal targets were the coastal waterways and roads and tracks across the Arakan Yoma (14) and the roads, railways and the rivercraft of the southern Irrawaddy (17) to harass the retreating Japs and foil attempts at reinforcement. In addition eight sorties, mainly at night, were flown in direct army co-operation to rocket targets selected by direct air support controllers. The delta was also a principal target with 16 sorties and other targets as follows: the main line south of Toungoo (7); Gulf of Martaban (8); Pegu-Moulmein (9); southern Shan, Karen States and Siam (5). Two of the longest sorties flown during the month landed at Akyab, which was now available, to top-up fuel on the outward flight.

These operations resulted in 6 locos damaged, 15 MT destroyed and 6 damaged, 25 power craft damaged or destroyed, including a 100-foot river steamer, and a similar-sized coaster, plus a large number of smaller rivercraft. Since January, and an increasingly intense effort in the delta, more small new river steamers or motor vessels were discovered, attacked and sunk. Once again there were no missing aircraft. The weather was mostly good but agricultural burning and forest fires combined to make all of southern Burma extremely hazy and particularly inhibited night patrols.

Some of the most productive sorties of February 1945 are described briefly, mostly from the ORB. On 16 February, Sgt G.I. Hook with F/S G.D. Robb once again found a significant, heavily camouflaged, two-decked river steamer two miles south of Ma-urbin on the east bank. The boat was attacked four times with pairs of 25 lb rockets; all but the first struck the boat and a column of steam rose to 400 feet. After four additional cannon attacks the ship was finished off, left blazing and sinking, with a cloud of black smoke rising to 2,000 feet (Figures 61 and 62).

W/O James Denny describes an operation with W/O N. Anderson that was one of their longest trips in a Beaufighter:

> This was a patrol of the railroad down the coast from Moulmein to Ye which is south of the turnoff to the Bangkok line at Thanbyu-zayat. It was at extreme range and so we were in the air six and a half hours. About half way along the railway I flew over some low trees to burst upon twenty to thirty Japanese soldiers at target practice in a field — I could see the targets at the far end. The Japs did not hear us until we were right upon them — no doubt this is why they christened the Beaufighter 'Whispering Death' . They knocked each other over in attempts to get to some cover. I made a steep left-hand climbing turn to get the height to attack them and managed two strafes before their remainder had disappeared under the trees. They were obviously not used to seeing ground attack air-craft so far south. I completed the trip to Ye without further inci-dent before turning back to Chiringa.

181

Figure 61 Rocket attack against a motor vessel in the delta (A.H. Rieck).

Figure 62 Direct hits destroyed the vessel (A.H. Rieck).

182

F/O K.S. Waldie, RCAF, with Sgt C.J.W. Whiteing were patrolling the Pegu–Martaban line on 19 February when they came upon six dispersed box cars at Thaton and made three attacks, each causing explosions. The cars were smouldering when they left to fly down the line and then patrol some roads into the hills. On return to Thaton the contents of some of the box cars were still exploding with frequent flashes; the other wagons were burned out with blue-grey smoke hanging over them that could still be seen 20 miles away. The cars must have contained ammunition.

On 20 February W/O G.S. Taylor with W/O C.B. Rainbow patrolled the same roads and railways as Waldie and encountered many vehicles. Two three-ton MTs and one fifteen-hundredweight MT were met just north of Pegu. Upon attack each was ignited and burned with a column of black smoke. Continuing along the railway, a tank car was attacked at Waw. Skirting Bilin a staff car was seen heading south and five attacks were made to destroy it. Nearer Martaban a bus was attacked three times and left smoking. The crew then crossed the Salween River and followed the road north where a fifteen-hundredweight lorry was seen on a raft at the west bank waiting to be ferried across the river. Hits were scored and it was claimed as damaged. Continuing north at the Sittang Bridge, a notorious centre of flak, some Bofors fire was encountered before breaking off from patrol.

F/O M.C.F. Elliott with W/O W.J. Perry were briefed to patrol the northern Siam railway from Lampang south of Chiengmai to Uttaradit, the second time this distant railway had been attacked. Soon they encountered four box cars which they strafed without visible results. At the station preceding Mea Phuak it was noticed that the railway signals were down and that there were people and freight on the platform. At Mea Phuak a loco with steam up was found at the head of a train of box cars, the rear end of which was still in the tunnel to the south of the station. The train appeared to be backing into the tunnel. Five attacks were made producing smoke after the first and steam in increasing quantity after the second. On the last attack one of the Beaus own cannons exploded without injuring the crew who returned safely.

On 28 February S/L R.H. Wood with F/L J.W. Harper was briefed to patrol the Gulf of Martaban coast. Nothing was seen on route to Kalegauk Island but just south of it a 100-foot metal coaster painted blue but covered with heavy camouflage netting was seen moored in a small bay. Five attacks were made causing oil to stream out at the stern and starting a small fire on the superstructure aft of the bridge (Figure 21). Before leaving the site the navigator was able to set the oil on fire with his rear gun. On the fifth attack one of their own cannons exploded. Too many pre-explosions were happening with the inferior ammunition sometimes being issued and it was needlessly endangering pilots and navigators.

Although no crews were lost during February it was a rough month for damage to our aircraft. On the 13th, F/O F.M. MacIntosh, RCAF, while returning from a patrol in the Moulmein area and flying at 30 feet received a direct hit in the port side of his tailplane by an AA shell. The explosion tore a hole in the top of the tail of approximately seven square feet which, together with some smaller holes, rendered his elevator control ineffective. The aircraft immediately went into a steep climb. Finding that pushing forward on the control column had no effect, MacIntosh worked with the elevator trim tabs and, by judicious use, got the aircraft under control. He then flew back to base, a distance of 350 miles, and with considerable skill, successfully landed without further damage to the aircraft. Command orders applauded this effort.

On 14 February, F/L O.E. Simpson with F/O N.F. Archer returned from the Pegu area and did a wheel landing not knowing one tyre was punctured by flak. The tyre completely separated, the Beau flipped on its back, the port engine was torn off and faced backwards and the port wing crumpled (Figure 63). Flames started to erupt but a fire tender and crash party quickly attended to it. Miraculously the crew escaped with only minor injury. Simmy must have been at the very least surprised, for when returning from a transit flight to Calcutta within a week his aircraft had another burst tyre after take-off at Alipore leading to another crash on landing at Chiringa.

In addition there was a belly landing on the first day of renewed operational flying. W/O Marsden with W/O A.E. Bush, after a sortie to Pegu in which they encountered LMG which they thought had only damaged the pitch control, found they could not lower their undercarriage. Also F/O Neil H. Boyd, RNZAF, with W/O E.E. Ruddell on a river and railway patrol of the southern Irrawaddy, had an engine failure but were able to climb to 1500 feet and then return on one motor.

Mike Hunt, who had finally left the squadron, was announced to have been awarded the Bar to his DSO and Jim Marquis also was awarded the DFC. W/O Eric Ruddell was commissioned Pilot Officer as of November.

Figure 63 Simmy Simpson and Gummy Archer survived this crash on 14 February 1945. The starboard tyre was shredded by flak, unknown to them, and the Beau flipped on touchdown. The port engine separated and the port wing crumpled but they walked away with minor injury (N. Boyd).

Crescendo

March 1945 was a climax for 177 Squadron as regards sorties and operational hours flown, as well as one of the larger game-bags. During the month 137 sorties, 26 at night, were flown for a total of 708 hours. This was believed to be a record for Beaufighter squadrons in the theatre. Part of the reason for the high number of hours was that the squadron was driven to fly ever more long-range missions to find viable Japanese targets. The squadron also had a fair number of relatively short army co-operation patrols. Many of the patrols in southwestern Burma were also long patrols as they included, say, the west coast, Taungup Pass, the Bassein railway and part of the delta. The latter sorts of patrols totalled 52. Patrols of roads in Karen State and roads and railways in Siam totalled 24; Pegu–Martaban roads and railways — 22, Gulf of Martaban and the Tavoy coast — 12, army co-op patrols at night — 11, Bangkok railway — 6, main line — 4, and some other operations such as intruder and searches. Three patrols were aborted for aircraft problems.

The month started with many army co-op patrols and multi-target southwestern Burma rhubarbs, but more and more long distance ops were carried out as the month progressed. The weather was mediocre and impeded night operations because of haze from slash burning and the start of the build-up of large local storms. An increase in LMG and LAA was noticed and was attributed to the increasing concentration of the enemy as they pulled back. Nevertheless, reserves were still pouring into Burma at the rate of 7–8000 troops per month. Tactics were modified again by increased application of rockets against a variety of new targets, such as just ripping up trackage as well as firing into loco shelters, railway stations and at bridges. Secret information provided some railroad schedules and these were applied with success. Also patrols did more doubling back to catch transport that thought the 'Churchill planes' were through for the day. W/C Nottage took the lead in devising new tactics and in carrying out long-range patrols.

These operations damaged 15 locos including 1 truck-loco, the most damage to prime movers for months. The operations also destroyed 25 MT and damaged 31; damaged or destroyed 41 powered river or sea-going craft, damaged 63 rivercraft, ignited pipelines three times; damaged trackage five times and damaged one Oscar on a remote landing ground southwest of Chiengmai. The sorties against the railway in northern Siam were particularly rewarding as they were not as prepared as the Burmese railways. Contrast the train in the open at mid-day in central Siam (Figure 64) with the passive and active defences of the main line in Burma (Figure 65). Thick-walled loco shelters forced attacks to be made along the tracks, simplifying the problems for the defending gunners.

The cost to 177 was not light; two aircraft went missing, and in addition two aircraft belly landed; one hit a Burmese powerline and was able to struggle home, and one was a write-off after landing with no brakes. Also twelve aircraft suffered flak damage, of which two were beyond repair. In addition three Beaus returned on one engine during March, and one aircraft then had to make a belly landing. None of the crews except those missing was seriously injured in these various misfortunes. F/O N.H. Boyd received a commendation from the AOC of 224 Group for returning from a sortie flying on one engine for two hours in February and, the day following receipt of this news, flying a local air test he was unable to unfeather a propeller and had to make another single-engine landing. Aircraft availability for the stepped-up operations was a real problem at the beginning of the month but finally some new Beaus arrived including a Very Long Range (VLR) aircraft fitted with a 200-gallon belly tank.

Figure 64 Column of steam issuing from a small loco travelling at midday south of Utteradit, central Siam, attacked by F/O N. Boyd with P/O Ruddell in 'B', KW399, 28 March 1945 (N. Boyd).

F/O J.E. Millis with F/O W.T. Jackson did not return from a sortie of the road from Tavoy to Ye on 12 March. It was their sixth trip. Chiringa Flying Control thought they heard a weak distress call from the aircraft but subsequent flights did not discover a crash. An experienced crew of F/S H.W.G. Hart with F/S H.H. Welsh failed to return to base on the 20th after being briefed to make a rocket attack at a suspected loco hide-out on a spur north of Thaton on the Pegu–Martaban line. Nothing was heard of the aircraft after take-off.

Two constant problems with squadron aircraft were rectified during the month. We saw the last of the KW series of Beaus that were built by a Rootes Group shadow factory. They had a very much worse serviceability record than any other series and we were glad to see the back of them. Another improvement is that an Armourer, LAC Burkitt, discovered a flaw in the breech of many cannons that was caused by the use of one type of ammunition. This flaw, a small ridge, caused extraction problems and stoppages and probably caused the pre-explosions that wounded two pilots and damaged five aircraft.

On the entertainment front there was considerable improvement. A new cinema was completed for the base and not only were good

Figure 65 Passive defences of Burma main line in 1945 are a strong contrast to the lack of them in Siam. Loco and train must be attacked along the line making the job easier for the defensive gunners. Note camouflaged shelter bottom left (A.H. Rieck).

current films now shown but visiting entertainers were more frequent, including the RAF Central Band. Another innovation that proved very popular was day trips to swim in the ocean at Cox's Bazar.

Many promotions came through during the month including eight aircrew and two groundcrew as follows: P/O J.B. Acton to F/O; W/O G.R. Taylor to P/O; F/S N.A. Bolitho to P/O; F/S E.G. Cooper to W/O; F/S E.E. Cheshire to W/O; Sgt A.B. Wilson to F/S; Sgt G.I. Hook to F/S; Sgt C.J. Whiteing to F/S; F/S G.H. Mitchell, Armourer, to W/O; Sgt A. Hay, Fitter, to F/S.

James Denny and (Hector) Norman Bolitho each comment on a series of operations they took part in during March. James reports that:

> On March 4th I made my 20th operational trip on 177 Squadron (129th overall). Compared to these 20 sorties the previous 109 on Bristol Bisleys and Hurribombers on 42 Squadron had been a much safer proposition. There were many hazards in long range, low level flights (usually by single planes) — ground fire, interception by Oscars, rapidly changing weather, mountain ranges to get over etc.

188

On this trip I flew south low over the sea a few miles off the Arakan coast for some 300 miles, then turned east over the Bassein delta and picked up the railway at Tikyii a few miles north of Rangoon. I followed the line northwards some 150 miles to Prome and then followed the roads westward over the Taungup Pass to the coast. We saw a fair amount of tracer coming up at us over the pass otherwise no sign of enemy activity. We then flew back up the coast to make a night landing at Chiringa.

On the 8th I did a similar patrol of the Martaban–Pegu rail and road. We ran into a storm over the Bassein delta on the way back and had to climb to 10,000 feet to get over it. F/O Millis with F/O Jackson did not return from a similar patrol the same day.

On 12th of March I wrote-off my one and only aircraft in my flying career! I went on patrol of the Pegu road and railway in the late afternoon. I heard something hit the Beau somewhere behind me when we were flying low along the railway. We arrived back at Chiringa after dark and while doing my pre-landing checks I found to my alarm that I had no air pressure for the brakes. I was horrified — landing a Beaufighter at night on a narrow strip with large trees on either side was tricky enough with all systems working but with no brakes I did not fancy my chances. However, there was nothing else for it — I had to try to get down in one piece. I made my normal approach under power and touched down as early as possible on the runway, cut the throttles and let the tail come down. Immediately she started to swing off to the right and full rudder would not hold it, I had to put on some starboard engine. This kept me on the hard surface but we were not decelerating much but were rapidly running out of runway. When we were about 50 yards from the last pair of paraffin flares and still doing 60 knots I whipped up the undercarriage lever, switched off both engines and prayed! The wheels did not come up until we hit a slight ridge at the end of the runway and then the plane went grinding along on its belly until we hit something with an almighty crash. The undercarriage warning horn was blaring as I called to Andy to get out quickly. We both scrambled out the top emergency hatches. We had crashed into a mass of drums of tar — there was tar everywhere and smoke rising from the engines so we did not linger at the scene. We were both unhurt apart from a bruise on Andy's head from hitting his cupola. I learned afterwards that a bullet had penetrated the compressed air reservoir cylinder quite near the navigator's seat. The aircraft was a write-off; the engines had taken the brunt of the collision and both wing spars had been twisted back.

Although the Beaufighter was one of the most reliable aircraft I ever flew (I never had an engine cut the whole time) we had two unusual malfunctions during my spell on 177. In one case the pilot was halfway down the runway on take-off when his rockets started firing in pairs in rapid succession. They had 60 pound explosive heads and all landed some half mile from the end of the runway, doing some damage to trees in the area and making a hell of a noise. The pilot, having done a quick circuit and landing, was ribbed unmercifully despite swearing he'd not touched the rocket firing button.

In the other case the pilot was unable to throttle back after take-off — both throttles were jammed wide open. He climbed rapidly to 10,000 feet and circled the strip at full speed trying to free them without success. Finally, as landing was out of the question, the CO ordered him to head the plane towards the sea, let the navigator bale out and then do the same himself. Both descended successfully but the plane started to turn and finished up doing a circuit several miles wide around the strip. It was also gradually losing height due no doubt to both hatches being open. Another Beaufighter was then sent up with orders to shoot it down as far away from the strip as possible. This was done with some difficulty after three attacks because of the speed of the unmanned Beau.

S/L Timber Wood with F/L Jack Harper had a similar unfortunate experience with rockets. According to them:

There was an occasion when we inadvertantly attacked Chiringa. We were scheduled for an operation and got in the aircraft that had just come from a major service. The riggers had done various jobs around the aircraft including plugging in the tail fuses of eight RPs. We were given the all clear to start the port engine. Timber duly pressed the starter button and eight rockets screamed off above the heads of the Sikh LAA gun post. Fortunately the aircraft was pointing out into the vacant fields and there was no comment received about damage. The Sikh gunners, however, wondered whose side we were on and demanded that they be relocated to a safer position.

Norman Bolitho relates a series of operational narratives for March which began on the 3rd. He states:

W/C Nottage and I set off in 'M', NE645, but after one hour 50 minutes we were back at base with an unserviceable aircraft, this was a rare problem but understandable as the Beaus were parked in the open suffering extremes of temperature and monsoon rain. Our 'erks' had to work in these conditions wearing boots, shorts and Bombay bowlers or bush hats. The metal of the aircraft was incredibly hot during the day and they performed wonders in these conditions. Spare parts were not always easily obtained so beware

190

any u/s kite as parts were cannibalised to keep the others flying. On the 4th we took off in 'F', NE613, at 04:00 hours for a patrol of four hours and 55 minutes from Pegu to Martaban. After flying two and a half hours in the dark we caught a lorry and then a loco with 20 box cars; none were much use to the Japs after we left them. I think this was one of the occasions when I burst the bag under my gun that collected spent cartridges; I did not see much sense in just sitting there and letting the opposition fire at me without giving back as much as I could. The only problem for me when the bag burst was that all the very hot shell cases cascaded in my lap which my private parts did not appreciate. On the 8th of March we were again airborne in 'F' when we flew for four hours and 50 minutes after taking off at 04:30 for a patrol of the railway from Swa to Pegu on the main line. We wrote off a lorry and also a Jap tank which we caught on a road alongside the railway.

On the 12th we took off in 'G', NE658, at 07:08 for a 6 hour and 50 minute flight along the road from Tavoy north to Ye. We attacked two Mergui or Tavoy schooners [Figure 22] and knocked their masts off and then four MT all of which burned. We diverted into Heinze Basin where tin was dredged from the shallow bottom and here the enemy gave us quite a welcome with a battery of 20 mm cannons. I returned fire with my .303 which did not put them off but cheered me up especially as their tracer was very near and quite impressive.

On the 14th the CO phoned the Sergeant's Mess and asked me to come over to the Officers' Mess. I was fairly used to such calls as he would often ask me to go over with my maps and then we would lay on an operation for the next day; these were invariably for a job that had suddenly arisen. However, this time it was to tell me my commission as a Pilot Officer had just come through although it was dated the 30th November 1944. I had a drink to celebrate and asked to go back to the Sergeants' Mess to stand everyone a round. This was well received except for one groundcrew NCO who would not accept a drink from an officer. What a pity!

A Walk in the Rain

April 1945 in Chiringa was a curious and frustrating month for all personnel of 177. The weather was rapidly changing for the worse, the bomb line was progressing rapidly further south, some operations had objectives that were not understood, the squadron was divided in two and, worst of all, another CO went missing.

The monsoon arrived a week early at the end of the month. The individual storms before it began became progressively worse and forced a number of aborted sorties. The early monsoon and the preceding storm rains could have been more serious than they turned out to be. The 14th Army's pursuit of the enemy could have been completely bogged down and the planned amphibious landings on the delta (Operation Dracula) could have been a disaster. However the pursuit continued and the landings at the very end of the month were unopposed.

During the month the squadron mounted 106 sorties of which 24 were at night. A further five operations were aborted because of weather. Initially operations were concentrated on targets at long range such as the Tavoy coast, Siam and the Salween but as the month progressed more and more were in the delta and particularly hunting for elusive Japanese motor torpedo boats (MTBs). Altogether 45 sorties were primarily along the delta waterways; 16 of these were principally search and destroy missions against MTBs about which the navy was very nervous. While admittedly MTBs could be easily camouflaged and hidden in the delta chaungs (creeks) they did not appear to be very numerous and only one was definitely destroyed. Another 14 sorties were flown primarily against Bassein–Henzada railway and roads to confound the Japanese retreat from the Arakan. A further 18 sorties targeted the southern main and Pegu to Martaban lines; 11 the Tavoy coast where, amongst other things, they encountered and were fired upon by Allied destroyers, a characteristic naval response; and 10 patrolled Siam roads, railways and the Salween river. Five complete missions had secret objectives and four of the delta patrols had somewhat similar objectives in part. These sorties included looking for signals laid out on the ground by V force, an intelligence unit that operated behind enemy lines, reconnoitring parachute drop zones and diversions for other clandestine operations. Three sorties to reconnoitre possible radar sites northeast of Pegu and near Moulmein had dramatically different results. The first two flown together on 25 April were the most successful operations of the month. On the next day the third sortie, flown by W/C George Nottage with P/O N. Bolitho, was the greatest disaster for they failed to return. One sortie the following day was a sea search for the CO in case he ditched.

The successful sorties by S/L R.H. Wood with F/L J.W. Harper and F/O A.C. MacDonald with F/S B.L. Fender started with a diversion around a large storm near Pegu and an inconclusive reconnaissance of the radar site. Coming back under thick monsoon clouds they soon encountered first a staff car, then a three-ton lorry and then another staff car. Before Timber Wood had got very far with attacking these targets he noticed his No.2 making attacks to the west. Timber relates:

192

...we came across a clearing in the trees and found some 50 or so lorries apparently parked along a track. Hardly believing our luck, we were able to set fire or severely damage well over half of the MT and probably put a few shells in most of the rest. It was rather difficult to go around close to the ground [confined by the cloud base] carefully toting up the numbers whilst small arms fire is coming up towards you. During the course of the action both aircraft were hit but it was not until a few minutes later, when turning for home, that the effect was discovered. I was starting to pull up to a higher altitude and went to adjust the trimming tabs to the elevators. Instead of a resistance the wheel just spun around; the connecting cable had been severed. Of itself, not a great hardship for the journey home, apart from wondering whether any other operating cables had been frayed or weakened. A slight difficulty arose [from the lack of trim control when landing] for it involved starting the circuit higher than normal and, after lowering the wheels, delaying the application of only half flap to reduce forward pressure on the control column. The approach was then at a higher than normal speed until touchdown and, with only one small bounce, was followed by full flap, brakes and a sigh of relief.

Actually Wood's aircraft, NV261, was also hit in his main port tank and MacDonald's, NV548, was hit in the starboard inner tank and twice in the rear cupola. Thank the Lord for self-sealing fuel tanks!

The squadron had an effective month in spite of many sorties that could not find any MTBs. The results included the following: 16 locos damaged; 25 MT destroyed and 31 damaged; 2 AFV (tanks) damaged; 2 seagoing craft destroyed including 1 MTB and 16 damaged; 35 barges damaged; 7 rivercraft destroyed and 46 damaged; 1 river steamer destroyed, 1 other damaged and 3 effective attacks of pipelines.

Although the apparent loss of another CO was a severe blow there was not much serious damage to squadron aircraft; only one belly landing by F/O A.H. Rieck with F/O T.N. Allen at night. In addition S/L P.A.S. Thompson with F/O Stoney returned from a sortie on one engine and made a successful night landing.

The end of the war in Burma was close but no-one could foresee it: not General Slim struggling to get to Rangoon before the rains, not the Supreme Commander anxious for the success of combined operations to do the same, nor the rank and file of the operational units. All expected the Japs under the code of the Samurai would make a bitter and stubborn defence for Rangoon before they could be driven into the sea.

Conflicting indications could be read in events at the squadron. At the end of the month six crews finished tours and five came as replacements, indicating a steady state. On the other hand, during the month the squadron was broken up into a Japanese-style organisation; aircrew and a score of technical groundcrew specialists remained as 177 whilst the remainder were removed on paper to 7177 Servicing Echelon. The EO, F/L K.J. Gardiner, became the commander of the Echelon. This change was very unwelcome by all but probably was done to theoretically make the squadron more mobile. Experience at Tulihul would suggest that, although the air component would be more mobile to move into Siam, Malaya or Indo-China, it would soon encounter serious maintenance problems. However the schism could also have indicated a preparation for the end of the squadron. In any case nothing really changed during April regardless of the paper reorganisation.

Humorous incidents were not rare and not a few related to the different backgrounds and language of American and British interacting in the SEAC theatre. Early in April F/L Simpson (Figure 66) was on his way back from a sortie to the far south of Burma. Because he was running very low on fuel he landed at an American fighter strip near Cox's Bazar and was outside the Operations Room when his engines finally coughed and gave up. Simmy walked into the Ops Room and there met the CO surrounded by some of his pilots.

'What can I do for you Bud?'

'Can you let me have some fuel. I'm right out,' replied Simmy.

'Where are you going?'

'Chiringa, about 40 miles north.'

'Couldn't you make Chiringa?'

'No,' said Simmy, 'The needle is banging zero, the red warning lights were on for several minutes and the engines have just quit.'

'How long have you been up?' asked the CO.

Simmy looked at his watch. 'About seven and a half hours.'

The American looked surprised. 'Good Lord where have you been?'

'Tavoy.'

One wall of the Ops Room was covered with a map of Burma. The 14th Army was advancing from Mandalay towards the airfields around Meiktila and it was obvious the Americans had been giving close support to the ground forces there, some 250 miles away. The CO walked over to the map and began running his finger over the Meiktila area, some inches above his head.

'Tavoy. Tavoy,' he said.

'No. No,' said Simpson. 'We've been on a shipping strike. Down here,' and lowered his small self on his hands and knees, and pointed to Tavoy on the map just above the floor.

'What!' exclaimed the CO and pointing to the Beaufighter outside, 'In that thing! *Give him a hundred gallons!*'

In much the same vein some of the VHF communication between Brits and Americans could be amusing. A conversation overhead by Sutherland Brown in December went something like this. American plane, *Tower, this is the meat ship* [presumably the ambulance plane]. *Permission to land.*

RAF control tower, *Land 350.*

Plane, *Roger and I need gas.*

Tower, *I'll send out the bowser.*

Plane, *OK, and send out the gas truck too.*

The secret and diversionary sorties which increased markedly in April are described by James Denny and Eric Ruddell. Denny describes a trip on 26 April which was called a diversionary patrol:

> This sortie involved flying up and down the road between Zigon and Padigon [in the delta] firing frequent bursts of cannon to divert Japanese attention from some supply dropping to nearby advance army units. (Not a very exciting trip.) On arrival back at Chiringa we received the bad news our much-liked CO, W/C Nottage, with P/O Hector Bolitho had failed to return from a mission that day. Happily about a month later they returned from their walk in the rain.

F/O Eric Ruddell describes his last operational trip, one of the secret missions:

> At about 06:00 on the 9th of April S/L P.A.S. Thompson headed his Beaufighter down the runway at Chiringa en-route for an unusual flight to the southeast of Burma. He was just airborne when the starboard engine cut. He was just clearing the jungle at the end of the runway but managed to bring the plane around on a circuit and land. Back in dispersal he transferred to another aircraft and set off again.
>
> All seemed to go well with the second take-off but the plane had just cleared the ground when the port engine cut. Thompson managed a right hand circuit and landed. Back at dispersal he said: 'That's it!' or words to that effect, and headed to the Mess.
>
> I was rather surprised to hear his voice in the next room when I awoke just before 07:00 and he came in to tell me what happened. As my pilot, Noel Boyd, and I were stand-by crew we met in the Mess within an hour for breakfast and briefing.
>
> We were given map references — a location south of Kawkareik which itself is 150 miles east-south-east of Rangoon — where we would find a field in the northwest corner of which some strips of

bamboo would be laid out. We were to photograph these and return. If there was nothing in the first field we were to fly further east to a second map reference. These I pinpointed on my large scale map of the area.

Down at Flights our hearts sank. The only aircraft available was 'D' — a slow plane with a reputation for being a bit thirsty for a long flight like this. 'D' was equipped with rocket rails but fortunately Noel insisted that these, and their heavy protective plates, be removed before we left. At 09:30 we lifted off the runway and headed south.

The journey down was uneventful. We crossed the coast near Gwa Bay where the Arakan Yoma is quite low and little climbing is required and flying at about 30 feet skimming the tree tops — skirted Rangoon heading for the Gulf of Martaban. Where we crossed the Gulf is only about 35 miles wide; a 10 minutes flight. We flew on another 50 miles and by following small streams and roads eventually arrived at the first map reference. There was nothing to be seen. After combing the area thoroughly for several minutes we carefully map read our way east for five miles to the second map reference and there in the northwest corner of a sizeable field, were seven or eight large pieces of bamboo laid out in a pattern. We crossed the field several times taking photographs with the nose camera.

This part of Burma was a sparsely populated country and as usual we saw nothing for the first 50 miles as we cruised quietly homeward. Crossing the railway south of Moulmein near the coast we noticed a wisp of smoke emerging from a train shelter. Closer inspection revealed an engine and several trucks and coaches. Noel made four or five runs down the line, raking the target with cannon fire — concentrating on the engine — and with one eye on the fuel gauges, turned for home.

The only real worry on the way home was the plane's fuel consumption but the ground war was moving down the Arakan coast and we crossed the bomb line into safe territory. After six hours and a half in the air we radioed Chiringa that we were out of fuel and would land at Nazir — a strip in the Cox's Bazar area.

As I ducked out of the navigator's hatch I was approached by a familiar figure — a fitter who had worked on 177 Squadron. 'Hello sir, I thought you and Mr. Boyd would have finished your tour by now.'

'We have,' I replied looking looking at my watch, 'twenty minutes ago.'

The Beaufighters of 224 Group were the 'Maids of all work' but even so, this was an unusual operation. Before leaving the Squadron I talked to Eric Lovett (IO) and he subsequently asked Group whether they were happy with the outcome of this trip and whether the photographs were satisfactory. There was no reaction. 'A wall of silence has descended on this one,' he said.

The following story of the 'Walk in the Rain', the forced-landing, evasion and escape of the CO and his observer, is a pastiche of a recent writing of W/C George Nottage and that of his observer, Norman (Hector) Bolitho, and summary in the ORB. Nottage records:

> It was 07:45 on the 26th of April that we were airborne in [RD376] from Chiringa on what turned out to be our last operational sortie with the task to locate and attack a suspected Japanese radar station [on Bilugyn Island] south of Moulmein. I opted to fly down the coast turning on an easterly course south of Cape Negrais. The weather had been good this far ... but as we approached Moulmein we could see heavy rain and 10/10th cloud down to the deck ahead. We crossed the coast south of Moulmein at what Hector calculated was within a mile of our target, it soon became obvious that we would be too busy avoiding hills to do any effective search so we decided to attack a target already sighted. This was a heavily laden lugger carrying Japanese troops and cargo. Six attacks were made using cannons and Norman's Browning. The Japs could be seen replying with rifle fire [so intensely that the ship became covered in a blue haze]. I broke off when Norman told me that our cannons were almost out of ammunition. Smoke was coming out of the engines of the lugger and it headed for shore apparently out of control.
>
> I headed north with the intention of returning to base, but we spotted two more heavily laden luggers heading south from the mouth of the Salween River. In view of my ammo position I should have ignored them, but as good targets were getting harder to find, I could not resist putting in one attack. After pulling out I checked my instruments and found I had zero oil pressure in the starboard engine. I started to climb as we had a long way to go and reached 2.000 feet where the engine gave a loud report and ceased to function. The propeller refused to feather and actually started windmilling in fine pitch creating maximum drag. [We were losing altitude rapidly] and it was certain we would have to force-land [well short of potentially friendly troops]. I headed northeast back to land.
>
> North of Moulmein there is a flat coastal plain about 10 miles wide [underlain by recent sediments]. I picked roughly the middle of the plain and belly landed at about 11:00. I had jettisoned the petrol on the starboard side and probably because the fuel was still coming out a fire started under this engine. This relieved us of the requirement to set fire to the aircraft. We grabbed our escape kit, evacuated the Beau and started walking away fast.

197

There was only one way to go. Moulmein lay to the south, the sea to the west and the railway to the east was garrisoned by the Japs. It had to be north (Map 6).

Almost at once there was a strange incident. In quick succession three groups of Burmese peasants passed us walking towards the aircraft. Each member of all three groups was looking down. It was apparent that they were setting up a situation to enable them to tell the Japs that we had escaped out of sight before they arrived. We were most grateful to them.

The fields were typical bare paddies with bunds only 4 inches high; clearly no concealment in them. We kept looking back and it was most depressing, not only could we see the peasants climbing over the aircraft, but also the Beau itself on its belly. Eventually we decided that the only answer was to get down on all fours and crawl. This we did even though we felt quite daft doing it. It may have saved us!

In the early afternoon we came to a large paddy field where in one corner there were higher bunds and some rice straw. We crawled into the corner, pulled the straw over ourselves, inspected one another to make sure we were concealed and lay still without talking. During the afternoon three groups passed on the other side of the wall, talking excitedly but we could not determine if it was Burmese or Japanese. Later we inspected our rations and found we had three emergency MK II, three AMF emergency rations, three complete K rations and eight assorted tins from K rations. We were both wearing Beadon (so-called escape) suits and Indian army ammunition boots.

As dusk came we had a good look around, and as all seemed quiet, we continued north. I remembered that another crew, Tony Rieck with Tommy Allen, were due to start patrol of the railway at Thaton at 19:00 so we stopped opposite the town and made a plan. Hector had a torch so we decided that we should flash, 'CO here' because it was easily sent and read. I was to stand so as to shield the flashes on the landward side. The Beau duly flew by on time, Hector signalled but it was not seen. As per the Beau's sobriquet, the aircraft was upon us so suddenly we had little time to react and we were not well placed in any case. It was a sad sight to see our last contact with 177 disappearing into the night.

Soon after the aircraft had flown by there was considerable activity on the railway. This was annoying. The enemy had obviously worked out that after a patrol they had an hour or so when it was safe to move trains before another aircraft came. The Japs were not fools. We had become too routine.

As soon as the activity died down we set off for Thaton. When we came to the road and railway it looked very open and we crossed with extreme caution. We found ourselves on the edge of a

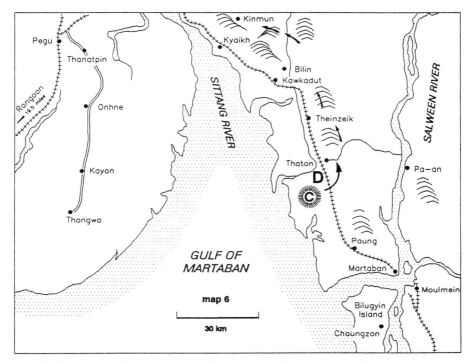

Map 6 Nottage and Bolitho's route for their 'Walk in the Rain', May 1945.
ⓒ = crash site.

village south of Thaton and as soon as we started to work our way around it, dogs started to bark and continued until we were free of it. We heard no people.

We came across a sunken road leading to the hills which we followed for a way. We then heard a muffled heavy explosion and in the moonlight determined that the pall of smoke was in the direction of our aircraft which had undoubtedly blown up. Soon after we found an empty space beside the road and flopped down and slept.

We awoke at first light, had a chat and were surprised to hear someone whistling an English tune, not what you would expect in the Burmese hinterland. We both wondered if it was a friendly agent trying to contact us but eventually decided not to chance it.

When the sun rose over the hills we found we had bottled ourselves up. The jungle on either side was too thick to make your way through without a lot of noise, the ground rose sharply to an unclimbable cliff in one direction and the road and railway were too open to tackle by day. We decided to spend the day resting and planning.

199

We did not know whether we were in friendly Karen territory so we decided to head north to the Bilin River, then over the hills and on due west across the Sittang River to contact the Allied patrols which should be in the area according to our briefing. We decided to walk by night and not on paths. We reckoned we could do this in 14 days although we soon changed that to 21 days. Basically it was not a good plan.

During the day we ate some Horlicks tablets and tried one of the K rations but couldn't swallow the latter. When it was dark we went down to the road. There we found water gushing from a pipe; evidently from a spring above. We filled our water bottles and carefully purified them. The water was very inviting and I was very thirsty so I drank directly from the pipe, stood up and promptly vomited. I was just recovering from dengue fever and at the time thought that was the cause although in retrospect I don't think so.

As soon as I recovered we started up the road to the east. It was still a fine night but at a point where the jungle to our left looked flat and not so thick, we turned into it. Right on time the monsoon clouds rolled over and the rain poured down. Almost at once we saw the only feral animal that appeared during our hike; a wild cat looking something like a lynx. It soon disappeared when it saw us.

We pressed on through the jungle which was thicker than expected and it was soon apparent there was no one about so we took an easier route. Even so our progress was slow and eventually we gave up after finding a grove of bamboo that gave us some shelter. We spent a thoroughly miserable night without sleep. The rain increased around dawn so we moved off. The ground became more difficult but we were travelling with the grain of the country but unfortunately we repeatedly had to cross ravines in which water was pouring off the hills. We were soon reduced to going down these on our backsides and climbing out on our hands and knees.

There were very few people about and we avoided these. On the fourth day (29th) we climbed out of a ravine to find a flat grassed area with a pool fed by a mountain stream. The rain had stopped so we stripped and laid our clothes to dry, flopped in the pool and eased our aches by swimming gently. We were looking forward to drying ourselves in the sun and getting into dry clothes. The fates decided otherwise. The clouds rolled over and the rain bucketed down. Miserably we pulled on our sodden clothes and moved on. We should have stayed sheltering under the overhang of the falls and rested the next day but we were unnecessarily bothered that we were behind our schedule.

On the fifth day we had an unpleasant experience. We camped near a pagoda on a hill and for the first time made some tea and then decided to spend the night there but had very little rest as we bedded down on a termites nest and got them into our hair and clothes and it was difficult to remove them. Meanwhile it rained.

On the eighth day we saw ahead part of the Bilin River but before reaching it we came across what had once been a cultivated field that in one corner still had some pineapples. Norman seized two and gorged himself on the first real food we had eaten.

On reaching the Bilin Norman did his sums and concluded we were averaging 6 miles a day. It seemed impossible that after all our efforts we were only doing that, but of course with the diversions to avoid people we were walking much further.

On the 9th day (May 4th) at the Bilin we came across a young man and asked him the best way to cross the river as it was wider and deeper than we expected. He led us about 200 yards up the river, took our kit on his head and waded across with us following. The river was about four feet deep and quite fast flowing. We rewarded him with 10 Burmese Rupees from our escape money belt and he seemed delighted. Across the river were cane fields with some huts used for pressing. We found a good one, dried our clothes and spent the best night so far.

The ORB continues:

On the next day, 5th May, they were approached by a small boy who was both intelligent and friendly. He seemed to want them to go to his village for food. Other children joined them and seemed genuinely warm towards them. The crew motioned to the children to go and fetch the food when they reached the edge of the jungle. When the children had gone they moved their position so they could observe what happened. Four men appeared with food and the crew revealed their location and were given native candy. The headman came to join them and made no bones of his dislike of the Japanese. He gave directions for the best way to avoid the enemy.

They moved on and later reached the Bilin–Papun road. It was a good road and they approached it with care, concealing themselves when two trucks came by in a southerly direction. While they were resting they watched about 10 Mosquitoes bombing and strafing the town of Bilin. They moved on following a cart track running north and later encountered a chaung full of clean water and decided to camp and make a shelter. Paradoxically it did not rain that night. They slept well after a meal of stew.

The next day (6th) they made an early start walking northwest over fairly open country [at first but it became more difficult, requiring frequent rests]... During the afternoon an elderly Burman appeared and produced a leaflet dropped by an Allied aircraft which told of the Japanese being in retreat and advising the natives to retreat to the hills. He sought confirmation of this from the crew.

Norman Bolitho continues the saga:

The elderly native kept saying 'chow' and with sign language seemed to be indicating coconuts and eating. He beckoned us to follow him and we did as the track was going northwest but became dubious as it turned south and we could see the outskirts of a village. However he led into a coconut grove and he sent some of his people up the palms and we were soon drinking the delicious milk and eating the meat of at least three nuts each. Another old man brought us boiled rice, oil and salt on a banana leaf. We ate with relish using vast amounts of salt to the amusement of the men... Heavy rain started again so they invited us into one of their huts to finish our food, concluding with 'chugri', a sugary sweet and green tea.

We tried to converse using the 'pointie talkie' from our escape kit without much success so all communication was achieved by sign language. Later the old chief indicated we should sleep on his raised verandah which we did. It became quite cold during the night. The chief climbed down from the verandah and we became suspicious until we realised he was lighting a small fire below us to keep us warm.

Next morning (7th May) they gave us tea and then the chief led us off along a northerly track. After half an hour he paused, indicated we should avoid going west as there were Japs in that direction, and left us. We made good speed but stopped after an hour for a brief rest as was our habit and opened another coconut. The track ended at a wide fast flowing chaung which, because of a distinctive bend we could identify as the Thebyuchaung. We took off our boots and socks and with poles started fording it heading for a sand bank which alarmed us as we sank up to our knees with every step. We were relieved to reach the other side and pushed off to the N.N.W. on the track which soon petered out in dense undergrowth and jungle.

About noon we rested and ate again in an open space on top of a hill. Soon after we pushed on through the jungle we saw eight Mosquitoes fly east over us. We found another highly rutted track going northeast and were so tired that for the first time we did not seek shelter while we rested. George Nottage suddenly said 'Aha' and when I looked around there was a line of men who looked Japanese lying on the top of a bank with rifles and a machine gun pointing at us. However we recognized Lee Enfield rifles and Bren guns which were hopeful signs. Their leader approached us and he realized we were not Japs and broke into smiles. Again we struggled with language but gathered there were British army officers in the area, a Major Luke and Capt. Clap. We asked for a guide who took off at an alarming rate for us but arrived at a basha surrounded by Burmese of which one spoke English. They did not

202

seem too hospitable so we pushed on with the guide thinking mean-while that the white men were myths. However eventually we came to a village where one basha had a pair of jungle boots and white socks outside drying in the sun. In the hut we found Major Lucas and Sgts. Lister and Shepherd of Force 136 and Capt. Pierce of 'E' Group, two clandestine organizations that operated behind the enemy. They fed us and brought us up to date on the news. We were still a long way behind the indefinite front between the Japs and the 14th Army.

The next day (8th May) we breakfasted with them on biscuits, marmalade and strong tea and then took off into the hills to their base camp at Pete Atet which had a wireless set. They signalled our presence to Calcutta. We fed and rested all day. On the 9th we went back with the CO and interpreter to the village to talk to the headman on whether they could clear a small landing strip (500 by 100 yards) so that we could be picked up by Westland Lysander. The chief agreed it could be done in four days.

A frustrating period began with waiting, false alarms and air drops but eventually on the 16th two Lysanders appeared. One landed and pranged; damaging his propeller and wing. We waved the other off. We now had the aircraft to camouflage and the pilot and another Force 136 Major as additional guests.

On the 18th we heard the Japs were getting very interested in the amount of air activity. The following day we went down to the little strip to improve it and noticed all the local people had disappeared. The interpreter discovered the Japs had seen us and were trying to encircle us. We ceased work and the seven of us moved off towards the hills. We had revolvers and a sergeant had a carbine but only seven rounds. Quite suddenly around a corner on the path we came face to face with one party of Japs, they dived off the path and most of us happened to dive to the same side. No one opened fire and the Japs retreated to the east at high speed. How different now they had had a bloody nose from the 14th Army! The Lysander pilot and I got separated from the others in this encounter and when we thought we spotted them in the trees we whistled 'Col. Bogey' and were reunited without any 'friendly fire'. The rumours indicated the Japs had spotted the Lysander so we had to guard it day and night, move our camp frequently to avoid the enemy, and recover supply drops. Several days were spent at the strip waiting for possible pick up by L5 (Fairchild Sentinel) light planes. At first the local Karens sat and waited with us but eventually they gave up. Finally on the 26th of May at about 11:00 four L5s arrived and landed safely, the pilots stopped their engines and calmly lit cigar-ettes while the Special Force people gave them their 'grocery lists'. Then the four guests took off for Pegu, with W/C Nottage and I continuing to Mingladon and on to Chiringa [Figure 66].

Figure 66 W/C George Nottage and P/O Norman Bolitho back at Chiringa after their 'walk in the rain' evading the enemy in Japanese-controlled terrain. F/L Simpson behind on the left with open shirt (N. Bolitho).

Rangoon

Early in May 1945 Rangoon was in Allied hands, although the war in Burma was not over because large groups of Japanese troops existed in the Pegu Yoma, and in the hills east of the Burmese plain. Many of these reacted with Bushido credo in tenacious attacks rather than the surprising melting away that occurred in Rangoon. General Slim and Lord Louis lost their race against the monsoon by a slim margin but were fortunate that General Kimura, Commander-in-Chief, Burma Area Armies, wanted no part in a suicide defence of the city. The Allied PoWs in Rangoon essentially freed themselves; the sick remaining at the gaol after the others were marched away by the Japanese as hostages to finally be abandoned near Pegu. Beaufighter and Mosquito crews were instrumental in the freeing of Rangoon. In spite of all it had done in prosecuting the war against Japan 177 Squadron ceased operations on 12 May and was rapidly disbanded. The end of the war in Burma was a ludicrous, anticlimactic event but not the less welcome for all that.

The 14th Army left elements to cope with clearing the south central plains of Burma after the victory at Meiktila at the end of March. One column advanced down the Irrawaddy but they took second place in the supply equation (Map 5). The main advance from Meiktila was slow with the Japanese putting up a village-by-village defence until at Pyawbwe, only 27 miles south of Meiktila, they fought the last major battle of the retreat. Once that was won on 11 April the advance, led by armour, rolled rapidly down the main line towards Toungoo. Karen irregulars played a vital role in blocking the Japanese from re-inforcing Toungoo from the east. By 29 April the 14th Army was attacking the enemy at Pegu. D-day for Dracula was 2 May and could not be delayed because of the expected arrival of the monsoon. The latter won the race, with the deluge starting on 1 May.

Meanwhile the Japanese abandoned Rangoon on 30 April. General Kimura surreptitiously left Rangoon by air for Moulmein on 23 April after long arguments with most of his staff and against his orders (Hudson, 1987, pp.202–210). Kimura and the Japanese had their prayers for the Kamikazi, the Divine Wind, answered in the form of an early monsoon but they had been too badly beaten to take advantage of it. Their decision was to hold Pegu as long as possible to allow escape of their forces in southern Burma to Moulmein and bolster the defence of the rest of southeast Asia but events, in the form of two atom bombs, intervened.

The Japanese adventure in Burma and their attempt to capture India had been an unmitigated disaster; their greatest defeat on land. Of the third of a million Japanese troops in Burma, 61 percent were killed. This contrasts with only 5500 killed in the capture of all South East Asia (Kinvig, 1992, p.198).

The freeing of Rangoon was an *opera bouffe*; it was feared it might have elements of tragedy but ended more like a comedy. The Allied PoWs in the Rangoon gaol widely believed they would all be shot by the Japanese after departure of the hostaged PoWs. Instead the prisoners found the Japanese had all departed on 30 April. Their next fear was that they would be bombed by the Allies. A cautious appraisal of the chaotic state outside the gaol made them think it was wiser to stay within and defend the gaol, waiting for the 14th Army that they knew was not too far away. They knew nothing of Operation Dracula.

On the next day, 1 May, they painted on a cell block roof, JAPS GONE, and on the other side BRITISH HERE (Hudson, 1987, pp.169–189). That day they saw a Beaufighter strafing in the vicinity and then fly over the gaol and recognise the signal. This plane was

Figure 67 Rangoon gaol on 1 May 1945 with the sign painted by the PoWs, JAPS GONE. S/L R.H. Wood photographed it. Presumably HQ thought it might be a ruse. The PoWs then painted the unmistakable RAF message, EXTRACT DIGIT (W. Benneworth).

S/L Wood's of 177 who took the picture, Figure 67. W/C L. Hudson, who was in nominal command of the PoWs, organised the traitor Indian National Army, INA, to turn over weapons to the PoWs and to act as police in the city. Also he tried to get the Burma Defence Army out of the city to pursue the Japanese. The BDA had started as a puppet army but slowly had transformed itself into secret and not so secret allies of the 14th Army. On 2 May the gaol was skip-bombed by a Mosquito and the inmates did not know whether the intention was to blast the gaol wall for them to escape or something more serious against the Japanese. In any case they decided to put up an unmistakable message in RAF argot, EXTRACT DIGIT. Later a Mosquito flown by W/C A.E. Saunders with F/L Stephens of 110 Squadron landed at Mingaladon but blew a tyre and had a small prang on the pockmarked runway. They were driven to the gaol by an INA colonel. Hudson and Saunders recognised the need to get word to Dracula not to flatten the city and the gaol. Saunders and Stephens then got a sampan and went down the river to meet the navy and turn off the bombardment. The next day, 3 May, the PoWs started work repairing the runways and the gaol received an air-drop of food, which they thought at first was a bombing run. Later the navy arrived to 'free the prisoners', greeted by some hoots of derision.

The Rangoon gaol had housed about 1000 prisoners before the departure of the 400 fit enough to be marched off as hostages. Most were Indian or Gurkha soldiers who refused to join the INA but there were several hundred British as well as Chinese, American and Dominion forces. The aircrew prisoners were separated and treated as criminals; confined to cells, housed with Burmese serious criminals such as murderers and generally refused medical attention. No notification was given to the International Red Cross, next of kin, or the Allied authorities of aircrew detained. Hudson (ibid.) clearly indicates that the gaol, brutal as it was, was a safer locale than the time between capture and incarceration. Hudson gives us little insight into the 177 aircrew and what happened to them except for W/C Hill. Perhaps this is because until the hostages were marched away and the cells opened at the end of April a man would only know his neighbours. Hudson makes a number of disparaging references to Hill that seem unlike the CO we knew. Hill was ill with beriberi and dysentery at the time (Figure 68). After release he was awarded the DSO in October 1945 and continued in the RAF until he retired as Group Captain in 1968. The others from 177 in the gaol were F/L J. McMichael and Sgt Dodd missing since detachment to 27 Squadron in March 1943; Sgt C.A. Grant missing on operations in December 1943; Sgt F. Jungalwalla since January 1944; F/O C.O. Kidd since August 1944; and F/O G.W. Broughton, Hill's navigator, and missing since October 1944.

The last 12 days of operations of 177 started with intense efforts to rocket the defensive gun positions at Rangoon. The main enemy on these sorties was the weather. On 1 May six Beaus took off at 13:00 led by S/L Woods acting CO with similar numbers of aircraft from 211 and 22 Squadrons. The latter had been in southern India until recently. One 177 aircraft crashed on take-off but the crew were unhurt. The others had some difficulty identifying the gun pits except for two crews but all launched their rockets at the map references. They were then briefed to strafe a neighbouring village which they did. Despite the fact, found out later, that the Japanese were supposed to have left, they encountered some flak. Twelve squadron Beaus took-off at 02:30 on the following night, 2 May, for the same target with some of the same crews but, in spite of a multitude of different approaches to get through to Rangoon, only two planes made

Figure 68. Some of the sick aircrew in the gaol. W/C Hill is in the centre at the back wearing a loincloth (Imperial War Museum, SE3991).

it — S/L P.A.S. Thompson with F/O J. Stoney and F/S A.B. Wilson with W/O E.F. Cheshire. Most admitted they had never flown in worse weather or heavier rain. The next week targets included the delta (10), Moulmein line (7), Siam and Karen (6), others (4). No aircraft were lost, one crashed and one, on the last operational sortie flown by the squadron — F/O S. Sinabaldi, RCAF, with F/O J.R. Hews — hit a trip wire which carried away the pitot-head, but the Beau landed successfully.

Normal targets were relatively few because of the nature of the missions, but a loco was damaged and a truck loco destroyed by F/O R.D. Robson, RCAF, with F/O D.R. Spackman. A number of barges and a small steamer were also destroyed.

James Denny describes the problems of flying on the operation that targeted the gun positions of Rangoon on the night of 1–2 May:

> [We took off to attack the Japanese guns on the Rangoon river at dawn.] Three squadrons, 36 aircraft in all, took part. Our course was south over the sea for about 300 miles and then east across

southeast Burma, all aircraft to proceed independently. There was a lot of cloud around Chiringa but the moon shone through some gaps. After half an hour over the sea at 2,000 feet I ran into massive towering black clouds with lightning flashes. I descended to try and get under them but found the cloud base was near the deck and it was raining heavily so I thought I would try the alternative. I started to climb and eventually reached 20,000 feet and could still see huge masses of cloud well above me. I couldn't get over the top in a derated Beau, so I descended to try getting underneath again... There were less gaps evident than before and more turbulence. By 1,000 feet I was still in cloud and beginning to worry when I came out in a small gap with towering clouds all around. Directly underneath was a cruiser which immediately opened up with all available guns — it could only be one of ours but I was not about to start flashing recognition signals! I put on full throttle and made a steep climbing turn back into the cloud. Buffeted around inside the cloud, I headed west then south and descended again, breaking out at about 500 feet in pitch darkness and heavy rain. I decided it was useless and asked Andy for a course for base; with all our blind manoeuvres he was only able to give a rough estimate so I set off on his course flying with heavy rain obscuring the windscreen and hoping it would let up before we were due to make a landfall in about in two hours. Finally the rain lessened and I was able to recognise Akyab and set a corrected course for Chiringa. Andy had not been far out. A grey dawn was breaking with lots of cloud and turbulence but nothing compared to most of the flight. I landed, taxied in and switched off with considerable relief after the worst weather I had experienced. Most of the 36 aircraft were also forced to turn back but there were no losses.

So the operational history of 177 Squadron ended, less with a bang than a whimper.

Denouement

The squadron ceased operations on 12 May 1945 and was disbanded on the 13th. Apart from the return of W/C Nottage and P/O Bolitho on 27 May to heroes' welcomes, the rest of the month and June were quiet with the squadron starting to disperse. 7177 Servicing Echelon (SE) was kept more or less intact but many aircrew (19) were tour-expired, and the others were eventually posted or repatriated. Chiringa was to be closed and notice was first given to the squadron to be ready to move on 24-hour notice on 14 May, probably to southern India. A series of changes and conflicting notices were issued over the next month but eventually, on 24 June, the remnants of 177 and 7177 SE were to move to Hathazari near Chittagong. There they found the station was full of units of various sizes waiting to move out of the Arakan but there was no RAF Station Administrative organisation. The squadron in the person of the Adjutant, F/L W. Benneworth, DFC, took over the task. Bill Benneworth, who was an operational Torbeau pilot in the UK, replaced F/L Ferguson when he left in January. Bill kept the records of the squadron fully and meticulously. He also seemed to have learned from Fergie, for in July, when he was one of only two officers left on the squadron and seemingly forgotten, he posted them both to Bangalore.

At the end of April and in May the following crews became tour-expired: S/L R.H. Wood and F/L J.W. Harper; F/L A.J. Rieck and F/O Allen; F/L O.E. Simpson and F/L N.F. Archer; F/O N.H. Boyd and P/O E.E. Ruddell; P/O R.F. Abel and W/O R. Loffill; W/O J.I. Munday and F/S F.J. Lumley; W/O F.J. King and W/O W.J. Perry; W/O N. Anderson and F/O M.F.C. Elliot.

The aircrew of 177 Squadron were dispersed all over the world. The Dominion aircrew were all repatriated to Canada, Australia or New Zealand. The aircrew remaining in South East Asia were dispersed variously. Many of the new crews (9) were posted to another Beaufighter unit, 22 Squadron; the tour-expired and experienced crews to a variety of jobs, some of which were quite interesting. W/C Nottage became OC of a Weapon and Attack Development Unit; other senior personnel became Liaison Officers, (S/L Thompson), or ADCs, (F/L Simpson), others on PRUs flying stripped-down Beaus, (F/L Rieck). A number ended up on Communications units. One crew on the latter job, W/O Munday with W/O Lumley, went missing and were later found to have crash-landed in the Irrawaddy delta and to have been attacked and shot there by dacoits (Loffill, 1989, Chapter 10, p.2). One of the most unusual jobs was the one Tony Rieck moved to after PRU. He was based in Saigon as OC of the Gremlin Task Force, whose job was to use surrendered Japanese aircraft and crews to handle the chaotic transportation in South East Asia (Figure 69). The Japanese aircraft were named by the RAF after P/O Prune and his colleagues who the Japanese interpreted as RAF heroes; Tony Rieck did not want to disabuse them.

Decorations to the squadron aircrew continued to accumulate in May and June. W/C G.R. Nottage was awarded the DSO; S/L P.A.S. Thompson, S/L R.H. Wood, F/L J.W. Harper, F/L A. Sutherland Brown, F/L A.H. Rieck, F/O T.N. Allen, and P/O N. Bolitho were awarded the DFC.

210

Figure 69 F/L A.J. Rieck in Saigon as OC of Gremlin Task Force in which Japanese aircrew and planes were used for transport in South East Asia (A.H. Rieck).

15

Epilogue

The Squadron's Accomplishments

Bill Benneworth concluded the ORB with the statement, 'It has been a good Squadron with a fine spirit of accomplishment and a reputation for efficiency... Good Luck indeed to the [former] members of the Squadron wherever they may be; we [also] remember those who were killed in our service; they shall never be forgotten. Nor will 177 Squadron by any who served in it.'

W/C Nottage received a personal message from the Allied Air Commander in Chief on 5 July 1945:

> Now that Germany has been finished off our forces must be reorganised to bring about the defeat of Japan with all possible speed. At the same time, in order to permit of us as great a measure of demobilisation as possible in 1945, the number of first line Squadrons in the Royal Air Force must be considerably reduced as early as possible. In so doing the Air Council have decided to retain in being the Squadrons which have been longest in existence and to disband those formed more recently. It is with this policy in view, yet with great regret, that I have had to issue instructions for the disbandment of your Squadron, especially in view of its magnificent record which I have before me. In the short history of its life I notice that your Squadron has been awarded two DSOs, twelve DFCs and two DFMs, [actually four DSOs, 14 DFCs, two DFMs and an MBE] and in addition, holds the distinction of having flown the longest sortie flown by Beaufighters in this Command. The contribution of your Squadron to the success of operations in Burma, culminating in the capture of Rangoon, has earned the admiration of your fellow airmen and soldiers in that great campaign. I wish you and all the personnel of your Squadron the best of luck in your new appointments.

Perhaps more telling because of its lack of the possible elements of soft-soap is the comment of Anthony Montague Browne (1995, p.26), the last private secretary of Winston Churchill. Browne was a pilot with 211 Squadron prior to his life with Churchill and in his recent

213

book, *Long Sunset*, states in his reminiscences of the RAF stage of his career, 'The third, and probably the best squadron of all [of 901 Wing] was 177, commanded by George Nottage.'

From the beginning, 177 Squadron carried its great offensive capabilities against a cruel and tenacious enemy with deadly effect. In less than two years the squadron of 16 aircraft flew 1830 sorties with a total of about 8000 hours of operational flying. It damaged 266 locomotives, many of which were irreparable. It destroyed 282 motor transports and damaged 391 others. It destroyed or damaged 273 barges, powercraft, river and seagoing ships (not counting the ones shared with 211 Squadron on the strike at Kalegauk Island). It destroyed 100 smaller rivercraft and damaged 2089 others. It destroyed one aircraft on the ground and damaged a further eight. It made 22 attacks against oil installations and pipelines on which major ignition was achieved. In the course of such wide-ranging sorties the squadron's aircrew glimpsed 'the old Moulmein Pagoda, looking lazy at the sea', became thoroughly familiar with the roads to Mandalay, marvelled (and cursed) the tropical weather and the dawns coming up like 'thunder outer China 'crost the Bay'.

Throughout these operations the aircrew were backed by a diligent, innovative and skilful groundcrew who kept the Beaufighters in their care at a high order of serviceability, often under appalling conditions of heat or tropical downpour. Typical of their work was the fact they were able to put 16 Beaufighters in the air at the beginning of the monsoon on 1–2 May 1945 within 13 hours for sorties that lasted up to 7 hours. Their innovation was evident in the adaptation of the Fairchild F24 mapping camera installed in the aircraft nose as an intelligence tool. They also converted the cupola of Squadron Beau VIs to house a rear-firing machine gun before the later model with this factory adaptation arrived. Also, they found and corrected the flaw that was damaging aircraft and pilots from premature explosion of cannon shells. Good fortune gave the squadron a groundcrew that consistently tried hard under the most adverse conditions. There was the comparative absence, too, of social distinctions which characterised the squadron throughout the Burma campaign — in Kipling's words 'neither East nor West, Border or Breed nor Birth' ever inhibited 177 from carrying the fight to the enemy.

Against this must be balanced the severe loss of aircrew and aircraft. The latter were quickly replaced; the former never — although their ranks were filled. Counting those lost while attached to 27 Squadron, 177 suffered 48 missing and presumed killed on operations, another 6 killed in action, 3 on non-operational flights, and 7 missing but subsequently discovered to be PoWs in the appal-

214

ling Rangoon gaol. Five others were wounded while on operations. This is a 40 percent casualty rate overall and with 33 percent killed in service. In addition, the first Adjutant and a photographer were killed in non-operational flights and two airmen died of tropical diseases. A high price indeed!

The question of whether it was worth it is a big part of the revisionist thinking of the 1990s. Certainly India did not have to suffer under the Japanese as most of South East Asia had to suffer. Burma has not been a happy country since it was freed and shortly thereafter achieved sovereign status. The decades of suffering that country has endured have only marginally been the result of the war and this because of the abundance of weapons left there which later encouraged insurgency. Finally and most importantly — the free world was in great danger of being engulfed in abhorrent despotisms that would possibly have lasted for generations, but it was saved this fate. And what role did 177 Squadron, Royal Air Force, have in these events? The only answer has to be a small but nevertheless significant part!

The Survivors

And where are they now, the survivors of this squadron that combined courage and discipline with egalitarian and elite attitudes? Many that outlived the hazards of war have been gathered in by the all-knowing IO in the Sky to the Great Debriefing. Surely they acquitted themselves no less well in life than on the squadron?

Many after the war dispersed without trace to conduct lives unknown to their former colleagues. Others lived lives that were known to some, but they are now gone. Then there are the survivors who have gathered together three times since the 50th Anniversary of the founding in 1943, after going without reunion except once soon after the war. Many of these survivors are pictured in Figure 70. These recent meetings were developed and arranged by Don Anderson of Perth, WA and Tony Rieck of London. Naturally all present are substantially retired now, although some worked until very recently. The careers of the survivors embraced a wide span of activities. Many retained some connection with the RAF, defence establishments or flying. Surprisingly for a group that was so audacious in war, many ended up as accountants, financial agents, school teachers and civil servants.

W/C Baldwin and W/C Nottage are still with us and shown in Figure 70. Philip Baldwin remained in the Service until 1967 and on retiring became a teacher of Spanish language and literature. George

Figure 70 Many of the survivors at the 50th anniversary reunion of the formation of the squadron at the RAF Club in London, January 1993. Back from the left; Tony Rieck, Alf Aldham, Atholl Sutherland Brown, Bill Benneworth, Kap Kappler, Eric Ruddell, Jim Marquis, Don Anderson, Norman Bolitho, Gee Herr, Tom Sagar; Front, Timber Wood, James Denny, George Nottage, P.H. Baldwin, Dick White, Chas Bateman (A.H. Rieck).

Nottage also remained in the RAF until retirement. John Hill remained in the Service until 1968 when he retired as a Group Captain. Mike Hunt also stayed in the RAF, took the Staff Course at Camberley, was awarded the AFC in 1950 but retired in 1962 to run a sailing school. Tragically, he drowned in a Scottish Loch a few years later trying to rescue a man overboard although he was not much of a swimmer himself. Willy Wills also stayed in the RAF but retired in 1952. Fergie Ferguson left the RAAF at the end of 1945 and disappeared from our view. He will be 95 if he is alive now. Gummy Archer stayed in the Air Force for five years and then was involved with the RAF Research and Development Establishment. Victor Valentine became a civil servant in the Air Ministry. James Denny was with the Air Ministry and then Customs and Excise. Bill Benneworth was with the Ministry of Defence and then became a school teacher. Noel Boyd in New Zealand also joined the Ministry of Defence and became Under Secretary. Don Anderson stayed in the RAAF for a few years and then became a commercial pilot until he retired. Eric Saint emigrated to Australia and became a flying doctor.

Timber Wood, Alec Kappler and Dickie White all became accountants or auditors. Gee Herr became an insurance agent in Winnipeg and Eric Ruddell a banker. Jim Marquis spent a working life in finance rising to chief financial officer of a development company and then retired to become an artist. Alf Aldham was a book and stationery agent. Norm Bolitho became an executive with Firestone Tyres. Tony Rieck took his family firm in industrial coatings to new levels. Ted Bellingham was in security and finance and Reg Fox stayed with the wireless field at the RAE. Blondie Newcombe when last seen was running a camera shop in Vancouver. Joe Van Nes became a computer expert with Hudson Bay Mining and Smelting in Flin Flon. Atholl Sutherland Brown became a government geologist and then a consultant in British Columbia.

The following have died of natural causes in recent years: Robin Cameron who was a financial expert with an investment firm in Perth, Australia; Rupe Horwood who was an administrator of the railways in Victoria, Australia; and Fred Burton who became a teacher and headmaster in the UK.

Most recently we lost Alec Kappler to a pedestrian accident in September of 1995. For such a stalwart member of the squadron who lived such a charmed life on operations to be taken this way seems ironic and tragic.

(Note added in proof) Two more aircrew in Figure 70 have died recently. George Nottage, our last, determined, innovative but gentle commander died on Christmas Day 1996 and Chas Bateman, intrepid survivor, early in the New Year. What enemy projectiles could not accomplish Time's arrows have done. This is why we want to tell our story while we can.

BIBLIOGRAPHY AND REFERENCES

Air Ministry (1946): *Pilot's Notes for Beaufighter TFX*, Air Publication 1721H-PN.

Aveyard, Ray (1976): We Guard by Night, in Bowyer, Chaz; *Beaufighter at War*, pp. 82–87, Ian Allan Ltd., London.

Baldwin, P.H. (1943): *Low Level Beaufighter Sorties during the Burma War*, Trustees of the Liddell Hart Centre for Military Archives, King's College London.

Bingham, Victor (1994): *Bristol Beaufighter*, Airlife, Shrewsbury, England.

Bowden,Tim (1984): *Changi Photographer, George Aspinall's Record of Captivity*, Times Editions, Singapore.

Bowyer, Chaz (1976): *Beaufighter at War*, Ian Allan Ltd., London.

Browne, Anthony Montague (1995): *Long Sunset*, Cassell PLC, London.

Burton, F.H. (1991): *Mission to Burma*, Fred H. Burton, 17 Davenport Fold Road, Harwood, Bolton, Lancs.

Churchill, Winston S. (1948–53): *The Second World War*, (VI Volumes), Houghton Mifflin Company, Boston.

Fraser, George MacDonald (1992): *Quartered Safe out Here*, Harvill, London.

Duff, Bill (1944): *Van and Matt Go Loco-Busting*, SEAC, 27 April.

Dunlop E.E. (1990): *The War Diaries of Weary Dunlop, Java and Burma–Thailand Railway 1942–1945*, Penguin Books, Australia Ltd., Ringwood, Victoria, Australia.

Dunmore, Spencer (1995): *Wings for Victory*, McClelland and Stewart Inc., Toronto.

Gardener, Charles (1945): Whispering Death, *Flight*, pp. 634–637.

Halley, James J. (1989): *The Squadrons of the Royal Air Force*, Air Britain, London.

Hartness, Brian (1976): Flying Elephants, in Bowyer, Chaz; *Beaufighter at War*, pp. 88–95, Ian Allan Ltd., London.

Hudson, Lionel (1987): *The Rats of Rangoon*, Leo Cooper, London.

Innes, David J. (1985): *Beaufighters over Burma*, Blandford Press, Poole, Dorset.

Kinvig, Clifford (1992): *The River Kwai Railway: The Story of the Burma–Siam Railway*, Brassey's, London.

Loffill, Reg (1989): *View from the Cupola*, unpublished manuscript.

Nu, Thakin (1954): *Burma Under the Japanese*, MacMillan & Co. Ltd, London.

Probert, Henry (1995): *The Forgotten Air Force, The Royal Air Force in the War Against Japan 1941–1945*, Brassey's, London.

Rawlings, John D.R. (1976): *Fighter Squadrons of the RAF and their Aircraft*, MacDonald and Janes, London.

Royal Air Force (1943–45): *177 Squadron Operations Record Book*, Air Historical Branch.

Saunders, Hilary St. George (1954): *Royal Air Force 1939–1945, Vol. III, The Fight Is Won*, HMSO, London.

Slim, William J. (1956): *Defeat into Victory*, Cassell, London.

Sutherland Brown, A. (1992): *Indian Days–Burmese Nights*, 546 Newport Avenue, Victoria, Canada.

Thomas, Andrew (1992): Burma Strikers, *Aviation News*, Vol.20, No.18, pp. 846–868.

Turner, C.C. (1936): Britain's New War Planes, in *War in the Air*, pp.759–763. The Amalgamated Press Ltd., London.

Welch, Edgar (1976): Burma Nav, in Bowyer, Chaz: *Beaufighter at War*, pp. 96–101, Ian Allan Ltd, London.

ACRONYMS, JARGON AND AIRMAN'S URDU

AA   Anti-aircraft fire
Adj   Adjutant
AFC   Air Force Cross
AFU   Advanced Flying Unit
AOC   Air Officer Commanding
basha   bamboo and palm-thatch hut
bofors   40 mm automatic AA
BORs   British Other Ranks
bowser   fuel tanker
char   tea
charpoy   string bed
chaung   creek or slough
CinC   Commander in Chief
CO   Commanding Officer
Cpl   corporal
DF   Direction Finding radio
DFC   Distinguished Flying Cross
DFM   Distinguished Flying Medal
DI   Daily (aircraft) Inspection
DR   Dead Reckoning navigation
DSO   Distinguished Service Order
EO   Engineering Officer
erk   mechanic
ETA   Estimated Time of Arrival
fitters   engine mechanics
flak   AA fire of all sorts
F/L   Flight Lieutenant
Flight   sub-squadron unit of eight aircraft
F/O   Flying Officer
F/S   Flight Sergeant
gharry   carriage, lorry
GR   General Reconnaissance school
HQ   Headquarters
IAF   Indian Air Force
IO   Intelligence Officer
knots   nautical miles per hour

LG   Landing Ground
LMF   Lack of Moral Fibre
LMG   Light Machine Gun
MBE   Medal of the British Empire
MO   Medical Officer
MT   Motor Transport
MTB   Motor Torpedo Boat
MU   Maintenance Unit
MV   Motor Vessel
NCO   Non-Commissioned Officer
ORB   Operational Record Book
Oscar   Japanese Army O1 fighter
P/O   Pilot Officer
PRU   Photo Reconnaissance Unit
RAF   Royal Air Force
RAAF   Royal Australian Air Force
RCAF   Royal Canadian Air Force
rigger   airframe mechanic
RNZAF   Royal New Zealand Air Force
R/T   Radio Telegraphy
SEAC   South East Asia Command
Sgt   Sergeant
Sigs   Signal Oficer
S/L   Squadron Leader
SLAIS   Special Low Attack Instructional School
TAF   Tactical Air Force
U/S   unserviceable
USAAF   United States Army Air Force
VHF   Very High Frequency voice radio
wad   bun
W/C   Wing Commander
W/O   Warrant Officer
W/T   Wireless Telegraphy

APPENDICES

Appendix 1: Evolution of the Beaufighter

The Bristol Aeroplane Company showed considerable foresight and initiative developing the Beaufighter in the uncertain prelude to the Second World War. As a company they had a history of developing designs independent of specifications issued by the Air Ministry. The Blenheim line of twin-engined fighters and light bombers were developed in the mid-1930s from an initiative of the company and Lord Rothermere to produce the type 142 (Turner, 1936) which certainly had resemblances to its successor, the Beaufighter (Figure 71). The origin of the Bristol Beaufighter (see Bingham, 1994, for extensive details) followed from the Air Ministry recognition in 1938 that they had a problem in having neither a cannon-armed fighter nor a night-fighter on the stocks. Bristol was in process of developing the Beaufort torpedo bomber and their new chief designer, Leslie G. Frise, made a proposal to the Ministry for the creation of two-seater,

Figure 71 Bristol type 142 in 1936; a direct precursor of the Blenheim I and, through the Beaufort, of the Beaufighter (*War in the Air*).

cannon-armed fighter. The original proposal in October 1938 envisaged development of this new fighter from major components of the Beaufort (wings, rear fuselage and tail unit) using the Beaufort's jigs. The proposal had the prospect of rapid development. Nevertheless the project languished for lack of Ministry decision, but Bristol pushed ahead with serious design work on a fighter powered with twin Bristol Hercules VI radial sleeve-valve engines and mounting four 20 mm Hispano-Suiza cannons within the fuselage firing forward. When decisions were made, the proposed aircraft was accelerated by reduction of normal staged procedures because of the component situation, the company's record and the progress of design.

Production of prototypes was delayed by unexpected difficulty in adapting Beaufort components and over-optimistic forecasts of availability of Hercules VIs. As a result not only prototypes but early production models were fitted with Herc IIs or IIIs. The first prototype, R2052, was not flown until 20 June 1939 and was followed by the first production order on 26 June. However a high production priority was not received until the end of 1939.

Initially it was proposed that Beaufighters would equip nightfighter squadrons on the basis of two to Fighter command to one for Coastal but this was quickly changed to delivery of the first 100 Beaus to four nightfighter squadrons. Delivery started at the beginning of September 1940.

Development and adaptation of armament, armour and radar proceeded in parallel with the development of the aircraft. The first Marks were heavily armed with four H-S 20 mm cannons and six .303 Browning machine guns firing forward. Later adaptations eliminated the machine guns in favour of long-range fuel tanks, fitted rocket rails for eight 60 lb high-explosive or 20 lb armour-piercing rockets, placed a rear-firing Vickers K machine gun with limited traverse in the cupola with the observer, developed Torbeaus to launch 18 inch Mark XV torpedoes, and some models to deliver two 500 lb bombs. Experiments were also made with mounting a Boulton Paul four-gun turret (Beau Mark V) and a prototype mounting two 40 mm cannons.

Other engines were considered or fitted to Beaufighters, most notably Rolls Royce Merlin XXs in Beau IIs, of which 450 were built and were used mostly as nightfighters. Generally pilots who flew Hercules-powered aircraft much preferred these to Beau IIs which were judged to be under-powered. Experiments were also made with Rolls Royce Griffons IIb and Wright Cyclone R2600s engines.

The Beaufighter was a heavy aircraft partly because it was fitted with considerable armour; a flat bulletproof windscreen, nonmagnetic armour plate in front of the instrument panel, under the pilot's and observer's seats, and doors behind the pilot and beside the rear wing spar protecting the fuel tanks. The engines themselves provided considerable protection to the pilot.

Aircraft-mounted radar grew up with the Beaufighter. The fourth Beaufighter prototype (R2055) was fitted with Airborne Interception (AI) Mark III radar that gave strong signals from targets three or four miles ahead. Development paralleled that of the sinister-looking, black-clad nightfighing Beau. Production models were fitted with the AI Mk IV to Mk 10s as these evolved.

Appendix 2: Performance and Handling of Beaufighters

The Bristol Beaufighter TFX (Torpedo Fighter Mark X) was a rugged aircraft of good but not superlative perfomance. They were not easy to fly because they needed constant attention, trim was always needing adustment, there was no hands-off flying and no autopilots except on some Australian models. These aircraft particularly needed attention during landing and take-off because a small error was quickly magnified. Otherwise, the Beaufighter was nice to handle, responsive, silent on approach, powerful and relatively fast at sea level. Novices feared these aircraft but experienced crews liked and trusted them.

Performance characteristics (Air Ministry, 1946) included: stalling speed of 110 mph with flaps and undercarriage up, and 86 mph with them down. Economic climbing speed was 172 mph. Cruising speed at medium loading for maximum endurance was 205 mph. Maximum speed at sea level was 305 mph. Normal landing speed was 110 mph The aircraft's tare weight (empty) was 15,592 lb and fully loaded 25,400 lb. Fuel capacity without external tanks was 682 imperial gallons. Maximum endurance with careful conservation was about seven hours. 177 pilots were constantly flying at the limits of endurance and found that this performance was enhanced by flying at low revs and high boost. This was later confirmed by Bristol engineers.

The Beaufighter had a very strong airframe, a remarkably well-planned, roomy cockpit with unexcelled visibility (Figure 4). The engines were trouble-free and kept on producing even with severe damage from enemy action. The Beaufighter was the only existing aircraft during the war that could deliver such an armament punch at low levels, day or night, over such extreme distances. They were the ideal aircraft for the ground attack war in Burma.

Appendix 3A: Aircrew of 177 Squadron, RAF, Phaphamau, 17 June 1943

PILOTS

W/C P.H. Baldwin
F/L H.B. Hunt, DFC
F/O A.P. Wills
F/O J.C. Van Nes, RCAF
F/O R.K. Weston, MBE
P/O T.C. Clayton
Sgt Boniface
Sgt G.A. Waddell
Sgt W.S. Watson
Sgt J. Ellis
Sgt W.G. Herr, RCAF
F/L H. Gandy, DFC
F/O H.W. Street
F/O W. Roberts, RCAF
F/O R.L. Bayard, RCAF
F/O H.S. Botell
Sgt H.I. Highfield
Sgt D.M. Anderson, RAAF
Sgt P.J. Kappler
F/S R. Horewood, RAAF
Sgt D.R. Rayner, RAAF

OBSERVERS

P/O G. Buckley
Sgt Read
Sgt J.H. Gibson
P/O T. Matthews
Sgt F.P. Smith
Sgt J. Walsh
Sgt F.H. Burton
Sgt B.B. Mearne
Sgt J. McKenzie
Sgt V.D. Valentine
Sgt J. Wilson
Sgt F. Jungalwalla
P/O J. Logan
P/O J.D. Marquis
P/O L.A. Seary
F/O R. Fletcher
F/O T.C. D.R. Hickie
Sgt R. White
Sgt C. Hennell
Sgt C. M. Bateman
Sgt G. Dinham

SURPLUS AIRCREW

P/O M. Adamson
P/O G.R. Taylor
P/O Wood
F/O J. Lottimer
P/O Haakenson, RCAF
Sgt Copeland
Sgt R.K. Cameron, RAAF
Sgt J. Wilson
Sgt Sharp
Sgt Moffatt
Sgt Goddard
Sgt T.W.Marsden

P/O D.J. Houston
P/O R.A. Watson
Sgt G.D. Pirie
Sgt Morris
Sgt Heywood
Sgt Ferguson
Sgt A. E. Bush
Sgt Davis
Sgt Sager
Sgt H.S. Marshall
Sgt Heyward
Sgt Kirk

Aircrew without initials did not return to 177 Squadron

ADMINISTRATION AND GROUND STAFF OFFICERS

F/L Westwood, Adjutant
F/O Scilley, EO
F/O Kay, Sigs

F/L Rutter, MO
vacant, IO

Appendix 3B: Aircrew Flying Operations, 177 Squadron, RAF, From Chiringa During August 1944; Ref. ORB

PILOTS	OBSERVERS
W/C J.E.S. Hill	F/O S.W. Broughton
S/L H.B. Hunt, DSO, DFC	P/O T.C.M. Marshall
S/L A.P. Wills, DFC	P/O J.H. Gibson
F/L J.C. Van Nes, DFC, RCAF	F/O J.T. Matthews, DFC
F/O W.G. Herr, RCAF	W/O F. Burton
F/O K.M. Reid, RAAF	W/O N. Anderson
F/O A. Sutherland Brown, RCAF	F/S A.J. Aldham
F/O J.A. MacKay	F/O A.J. Ede
P/O D.M. Anderson	W/O R. White
P/O N. M. Boyd, RNZAF	F/S E.E. Ruddell
W/O P.A. Hawkins	W/O D.A.S. Hollay
W/O J. Ellis	F/S E.G. Cooper
W/O R. Welsh	W/O L. McNulty
W/O J.F. Denny	F/S J. Yates
W/O T.N. Marsden	W/O A.E. Bush
W/O J.C. Forbes	W/O L.F. Reynolds
W/O J.F. King	F/S R.G. Harrison
F/S A.J. Kappler, DFM	F/O J.D. Marquis
F/S J.I. Munday	F/S F.J. Lumley
F/S H.W.G. Hart	F/S R.N. Welsh
F/S R.E. Wiscome	F/S N. Kelly
F/S G.D.S. Taylor	F/S C.B. Rainbow
F/S R.V. Conibear	F/S A.W. Claridge
	P/O R.F. Martin

ADMINISTRATION AND GROUND STAFF OFFICERS

F/L W.S. Ferguson, RAAF, Adjutant
F/O E.G.T. Lovett, IO
F/O Z.A. Aziz, IAF, Sigs

F/L P. Hallas, EO
F/L Rutter, M/O

Appendix 3C: Aircrew Flying Operations, 177 Squadron, RAF, From Chiringa During April 1945

PILOTS	OBSERVERS
W/C G. Nottage, AFC	P/O N.A. Bolitho
S/L R.H. Wood	F/L J.W. Harper
S/L P.A.S. Thompson	F/O J. Stoney
F/L O.E. Simpson	F/O N.F. Archer
F/L K.J. Gibbons	F/O J. Acton
F/O A.H. Rieck	F/O N.T. Allen
F/O A.C. MacDonald, RCAF	Sgt B.L. Fender
F/O F.M. MacIntosh, RCAF	F/O F.N. Royle
F/O N.H. Boyd, RNZAF	P/O E.E. Ruddell
F/O M.F.C. Elliott	W/O W.J. Perry
F/O K.S. Waldie, RCAF	F/S C.J.W. Whiteing
F/O S. Sinibaldi, RCAF	F/O J.R. Hews
F/O R.D. Robson, RCAF	F/O D.R. Spackman
F/O L.E.H. Scotchmer	F/O A.L. Murphy
F/O M.T. Barber	F/O. J.H. Priddle
P/O R.F. Abel	F/S R. Loffill
W/O J.I. Munday	F/S F.J. Lumley
W/O T.J. Denny	W/O N. Anderson
W/O F.J. King	W/O J. Yates
W/O R.A. Jaensch, RAAF	F/S R.D. Crook
F/S G.I. Hook	F/S G.D. Robb
F/S A.B. Wilson	F/S E.F. Cheshire
F/S L.W. Lorraine	W/O H.B. Lendrem
Sgt G.P. Large	F/S H.G. Davey

ADMINISTRATION AND GROUND STAFF OFFICERS

F/L W.A. Benneworth, DFC, Adjutant	F/L K.G. Gardiner, EO
F/L E.G. Saint, MO	F/O L.D. Green, IO
F/O Z.A. Aziz, IAF, Sigs	

Appendix 4A: Aircrew Who Flew on Operations with 177 Squadron

Listed in the approximate order, from top to bottom, in which they first flew on operations with 177 Squadron. Rank and decorations on joining. P = Pilot. O = Observer. * = Missing or killed on Active Service with the squadron. + = PoW. Ph = Photographer.

| W/C P.H. Baldwin | P | F/O T.C. Clayton | P |
| F/O J.C. Van Nes, RCAF | P | F/O T. Matthews | O |

228

F/O H.W. Street	P*	Sgt F.H. Burton	O
Sgt P.J. Kappler	P	Sgt C. Hennell	O
F/S R.K. Cameron, RAAF	P	Sgt H.S. Marshall	O
F/O M. Adamson	P*	P/O D.J. Houston	O*
P/O J. Logan	O*	Sgt J.Walsh	O
P/O R.K. Weston, MBE	P	F/O T.C. Hickey	O*
F/S R. Horwood, RAAF	P	Sgt C.M. Bateman	O
F/L H. Gandy, DFC	P	Sgt F. Jungalwalla	O+
Sgt G.A. Waddell	P	Sgt B.B. Mearne	O
F/S H.I. Highfield	P*	F/L H.B. Hunt, DFC	P
Sgt J.H. Gibson	O	P/O G.R. Taylor	P
Sgt V.D. Valentine	O	P/O G. Buckley	O*
F/S D.M. Anderson, RAAF	P	Sgt T.W. Hall	O*
Sgt M.H. Crossing, RAAF	P*	F/O H.S. Botell	P*
F/O R. Fletcher	O	F/O R.L. Bayard, RCAF	P*
F/O L.A. Seary	O*	Sgt G.D. Pirie	O
F/L D.C. Nicholl	P	Sgt M.H. Bunn	O
Sgt W.G. Herr, RCAF	P	Sgt J. Wilson	O
F/O W. Roberts, RCAF	P*	F/O J.D. Marquis	O
F/S D.R. Rayner, RAAF	P*	Sgt G. Dinham	O*
Sgt R. White	O	Sgt F.P. Smith	O
Sgt J. McKenzie	O	F/O L.A. Clark	O
Sgt W.S. Watson	O*	F/L A.P. Wills	P
F/L L.G. Caen	P	F/O J. Lottimer	P
F/O R.A. Watson	O*	Sgt J.C. Forbes	P*
Sgt L. Reynolds	O*	Sgt R. Welsh	P*
Sgt L. NcNulty	O	Sgt C.A. Grant	P*
Sgt C.S. Morgan	O*	F/S K.T. Barwick	P
F/S P. Mead	O	F/O M.S. Gurski, RCAF	P*
F/O R.F.M. Hacker	O*	W/C J.E.S. Hill	P+
Sgt W.V. Humphries	O*	F/S A. Beanlands	P*
F/O G.W. Broughton	O+	F/S G. Bloom	P*
F/S N. Kelly	O	F/S R.E. Wiscome	P
F/O A.F. Crebbin	O*	F/S A. J. Aldham	O
F/S T.W. Marsden	P	F/S A.E. Bush	O
F/O A. Sutherland Brown, RCAF	P	F/O A.J. Platt	P*
F/O C.O. Kidd	O+	F/O S. Lindsell	P*
F/S L.E. Willis	O*	W/O P.A. Hawkins	P*
W/O D.A.S. Hollay	O*	W/O J. Ellis	P
F/S E.G. Cooper	O	F/S H.W.G. Hart	P*

F/S R.H. Welsh	O*	F/S J. Munday	P*
F/S F.J. Lumley	O*	P/O T.C.M. Marshall	O
F/O J.A. MacKay	P*	F/S G.D.S. Taylor	P
F/S C.B. Rainbow	O	F/O A.J. Ede	O*
P/O R.M. Martin	O	W/O T.J. Denny	P
F/S J. Yates	O	W/O F.J. King	P
F/S R. Harrison	O	P/O N. Boyd, RNZAF	P
F/S E. Hall	P*	F/S K. Haigh	O*
F/S E.E. Ruddell	O	F/S R.V. Conibear	P
F/O R.N. Peever, RCAF	P*	F/S A.W. Claridge	O
P/O K.M. Ried	P	F/L R.H. Wood	P
W/O N. Anderson	O	F/L O.E. Simpson	P
F/O J.W. Harper	O	F/O N.F. Archer	O
P/O M.F.C. Elliot	P	W/O R.F. Abel	P
F/S W.J. Perry	O	F/O S.J. Emery, RCAF	P*
F/S R. Loffill	O	F/S R.G. James	O*
P/O A.E. Stuart-Cox	P*	F/S W.J.H. Hudson	P*
F/S P.C. Woods	O*	F/O A.H. Rieck	P
F/S J.K. Smith	O*	F/O T.N. Allen	O
W/C G.R. Nottage, AFC	P	Sgt D.W. Buckman	O*
F/O B.N. Jacobson, RNZAF	P*	F/O F.M. MacIntosh, RCAF	P
F/O S. Sinibaldi, RCAF	P	Sgt G.I. Hook	P
F/O J.R. Hews	O	F/O F.N. Royle	O
Sgt G.D. Robb	O	F/O K.S. Waldie, RCAF	P
Sgt C.J.W. Whiteing	O	F/L R.J. Newcombe, RCAF	P
F/S N.A. Bolitho	O	F/O J. Stoney	O
S/L P.A.S. Thompson	P	Sgt B.L. Fender	O
F/O A.C. MacDonald, RCAF	P	Sgt A.B. Wilson	P
F/L K.J. Gibbon	P	F/S L.W. Lorraine	P
P/O J.B. Acton	O	W/O H.B. Lendrem	O
F/S R.H. Welsh	O*	F/O J.E. Millis	P*
F/S E.F. Cheshire RCAF	O	F/O R.B. Robson,	P
F/O W.T. Jackson	O*	F/O D.B. Spackman	O
F/S H.V. Davey	O	Sgt G.P. Large	P
F/O M.T. Barber	P	F/O J.H. Priddle	O
F/O A.L. Murphy	O	F/O L.E.H. Scotchmer	P
F/S R.D. Crook RAAF	O	W/O R.A. Jaensch,	P
F/S T. Gorton	O	Sgt J.F. Sutherland	P

Appendix 4B: List of Casualties of 177 Squadron

PERSONNEL MISSING ON OPERATIONS INCLUDING 27 SQUADRON DETACHMENT

F/O M. Adamson	P	31.12.43	F/S P.G. Bloom	P	25.02.44
F/O R.L. Bayard	P	10.10.43	F/S D.W. Buckman	P	01.12.44
F/O G. Buckley	O	08.03.44	Sgt J.A. Clough	O	04.04.43
F/O A.J. Ede	O	27.09.44	Sgt M.H. Crossing	P	10.10.43
F/O R.F.M. Hacker	O	22.04.44	F/S G. Dinham	O	23.02.43
F/O D.J. Houston	O	31.12.43	Sgt F. Ensor	P	04.04.43
F/O W.T. Jackson	O	12.03.45	W/O J.C. Forbes	P	15.09.44
F/O B.N. Jacobson	P	01.12.44	Sgt C.A. Grant	P	27.12.43
F/O M.S. Gurski	P	22.04.44	Sgt T.W. Hall	O	10.10.43
F/O S. Lindsell	P	05.04.44	F/S H.W.G. Hart	P	20.03.45
F/O J. Logan	O	25.11.45	W/O R.A. Hawkins	P	01.12.44
F/O J.A. MacKay	P	27.09.44	Sgt J. Heywood	O	29.05.43
F/O J.E. Millis	P	12.03.45	F/S G.I. Highfield	P	29.01.44
F/O R.N. Peever	P	09.05.44	W/O D.A.S. Hollay	O	01.12.44
F/O A.J. Platt	P	14.08.44	W/O W.J. Hudson	P	24.11.44
F/O L.A. Seary	O	10.10.43	Sgt W.V. Humphries	O	24.02.44
F/O H.W. Street	P	25.11.43	Sgt C.S. Morgan	O	27.12.43
P/O A.E. Stuart-Cox	P	15.10.44	W/O D. Rayner	P	23.02.43
F/O D.G. Sturrock	P	29.05.43	W/O L. Reynolds	O	15.09.44
F/O R.A. Watson	O	09.05.44	F/S J.K. Smith	O	24.11.44
W/O W. Watson	P	08.03.44	F/S R.H. Welsh	O	20.03.45
F/S L.E. Willis	O	05.04.44	F/S P.C. Woods	O	15.10.44

PERSONNEL KILLED ON OPERATIONAL FLIGHTS

F/O W. Roberts	P	04.11.43	F/L T.C. Hickey	O	04.11.43
F/S A. Beanlands	P	08.05.44	F/O A.F. Crebbin	O	08.05.44
F/O S.J. Emery	P	17.10.44	F/S R.G. James	O	17.10.44

PERSONNEL KILLED ON NON-OPERATIONAL FLIGHTS

F/O H. Botell	P	02.01.44	F/L W.J. Westwood	Adj	02.01.44
F/S E. Hall	P	28.08.44	F/S K. Haigh	O	28.08.44
Cpl N.R. Morris	Ph.	28.08.44			
W/O J.I. Munday	P	July 1945	F/S F.J. Lumley	O	July 1945

PERSONNEL WHO DIED FROM ILLNESS

LAC N. Naylor	FME	04.04.44	AC2 D.E. Clements	W/ Mech	28.05.43

Appendix 5: Personnel Awarded Decorations Whilst on 177 Squadron

W/C J.E.S. Hill	Pilot	DSO
W/C G.R. Nottage, AFC	Pilot	DSO
S/L H.B. Hunt, DFC	Pilot	DSO and Bar
S/L P.A.S. Thompson	Pilot	DFC
S/L A.P. Wills	Pilot	DFC
S/L R.H. Woods	Pilot	DFC
F/L W.S. Ferguson	Adjutant	MBE
F/L J.C. Van Nes	Pilot	DFC
F/L J. Lottimer	Pilot	DFC
F/L G.R. Taylor	Pilot	DFC
F/L J.D. Marquis	Observer	DFC
F/L J.W. Harper	Observer	DFC
F/L A. Sutherland Brown	Pilot	DFC
F/O J.T. Matthews	Observer	DFC
F/O A.H. Rieck	Pilot	DFC
F/O T.N. Allen	Observer	DFC
P/O D.M. Anderson	Pilot	DFC
P/O J.H. Gibson	Observer	DFM
P/O R.S. Horwood	Pilot	DFC
P/O A.J. Kappler	Pilot	DFM
P/O N.A. Bolitho	Observer	DFC

Appendix 6A: List of Groundcrew on 177 Squadron on Move to the Arakan on 16 August 1943

W/O Lambdin	400 Clewlow	056 Gronow	705 Morris
Sgt Bazeley	034 Clissold	209 Hall	741 Moulder
Sgt Balls	665 Cole	745 Hallums	353 Munday
F/S Carvell	218 Colledge	342 Hamilton	347 Mills
Sgt Chambers	934 Collier	Cpl Harris	825 Meadows
Sgt Elcoate	839 Conlan	809 Hawkins	228 Navey
Sgt Flower	513 Cook	113 Higgins	845 Naylor
Sgt Griffin	428 Cook	Cpl Higson	Cpl Nelson
Sgt Iddon	Cpl Cooper	850 Hill	Cpl Peterson
Sgt McHendry	995 Cowie	664 Hill	Cpl Parkin
Sgt Mitchell	892 Crampin	Cpl Hinkins	Cpl Pratt
F/S Ralphs	510 Crichton	816 Howard	583 Prescott
Sgt Watkins	Cpl Cummings	658 Howett	643 Rowbotham
Sgt Wilkins	822 Curties	Cpl Hudson	381 Read
F/S Boniface	529 Carpenter	Cpl Hush	120 Reeder
748 Adkins	541 Davidson	523 Inger	960 Reid
730 Aitkins	248 Day	332 Irving	290 Reilly
Cpl Alexander	544 Dearnley	858 James	690 Robertson

607 Anderson	757 Denny	927 James	691 Robertson
022 Archer	745 Dickson	380 Joseph	620 Robinson
790 Asbury	642 Disley	125 Kirk	200 Sainsbury
150 Banks	277 Dodds	877 Kornblum	950 Sakne
815 Barlow	149 Eades	200 Lambert	719 Scholes
168 Barnett	Cpl Evans	Cpl Jennings	465 Swartz
181 Barrell	676 Fairbotham	290 Lawson	707 Selmes
565 Baynes	144 Farrell	Cpl Le Duc	Cpl Sheard
148 Bellingham	201 Fearman	114 Ledward	Cpl Shimmin
282 Bicker	441 Fenn	700 Longbottom	723 Shuck
540 Brooks	873 Ferguson	Cpl Lovegrove	699 Simpson
938 Burgoyne	592 Fisher	105 Lovett	571 Smith
Cpl Bushnell	553 Fox	Cpl MacAlpine	948 Sowerby
328 Butler	656 Frew	021 McCabe	Cpl Spittle
535 Baker	360 Fuller	652 McConnell	Cpl Stemier
956 Calderon	852 Gaskell	732 McGibbon	818 Stevens
292 Carr	Cpl Gentleman	024 McCarter	846 Stokeley
510 Carter	Cpl Gothorp	403 Mack	575 Swanson
806 Cessford	945 George	791 Maidment	652 Smith
501 Chapman	744 Gibson	889 Mason	291 Shedden
254 Chesney	537 Goldthorpe	178 Maycock	363 Taylor
884 Chew	868 Gould	024 Merralls	191 Thomson
528 Clark	014 Griffiths	393 Metheringham	Cpl Vallee
Cpl Wadsworth	Cpl Topham	653 Wharton	933 Wright
853 Woodward	031 Yates	461 York	

From the Movement Order of Main Party of 177 Squadron on 12 August 1943 by train from Phaphamau to Chittagong under P/O Adamson.

Forward Party to movement by train on 29 July 1943 under F/O Street included the following:

F/S Harrison	Sgt Woods	Sgt Shoesmith	Cpl Chappelow
Cpl Burrows	Cpl Naylor	Cpl Ryan	Cpl Balls
Cpl Smith	Cpl Booth	Cpl Wheeler	363 LAC Taylor
189 AC Gourlay	123 LAC Edge	771 LAC Currie	744 LAC Reid
966 LAC Page	567 AC Broadhead	184 AC McLaren	247 LAC Halliday
619 LAC Eason	035 LAC Hadwell	334 LAC Venables	166 LAC Coster
078 LAC Ferguson	920 AC Pratt	411 AC Dickens	996 LAC Edgar
405 LAC Kesterton	540 AC Cooper	628 AC Hughes	628 AC Edwards
570 LAC Long	025 LAC Edgcombe	373 LAC Chapman	941 LAC Carter
360 AC George	416 LAC Nutbrown	296 AC Kilpatrick	944 LAC Hayes
409 LAC Cox	442 AC Scarr	602 AC Coleman	583 AC Sefton
650 AC Wright			

Rear Party under F/L Gandy to move as soon as possible after the Main Party included the following:

Sgt Jones	966 Day	771 Lowin	508 Dyble
009 McNeill			

No initials or rank of airmen listed in ORB source for main body, only last three digits of RAF Number.

Appendix 6B: Groundcrew of 177 Squadron and 7177 Servicing Echelon, 1 July 1945

SPECIALISTS AND SERVICE PERSONNEL WITH 177 SQUADRON

LAC K.E. Archer	LAC G.S. Arden	Sgt L. Bugg	AC1 H.J. Crane
LAC J.H. Edgar	LAC H.D. Haynes	F/S E. Hodgson	Cpl W. Hook
Sgt R.H. Iddon	LAC B.W. Jones	Cpl J.M. Lawson	LAC F.J. Lay
LAC F.T. Lynham	LAC F.J. McDonald	AC2 J.V. Mills	Cpl P.E. Parsons
Cpl G.J. Roberts	Cpl P.G. Smart	LAC A.D. Wharton	Sgt J.A. Wilkins

7177 SERVICING ECHELON BY TRADES (GENERALISED)

Administration and General Duties:

W/O J. Charlton	Cpl A. Stokely	Cpl R.D. Taylor	Cpl H. Whittington
Cpl F.Hughes	Cpl W.F. Lee	Cpl C.R.H. Long	Cpl A.E. Teasdale
Cpl F.H Wansbury	LAC H.C. Day	LAC W.J. Fisher	LAC E. McNeill
LAC H.W. Meadows	LAC S.W. Worley		
LAC V.S. French	LAC A.D.B. Higgs	LAC A.E. Pritchard	LAC S.H. Wallis
LAC E.H.Wood	AC1 K.D. Donovan	AC1 A. Jones	AC1 J. Pelnam
AC1 W.D. Watson	AC1 J. Dixon	AC2 G.E. Richardson	

Armourers:

W/O G.H.W. Mitchell	Sgt J. Dent	Sgt J. Hush	Cpl L. Sakne
LAC A. Foster	LAC R.D. Heathcote	Cpl H.M. Bender	LAC C.C. Brown
LAC R.V. Gower	LAC W.M. Kilpatrick	LAC N.J.F. Conlan	LAC P.L. Beecroft
LAC J.H.C. Burgoyne	LAC H. Fenn	LAC C.J.H. French	LAC W. Hall
LAC R.E. Maidment	LAC L. Metheringham	LAC G. Mills	LAC K.Nutbrown
LAC S. Thompson	LAC H.Burkitt	LAC J.W. Sowerby	

Cooks:

Cpl E. Bessant	LAC D.M. Clark	LAC D.A. Harris	LAC T. Currie
LAC W.A. Chesney	LAC J. Carpenter		

Motor Transport:

F/S W.T. Warrilow	Cpl J.W. Allen	LAC F. Cardwell	LAC A.K. Coakley
LAC S.F. Cox	LAC G.W. Stringer	LAC J. Atkinson	LAC C.G. Lowin
LAC A. Maycock	LAC H.K. Mills	LAC A. Spanton	LAC J.H. Chew
LAC R.G. Reed	LAC H.J. Chapman	LAC G. Clewlow	Cpl J.W. Lanagan
LAC W. Kelsall	LAC W. Terry	AC2 J.McRoberts	LAC J. Cairns
LAC H.H. Scott	LAC B.C. Tucker	LAC C.W. Woodhams	

Airframe Mechanics:

F/S R.A. Dungay	Sgt A.W. Crossley	Sgt L. King	Cpl R. Barrnett
Cpl T.W. Black	Cpl B.G. Cook	Cpl D.M. Crichton	Cpl R. Asbury
Cpl L.A.H. Cooper	Cpl P. Burrow	Cpl J. Alexander	LAC C. Fairhurst
LAC J. Murray	LAC F. Prescott	LAC E.G. Read	LAC R.E. Rendle
LAC G.T. Tildesley	LAC N. Wood	LAC D.B. McLaren	LAC W.J. Hill
LAC S. Broadhead	Cpl W. Lawson	LAC T. Clark	LAC L.S. Cockett
LAC I.W. Eason	LAC N. Farrell	LAC A.C. Fermor	LAC F.J. Hicks

LAC R.J. Hocking LAC W.E.S. Howells LAC E.G. Hughes LAC C.D. Lockerbie
LAC R. Milne LAC J. Paton LAC H. Pope LAC V.A.F. Price
LAC T.H. Prior LAC J.J. Robinson LAC W.T. Stuart LAC H. Gaskill
LAC A.J. Cooper

Engine Mechanics:

F/S A. Hay Sgt J. Amstrong Sgt J.M. Sykes Cpl L. Brine
Cpl W.J. Burnett Cpl V.J. Hallams Cpl E.S. Harding Cpl H. G. LeDuc
Cpl E.V. Morgan Cpl F. Rennie Cpl G.A. Yeates Cpl J.R. Ryan
Cpl G.E. Nelson LAC E.T. Brandrick LAC A.R. Davidson LAC H. Howard
LAC J.D. McIntosh LAC A. Tapper LAC H. Williams LAC H. Lowe
LAC S. Longbottom LAC Holden LAC N.W. Beeby LAC D.H. Collister
LAC R.A. Cowie LAC J.W. Curley LAC L. Dearnley LAC J.R. Denny
LAC H. Dickens LAC F. Dickson LAC C.A. Disley LAC G. Eden
LAC J.H. Falconbridge LAC W.D. Ferguson LAC R.H. Frost LAC B. Goldthorpe
LAC F. Griffiths LAC S.C. Hadwell LAC R.D. Hawkins LAC A.W.J. Huckell
LAC N.J. Kesterton LAC J.R. Kirk LAC R.S. Ley LAC D. Livings
LAC E.E. Markland LAC G.P. Nash LAC C. Reilly LAC H.W. Richman
LAC W.E. Searle LAC J. Smith LAC J. Stevens LAC F.A. Syrett
LAC C.E. Taylor LAC C.E. Weale LAC I.H. Venables AC2 L.E. Conway
AC2 A. McCabe

Electrical:

F/S J.R. Thaton Cpl J.S. Taylor LAC J. Sefton LAC L.H. Merralls
AC1 R. Giddons LAC E.G.W. Wright LAC J.F. Smith LAC J. Johnstone
LAC G.A.W.Coleman LAC G.J.Brown LAC W.A.C. Cunningham
LAC L.C. York AC1 A.G. Gowlett

Equipment:

F/S A. Burkitt Cpl F. Page LAC T.W. Walters LAC W.E. Dodd

Instruments:

Sgt S.P. Smith Cpl H.J. Hamilton Cpl R.J. Hill LAC E.C. Pearce
AC1 D.O. Thomas LAC P.B. Schwartz LAC G.E. Grubb LAC H. Carter
LAC J. Carr

Photography:

Cpl Stowe LAC H.J. Hancock LAC D.F. Muggleton LAC G.W. Semley
LAC E. Stafford LAC D. Wilson AC1 S.H. Stott

Wireless:

F/S A. Pratt Sgt C. Wheeler Cpl B. Draper Cpl C.R. Fox
Cpl G. Kyle Cpl F. Ward LAC H.G. Woodhouse Cpl C. Cox
LAC P. Barnett LAC K.J. Clissold AC R. James LAC H. Lambert
LAC J.H. Mason LAC J.W. Maynard LAC J. Walton LAC J.A. Weir
LAC D.M. Ferguson Cpl Knight

Special and Other Trades:

Sgt M. Samuels Cpl J. Adkin Cpl J.E. Harris Cpl C.S. Spittle
LAC S. Woodward LAC L. Barlow Cpl S.T. Hawkins LAC G. Worrall
LAC E.A. Youles LAC H.H. Gould AC1 J. Plummer Cpl S. Ledward
AC1 L. Binnington AC2 A. Mathews

235

Appendix 7A: "Then" by LAC

On a cold wintry day some sixteen hundred years ago two Roman Legionaries of the one hundred and seventy-seventh squadron sat upon Hadrian's Wall and surveyed the rolling Uplands of the Scottish Border. A drizzling mist was rolling down from the hills and their faces were blue and nipped with cold. They sat in moody silence for some time while below them a crowd of Britons laboured noisily.

Then one whose name was Gaius spoke, his voice pregnant with disgust, 'What a country! I am frozen stiff.'

'My feet and hands are numb,' growled his companion whose name was Lucius. 'How do those old fools in Rome expect us to last four years out here?'

'They would know better if they had to do it,' said Gaius.

'They ought to bring it down to two years,' continued Lucius. 'I am getting rheumatics with all this cold.'

'I'm going sick in the morning,' Gaius declared, 'I'm cheesed off with this. Then I'll get a warm bed.'

They were silent for a while until along the wall they perceived a Briton approaching carrying on his shoulder an earthen jar. Both faces brightened up immediately and as if impelled by the same force, they yelled in unison, 'Come on ale-fellow. Hurry up. Where have you been?'

'Coming, sir, coming,' said the old man and when he reached the spot where the legionaries sat, 'Plenty of ale; plenty of oat cakes.'

The ale was poured out into earthen vessels and each took two oat cakes.

'How much old man?' asked Lucius.

'The ale one denarius each . . .' began the old man.

'What!' exclaimed Gaius. 'A denarius!!!! A whole denarius for that small amount. You robbing old mountain goat!! You grey beard rascal!!'

'No, sir, no,' pleaded the old man. 'Ale is scarce and my oats this year were burned by the Scots, and I am very poor man.'

'Poor man,' said Lucius, 'Here we are protecting you from the barbarians in the mountains and all you can do in return is to rob us.'

Appendix 7B: Phaphamau Saga

1. There's a little sand-swept desert
   To the south of Pha-Pha-Mau,
   Where the pie-dogs, snakes and vultures

236

Roam the plains:
How they lived was hard to tell,
For this last outpost of Hell
Offered nought but grim stark death
In its domains.

2. It was known as Pha-Pha-Mau,
   And, 'tis said that once a war
   Brought some airmen and their planes
   Therein to fly.
   But the kites ne'er left the ground,
   And their crews just moped around,
   Decaying as the years went rolling by.

3. They were wrecks, just skin and bone,
   Forgotten by folks at home,
   In dreams they had their wisps of heaven.
   One might find the place perhaps
   Along desert camel tracks,
   To see the remnants of that crowd '177'.

4. Natives say at dead of night,
   In the distance ghostly lights
   Illuminate the runways and the trees;
   While a high-pitched ghostly roar,
   Fills the skies o'er Pha-Pha-Mau,
   As some ghostly pilot rev's his Hercules.

INDEX

240

242